Sir John Lyons has been Master of Trinity Hall since 1984. He was born in 1932 and educated at St Bede's College, Manchester, and at Christ's College, Cambridge, where he took his first degree in Classics in 1953 and the Diploma in Education in 1954. After two years' national service in the Royal Navy, during which time he was trained as an interpreter in Russian, he returned to Cambridge as a PhD student in 1956, and the following year he was appointed to a Lectureship at the School of Oriental and African Studies, University of London. In 1961, he took up a University Lectureship in General Linguistics in Cambridge and a Fellowship in Classics at Christ's College. From 1964 to 1976 he was Professor of General Linguistics at Edinburgh, and from 1976 to 1984 Professor of Linguistics at the University of Sussex. He has also held visiting appointments at several universities in the United States (including Indiana University, where he taught linguistics and worked on a machine-translation research project, in 1960–1 and in 1963) and at the University of Paris. He has lectured in many different countries.

He received a LittD in Linguistics at the University of Cambridge in 1987 and has been awarded honorary doctorates by the universities of Louvain, Reading, Edinburgh and Sussex. He is a Fellow of the British Academy and an Honorary Member of the Linguistics Society of America. He was knighted in 1987 for services to linguistics.

He was the first editor of the *Journal of Linguistics* (1965–9); and his publications (many of which have been translated into several languages) include *Structural Semantics* (1963), *Introduction to Theoretical Linguistics* (1968), *Language and Linguistics* (1981), *Language, Meaning and Context* (1981; 2nd edn, 1991) and *Natural Language and Universal Grammar* (1991). He is married, with two daughters and two grandchildren.

Modern Masters

Chomsky

THIRD EDITION

John Lyons

FontanaPress
An Imprint of HarperCollins*Publishers*

First issued in 1970 by Fontana,
an imprint of HarperCollins Publishers,
77–85 Fulham Palace Road,
Hammersmith, London W6 8JB

Second Edition published in 1977

This Third Edition first published by Fontana Press in 1991

9 8 7 6 5 4 3 2 1

Phototypeset by Intype, London
Printed and bound in Great Britain by
HarperCollins Book Manufacturing, Glasgow

Contents

Preface to the Third Edition

Unlike many scholars who have revolutionized their field of study while still young and have been recognized more widely, within a very short time, as 'masters of modern thought', Chomsky continues to be, at the age of sixty-two, as active and as productive as he was in his youth. His academic reputation stands as high today as it did twenty or twenty-five years ago. His current work in linguistics (with excursions into philosophy, psychology and related disciplines) no longer carries with it the shock of the new. But it is still regarded by specialists, even by those who disagree with him, as uniquely authoritative. And it is still, of course, controversial.

My main purpose in writing this book (as I said in the Preface to the First Edition) was to provide readers with enough of the historical and technical background for them to go on afterwards to Chomsky's own works. I did not, and do not, believe that it is possible to understand even Chomsky's less technical works or to appreciate the impact that his ideas have had in a number of different disciplines without going into some of the details of the systems of generative grammar that he has constructed. The fact that Chomsky himself was kind enough to read and comment upon the typescript of the first edition in advance means that it can be assumed to have given a reasonably fair and reliable account of his views at the time (1970). Wherever Chomsky did not express himself as being in agreement with what I had to say about matters of fact or about my interpretation of them, I made this clear in the text itself or in the notes that I added to the text. The first edition was widely, and for the most part favourably, reviewed.

Chomsky's thought has not changed fundamentally since at least the early 1960s. But it has been continuously refined and modified over the years, in a succession of books, articles, lectures and interviews addressed to readers and audiences of the most diverse backgrounds and interests. This presents his expositors and interpreters with a problem. If they try to take full account of all the changes of detail that have been introduced into the theory of generative grammar in the last thirty years, they will make it impossible for even the most assiduous and best-intentioned of non-specialists to follow the argument. If they limit themselves to Chomsky's most recent publications and adjust their selection of material and their terminology accordingly, the book that they produce will be of very restricted usefulness. For it is Chomsky's earlier work – his work of what we may now think of as the middle, or 'classical', period (from the mid-1960s into the early 1970s) – which has had the widest influence outside linguistics and which has provided the terminology which non-linguists have adopted and with which they still discuss the issues of philosophical and psychological significance which he first brought into prominence. Moreover, although Chomsky still contributes actively to linguistic research in his own chosen domain and, in that domain, as I have said, speaks with unique authority, the particular system of generative grammar with which he is currently associated is but one of many competing, broadly Chomskyan, systems; and it is one which only a minority of practising linguistics have espoused. There is a sense, therefore, in which even for linguists an introduction to Chomsky's work should concentrate on the earlier period. And yet one cannot, of course, neglect the very important and influential work that he has done in the last twenty years!

When I prepared, in 1977, the second (revised and enlarged) edition of the present work, the problem was by no means as acute as it is now. As a matter of principle, however, I left the first seven chapters almost unchanged (except for the correction of some misprints and minor errors). But I brought the Introduction up to date by adding a little material and changing a few phrases; and I inserted one or two footnotes drawing the reader's attention to the two new Appendices. I also added a new Chapter 8, on developments that had been taking place in the field of generative grammar between the late 1960s and the mid-1970s, and I made extensive additions to what then became Chapters 9–11.

In the first of the Appendices, I provided (for the benefit of students) a fairly technical account of the formalism upon which Chomsky based his system of generative grammar (of the 'classical' period) and, no less important, some cautionary comments about the complexity of the relationship between generative grammars and natural languages, on the one hand, and about some of the assumptions that Chomsky had built into the formalism, on the other. In the second, shorter, Appendix, I took the opportunity to correct what many reviewers and readers of the first edition of my book had taken to be a certain imbalance, not to say prejudice, in my presentation of Chomsky as a 'modern master'. I drew attention to the published version of Chomsky's *Logical Structure of Linguistic Theory* (1975), which made it clear that there may have been less difference than I thought (on the basis of his published work) between Chomsky's earlier and later views. At the same time, I said that, on the whole, I stood by my own assessment of the significance of Chomsky's work in linguistics and its relation to that of his predecessors. I also included in

Appendix 2 a reply to criticisms made by Dell Hymes in his long and informative review of the first edition of my book, recommending the review for the background information that it contained about American linguistics and American academic life and attitudes in the 1960s, when Chomsky emerged as a political thinker and activist.

In preparing this further revised, updated and enlarged edition I have now left the first eleven chapters unchanged (from the second edition): I have, however, made slight changes in the titles of Chapters 8 and 11. I have also left unchanged the two Appendices. But I have added a completely new Chapter 12, entitled 'The Chomskyan Revolution: a Progress Report (1991)', and I have completed revised and updated the Biographical Note, the Bibliography and the Suggestions for Further Reading.

It would have been impossible to cover in detail in a single short chapter the most recent developments in Chomsky's theory of grammar and in his own system of grammatical description (commonly referred to, rather unsatisfactorily, as 'Government-Binding Theory'). What I have attempted to do in Chapter 12 is to pick out what are generally agreed to be the most significant developments of the last decade or so, to relate them succinctly and non-technically to the ideas that Chomsky was expounding in the 'classical' period of the so-called 'standard theory' of transformational grammar and to comment critically upon them in the context or more general theoretical and empirical considerations. This is all the more important at the present time, it seems to me, in that it is very difficult even for well-trained linguists, let alone non-linguists, to see the wood for the trees and, among the trees, to pick out the genuinely new species from the large number of sports and hybrids that are now growing in the wood. Even the best of the currently available textbooks and introductions to generative grammar or to Chomsky's philosophy of linguistics fail to discuss his ideas from a sufficiently general point of view and tend to be historically unreliable. For convenience of reference, I have organized my comments in Chapter 12 under such headings as 'Chomsky's linguistics and Chomskyan linguistics', 'Generative grammar and "the generative enterprise" ', 'Plato's problem, and Chomsky's solution: genetic anamnesis', 'I-language and E-language', 'Deep structure', 'Modularity of mind and language', 'Modular (neurolinguistic) parallelism?', 'Universal grammar: principles and parameters; core and periphery', 'Languages and grammars: reductionism and the unity of science', 'Government-Binding Theory' and 'Rationalism, rationality and rationalization'. And in the new Suggestions for Further Reading I have given as much guidance as I could for different kinds of readers.

A final word now about Chomsky's political writings. As I said in the Preface to the Second Edition of my book, I had deliberately said very little about these, because I did not feel qualified (by nationality or experience) to do so. I also ventured the opinion that 'important though Chomsky's political ideas are in any portrayal of him as man, it is his theory of language that makes him a "master of modern thought" ', I still incline to the same opinion. It must be admitted, however, that Chomsky's publications in the field of political theory and political commentary have equalled, if not outnumbered, his publications on language in the last ten years. I have listed the more important and the more accessible of these in the Bibliography and have included in the Suggestions for Further Reading some guidance for those who are particularly interested in Chomsky's political views.

Cambridge, March 1991   J.L.

1 Introduction

Chomsky's position is not only unique within linguistics at the present time, but is probably unprecedented in the whole history of the subject. His first book, published in 1957, short and relatively non-technical though it was, revolutionized the scientific study of language; and for many years he has spoken with unrivalled authority on all aspects of grammatical theory. This is not to say, of course, that all linguists, or even the majority of them, have accepted the theory of transformational grammar that Chomsky put forward some twenty years ago in *Syntactic Structures*. They have not. There are at least as many recognizably different 'schools' of linguistics throughout the world as there were before the 'Chomskyan revolution'. But the 'transformationalist', or 'Chomskyan', school is not just one among many. Right or wrong, Chomsky's theory of grammar is undoubtedly the most dynamic and influential; and no linguist who wishes to keep abreast of current developments in his subject can afford to ignore Chomsky's theoretical pronouncements. Every other 'school' of linguistics at the present time tends to define its position in relation to Chomsky's views on particular issues.

However, it is not so much Chomsky's status and reputation among linguists that has made him a 'master of modern thought'. After all, theoretical linguistics is a rather esoteric subject, which few people had even heard of and still fewer knew anything about until very recently. If it is now more widely recognized as a branch of science which is worthwhile pursuing, not only for its own sake, but also for the contributions it can make to other disciplines, this is very largely due to Chomsky. More than a thousand university students and teachers are said to have attended his lectures on the philosophy of language and mind in the University of Oxford in the spring of 1969. Few of these could have had any previous contact with linguistics, but all of them presumably were convinced, or prepared to be convinced, that it was worth making the intellectual effort required to follow Chomsky's at times quite technical argument; and the lectures were widely reported in the national press.

Readers who are not already familiar with Chomsky's work may well be wondering at this point what possible connexion there might be between a field of study as specialized as transformational grammar and such better known and obviously important disciplines as psychology and philosophy. This is a question we shall be discussing in some detail in the later chapters of this book. But it may be worth while attempting a more general answer here.

It has often been suggested that man is most clearly distinguished from other animal species, not by the faculty of thought or intelligence, as the standard zoological label 'homo sapiens' might indicate, but by his capacity for language. Indeed, philosophers and psychologists have long debated whether thought in the proper sense of the term is conceivable except as 'embodied' in speech or writing. Whether or not this is so, it is obvious that language is of vital importance in every aspect of human activity and that, without language, all but the most rudimentary kind of communication would be impossible. Granted that language is essential to human life as we know it, it is only natural to ask what contribution the study of language can make to our understanding of human nature.

But what is language? This is a question that few people even think of asking. In one sense of course we all know what we mean by 'language'; and our use of the word in everyday conversation depends upon the fact that we all interpret it, as we interpret the other words we use, in the same or in a very similar way. There is, however, a difference between this kind of unreflecting and practical knowledge of what language is and the deeper or more systematic understanding that we should want to call 'scientific'. As we shall see in the following chapters, it is the aim of theoretical linguistics to give a scientific answer to the question 'What is language?' and, in doing so, to provide evidence that philosophers and psychologists can draw upon in their discussion of the relationship that holds between language and thought.

Chomsky's system of transformational grammar was developed, as we shall see, in order to give a mathematically precise description of some of the most striking features of language. Of particular importance in this connexion is the ability that children have to derive the structural regularities of their native language—its grammatical rules—from the utterances of their parents and others around them, and then to make use of the same regularities in the construction of utterances they have never heard before. Chomsky has argued, in several of his publications, that the general principles which determine the form of grammatical rules in particular languages, such as English, Turkish or Chinese, are to some considerable degree common to all human languages. Furthermore, he has claimed that the principles underlying the structure of language are so specific and so highly articulated that they must be regarded as being biologically determined; that is to say, as constituting part of what we call 'human nature' and as being genetically transmitted from parents to their children. If this is so, and if it is also the case, as Chomsky maintains, that transformational grammar is the best theory so far developed for the systematic description and explanation of the structure of human language, it is clear that an understanding of transformational grammar is essential for any philosopher, psychologist or biologist who wishes to take account of man's capacity for language.

The significance of Chomsky's work for disciplines other than linguistics derives primarily, then, from the acknowledged importance of language in all areas of human activity and from the peculiarly intimate relationship that is said to hold between the structure of language and the innate properties or operations of the mind. But language is not the only kind of complex 'behaviour' that human beings engage in; and there is at least a possibility that other forms of typically human activity (including perhaps certain aspects of what we call 'artistic creation') will also prove amenable to description within the framework of specially constructed mathematical systems analogous to, or even based upon, transformational grammar. There are many scholars working now in the social sciences and the humanities who believe that this is so. For them, Chomsky's formalization of grammatical theory serves as a model and a standard.

From what has been said in the last few paragraphs it will be clear that Chomsky's influence is now being felt in many different disciplines. So far, however, it is the study of language that has been most profoundly affected by the 'Chomskyan revolution'; and it is from current research on the grammatical structure of English and other languages that Chomsky draws most of his more general philosophical and psychological views. It is for this reason that we shall give so much attention in the present volume to the linguistic background of Chomsky's thought.

Chomsky's current fame and popularity is not due solely, or even mainly, to his work in linguistics and the effect that this is having on other disciplines. In the 1960s, he became widely known as one of the most outspoken and most articulate critics of American politics in Vietnam—a 'hero of the New Left', who risked imprisonment by refusing to pay half his taxes and gave support and encouragement to young men refusing to undertake military service in Vietnam. It is undoubtedly for his political writings and his political activity that Chomsky is now most famous, especially in the United States—for his condemnation of American 'imperialism' and of those academic advisers to the American Government who, posing as 'experts' in a field where there is no such thing as scientific expertise and where considera'ions of common morality should have prevailed, have been guilty of deceiving the public about the character of the war in Vietnam, American involvement in Cuba and other issues. Cho nsky's political writings continue to attract attention (*American Power and the New Mandarins, For Reasons of State, The Backroom Boys, At War with Asia, Peace in the Middle East?*); and he is still an active supporter of radical social change in the United States.

Although this book is mainly about Chomsky's views on language, it should perhaps be emphasized here that his theory of language and his political philosophy are by no means unconnected, as they might appear to be at first sight. As we shall see in the chapters which follow, Chomsky has long been an opponent of at least the more extreme form of behaviourist psychology—'radical behaviourism', according to which all human knowledge and belief, and all the 'patterns' of thought and action characteristic of man, can be explained as 'habits' built up by a process of 'conditioning', lengthier and more complex no doubt in its details, but not qualitatively different from the process by which rats in a psychological laboratory 'learn' to obtain food by pressing a bar in the cage in which they are housed. Chomsky's attack on radical behaviourism was first made in a long and well-documented review of B. F. Skinner's *Verbal Behavior* in 1959, in which he claimed that the behaviourists' impressive panoply of scientific terminology and statistics was no more than camouflage, covering up their inability to account for the fact that language simply is not a set of 'habits' and is radically different from animal communication. It is the same charge that Chomsky has made in his political writings against the sociologists, psychologists and other social scientists whose 'expert' advice is sought by governments: that they 'desperately attempt . . . to imitate the surface features of sciences that really have significant intellectual content', neglecting in this attempt all the fundamental problems with which they should be concerned and taking refuge in pragmatic and methodological trivialities. It is Chomsky's conviction that human beings are different from animals or machines and that this difference should be respected both in science and in government; and it is this conviction which underlies and unifies his politics, his linguistics and his philosophy.

Chomsky's message is familiar enough, and it will find an immediate response in all those who subscribe to a belief in the brotherhood of man and the dignity of human life. Only too often, however, the defence of these traditional values is left to scholars who by academic training are unfitted for the kind of argument which appeals to hard-headed 'pragmatists'. Chomsky cannot be written off quite so easily as a 'woolly-minded liberal'. He is as well read in the philosophy of science as his opponents are, and he can manipulate the conceptual and mathematical apparatus of the social sciences with equal ease. His arguments may be accepted or rejected: they cannot be ignored. And anyone who wishes to follow and evaluate these arguments must be prepared to meet Chomsky on his home ground: linguistics, or the scientific investigation of language. For Chomsky believes (as I said earlier) that the structure of language is determined by the structure of the human mind and that the universality of certain properties characteristic of language is evidence that at least this part of human nature is common to all members of the species, regardless of their race or class and their undoubted differences in intellect, personality and physical attributes. This belief is quite traditional (and Chomsky himself, we shall see, explicitly relates his views to those of the rationalist philosophers of the seventeenth and eighteenth centuries). What is new is the way in which Chomsky argues his case and the kind of evidence that he adduces in support of it.

It is appropriate, and symbolic of his position and influence, that the institution in which Chomsky carries out his research into the structure of language and the properties of the human mind should be that citadel of modern science, the Massachusetts Institute of Technology, but the views he expresses in summarizing his research should be those more characteristic of the humanities departments of a traditional university. The contradiction is only apparent. For Chomsky's work suggests that the conventional boundary that exists between 'arts' and 'science' can, and should, be abolished.

2 Modern Linguistics: Aims and Attitudes

For many readers of this book, and possibly the majority, linguistics will be a completely new subject. I will begin therefore by explaining, in very general terms, what linguistics is. We can then move on, in the next chapter, to consider those aspects of the subject which have been of particular importance in the formation of Chomsky's own thought.

Linguistics is commonly defined as the science of language. The word 'science' is crucial here, and in our discussion of Chomsky's work we shall be very much concerned with the implications of this term. For the moment, however, we may say that a *scientific* description is one that is carried out systematically on the basis of objectively verifiable observations and within the framework of some general theory appropriate to the data. It is often said that linguistics properly so called is of relatively recent origin and that the investigation of language as practised in Europe and America before the nineteenth century was subjective, speculative and unsystematic. Whether this sweeping condemnation of past linguistic research is historically justifiable is a question that we need not go into here. The important point to note is that linguistics as we know it today was developed in conscious opposition to the more traditional approaches to the study of language characteristic of earlier centuries. As we shall see, this deliberate break with the past was sharper and more definitive in America than it was in Europe. Nowhere was the rejection of traditional grammar more vehemently expressed than it was by the 'Bloomfieldian' school of linguistics, dominant in the

United States in the years following the Second World War—the school in which Chomsky was trained and against which, in due course, he reacted.

We will not discuss here all the characteristics of modern linguistics which distinguish it from traditional grammar, but only those that are relevant to the theme of this book. The first of these, which is often regarded as a direct consequence of the scientific status of linguistics, is its *autonomy*, or independence of other disciplines. Traditional grammar, which like so much else in Western culture originated in Greece of the fifth century B.C., has since its beginnings been intimately connected with philosophy and literary criticism. At various times either the literary or the philosophical influence has been predominant, but they have both been present to some degree in all periods and together they have shaped the attitudes and presuppositions with which scholars have for centuries approached the study of language. It is worth remembering also that these attitudes and presuppositions are now so pervasive and so deeply entrenched in our culture that not only the scholar trained in traditional grammar, but also the man in the street, tends to accept them without question. When the linguist claims 'autonomy' for his subject he is asking to be allowed to take a fresh and objective look at language without prior commitment to traditional ideas and without necessarily adopting the same point of view as philosophers, psychologists, literary critics or representatives of other disciplines. This does not mean that there is not, or should not be, any connexion between linguistics and other disciplines concerned with language. Indeed, as we shall see in the later chapters of this book, there is at the present time a remarkable convergence of interest among linguists, psychologists and philosophers. But the present rapprochement has come about as a consequence of the development of 'autonomous' linguistics; and it is linguistics (and more particularly the work of Chomsky) that has provided the inspiration for the alliance of the three disciplines.

Reference has been made above to the literary bias of traditional grammar. That bias, which derived from the fact that the earliest Western grammarians were mainly concerned with the preservation and interpretation of the texts of the classical Greek writers, manifested itself in various ways. Scholars tended to concentrate upon the written language and to ignore the difference between speech and writing. Although it was not entirely neglected by traditional grammarians, the spoken language was only too often regarded as an imperfect copy of the written language. By contrast, most linguists today take it as axiomatic that speech is primary, and that the written language is secondary and derived from it: in other words, that sound (and more particularly the range of sounds that can be produced by the so-called 'speech organs') is the *medium* in which language is 'embodied' and that written languages result from the transference of speech to a secondary, visual medium. Every known language existed first as a spoken language, and thousands of languages have never, or only very recently, been committed to writing. Furthermore, children acquire a command of the spoken language before they learn to read and write, and they do so spontaneously, without any training; whereas reading and writing are special skills, in which the child is normally given special instruction based upon his prior knowledge of the corresponding spoken language. Although nothing will be said about phonetics in this book and we shall cite all the illustrative material in its normal written form, it must be constantly borne in mind that we are mainly concerned with the spoken language.

It should be emphasized that adherence to the principle of the primacy of speech over writing does not imply a lack of interest in, still less a contempt for, written languages. Nor does it necessarily imply (although many linguists, it must be admitted, have failed to make this qualification) that the written language is wholly derivative. The conditions in which it is used are different from the conditions in which the spoken language is employed: since there is no direct face-to-face confrontation of speaker and writer, information that is normally carried by the gestures and facial expressions accompanying speech and by a complex of other features that we may subsume here under the impressionistic term 'tone of voice' must be conveyed in writing, if at all, by other means. The conventions of punctuation and the practice of italicizing words for emphasis are incapable of representing all the significant variations of pitch and stress that are present in spoken utterances. There will always be some degree of independence, therefore, in the written language. In many instances, as in the case of English, the difference between the spoken and the written forms of the 'same' language has been increased by the conservatism of the orthographic conventions, established some centuries ago and maintained to this day despite the changes that have since taken place in the pronunciation of the language in different parts of the world.

One further point should be made in this connexion. It is often said that none of the 'speech organs' has as its sole, or indeed its primary, function the part it plays in the production of speech—that the lungs are used in breathing, the teeth in the mastication of food, and so on—and that the 'speech organs' do not constitute a physiological system in the normal sense of this term. It should not be forgotten, however, that the faculty of speech is as characteristic of human beings, and as natural and important to them, as walking on two feet, or even eating. Whatever may have been the cause of this, in some remote period of man's evolutionary development, it is a fact to be accounted for that all human beings make use of the same physiological 'apparatus' in speech. It is at least conceivable that they are genetically 'programmed' to do so. The relevance of this point to the ideas of Chomsky will become clear in a later chapter.

Traditional grammarians were concerned more or less exclusively with the standard, literary language; and they tended to disregard, or to condemn as 'incorrect', more informal or colloquial usage both in speech and writing. Also, they often failed to realize that the standard language is, from a historical point of view, merely that regional or social dialect which has acquired prestige and become the instrument of administration, education and literature. Because of its more widespread use, by a greater number of people and for a wider range of activities, the standard language may have a richer vocabulary than any of the co-existent 'substandard' dialects, but it is not intrinsically more correct. The distinction between 'language' and 'dialect' is commonly drawn on political grounds. There is less difference between Swedish, Danish and Norwegian, for example, which are usually referred to as distinct 'languages', than there is between many of the so-called 'dialects' of Chinese. The important point is that the regional or social dialects of a language, say English, are no less systematic than the standard language and should not be described as imperfect approximations to it. This point is worth emphasizing, since many people are inclined to believe that it is only the standard language taught in school that is subject to systematic description. From a purely linguistic point of view all the dialects of English are worthy of equal consideration.

Traditional grammar was developed on the basis of Greek and Latin, and it was subsequently applied, with minimal modifications and often uncritically, to the description of a large number of other languages. But there are many languages which, in certain respects at least, are strikingly different in structure from Latin, Greek and the more familiar languages of Europe and Asia. One of the principal aims of modern linguistics has therefore been to construct a theory of grammar which is more *general* than the traditional theory—one that is appropriate for the description of all human languages and is not biased in favour of those languages which are similar in their grammatical structure to Greek and Latin.

One should perhaps mention at this point that linguistics provides no support for those who believe that there is a fundamental difference between 'civilized' and 'primitive' languages. The vocabulary of a language will, of course, reflect the characteristic pursuits and interests of the society which uses it. One of the major world languages, like English, French or Russian, will have a large number of words relating to modern science and technology which will have no equivalent in the language of some 'underdeveloped' people. Conversely, however, there will be many words in the language of, let us say, some remote and backward tribe in New Guinea or South America which cannot be translated satisfactorily into English, French or Russian, because they are words which refer to objects, flora, fauna or customs unfamiliar in Western culture. The vocabulary of one language cannot be described as richer or poorer than the vocabulary of some other language in any absolute sense; every language has a sufficiently rich vocabulary for the expression of all the distinctions that are important in the society using it. We cannot therefore say, from this point of view, that one language is more 'primitive' or more 'advanced' than another. The point is even clearer with respect to the grammatical structure of languages. Differences there are between any particular 'primitive' language and any particular 'civilized' language. But these are no greater on the average than the differences between any random pair of 'primitive' languages and any random pair of 'civilized' languages. So-called 'primitive' languages are no less systematic, and are neither structurally simpler nor structurally more complex, than are the languages spoken by more 'civilized' peoples. This is an important point. All human societies of which we have knowledge speak languages of roughly equal complexity; and the differences of grammatical structure that we do find between languages throughout the world are such that they cannot be correlated with the cultural development of the people speaking them and cannot be used as evidence for the construction of an evolutionary theory of human language. The uniqueness of language to the human species and the fact that no languages seem to be more primitive than any others, or closer to systems of animal communication, are points that have been given particular prominence in Chomsky's more recent work.

What are the features of human languages, then, which distinguish them from the systems of communication used by other species? This question will occupy us in greater detail later. But two particularly striking properties of human language may be mentioned here. The first of these is *duality of structure*. Every language so far investigated (and we may confidently assume that this will also be true of any language yet to come to the attention of linguists) has two *levels* of grammatical structure. There is, first of all, what we may call the 'primary', or *syntactic*, level of analysis, at which sentences can be represented as combinations of meaningful units: we will call these *words* (and gloss over the fact that not all the minimal syntactic units in all languages are words in the usual sense of this term). And there is also a 'secondary', or *phonological*, level, at which sentences can be represented as combinations of units which are themselves without meaning and serve for the identification of the 'primary' units. The 'secondary' units of language are sounds, or *phonemes* (to use a more technical term). If we take as an example the sentence *He went to London* (and, purely for the purpose of exposition, make the simplifying assumption that each letter represents one and only one phoneme), we can say that the sentence is composed of four words and that the first of these 'primary' units is identified by the combination of the 'secondary' units *h* and *e* (in that order), the second of the 'primary' units by the combination *w*, *e*, *n* and *t*, and so on. It should be noted that there is nothing that is particularly novel in the principle of duality of structure, as I have described it here. It was recognized in traditional grammar. But one point should be stressed. Although I have said that the 'primary' units, unlike the 'secondary' units, convey meaning (and this, in general at least, is true), it is not the defining characteristic of words that they have meaning. As we shall see, it is possible to analyse language at the syntactic level without reference to whether the units established at this level have meaning or not; and there are some words at least that have no meaning (e.g. *to* in *I want to go home*). We must be careful, therefore, not to describe the duality of structure that is being referred to here in terms of the association of sound and meaning.

Granted that every language manifests the property of duality of structure, we may expect that the description, or *grammar*, of every language will consist of three interrelated parts. The part which accounts for the regularities governing the combination of words is *syntax*. It is by means of syntactic rules, for example, that we specify that *He went to London*, by contrast with **Went to he London*, is a grammatical sentence. (The asterisk prefixed here to *Went to he London* indicates that this sequence of words is ungrammatical. We shall use this standard notational convention throughout.) That part of grammar which describes the meaning of words and sentences is *semantics*. And the part of grammar that deals with the sounds and their permissible combinations (e.g. the fact that *went*, but not *twne, is a possible English word) is *phonology*.

At this point, I should perhaps warn the reader that there is a certain amount of terminological confusion and inconsistency in linguistics. In the previous paragraph, I have introduced the term 'grammar' to refer to the whole of the systematic description of language, including both phonology and semantics, as well as syntax. This is the sense in which Chomsky uses the word 'grammar' in his more recent writings; and I will adhere to this usage throughout the present book, except in those sections where I explicitly draw the reader's attention to the fact that I am employing the term in a somewhat narrower sense. Many linguists describe as 'grammar' what we are calling 'syntax' and give a correspondingly restricted interpretation to 'syntax' (opposing it to 'morphology'). There are certain points of substance involved in the choice of terminology. But we need not go into these in this brief, and necessarily somewhat superficial, account of the aims and attitudes of modern linguistics. In this book we shall be mainly concerned with the theory of syntax, since this is the field where Chomsky has made his major contribution to the more technical side of linguistics.

The second general property of human language to be mentioned here is its *creativity* (or 'open-endedness'). By this is meant the capacity that all native speakers of a language have to produce and understand an indefinitely large number of sentences that they have never heard before, and which may indeed never have been uttered before by anyone. The native speaker's 'creative' command of his language, it should be noted, is in normal circumstances unconscious and unreflecting. He is generally unaware of applying any grammatical rules or systematic principles of formation when he constructs either new sentences or sentences he has previously encountered. And yet the sentences that he utters will generally be accepted by other native speakers of the language as correct and will be understood by them. (We must make allowance, as we shall see later, for a certain amount of error—hence the qualification implied by 'generally' in the previous sentence—but this does not affect the principle that is under discussion here.) As far as we know, this creative command of language is unique to human beings: it is *species-specific*. Systems of communication employed by other species than man are not 'open-ended' in the same way. Most of them are 'closed', in the sense that they admit of the transmission of only a finite and relatively small set of distinct 'messages', the 'meaning' of which is fixed (rather as the messages that one may send by means of the international telegraphic code are determined in advance), and it is not possible for the animal to vary these and construct new 'sentences'. It is true that certain forms of animal communication (for example, the signalling 'code' that is used by bees to indicate the direction and distance of a source of honey) incorporate the possibility of making new 'sentences' by systematically varying the 'signal'. But in all instances there is a simple correlation between the two variables—the 'signal' and its 'meaning'. For example, as K. von Frisch discovered in his celebrated work on the subject, it is by the intensity of their body movements that bees signal the distance of the source of honey from the hive; and this parameter of 'intensity' is subject to infinite (and continuous) variation. This kind of continuous variation is also found in human language: for instance, one can vary the 'intensity' with which the

word *very* is pronounced in a sentence like *He was very rich.*
But it is not this feature that is being referred to when one
talks of the creativity of human language. It is the ability
to construct new combinations of discrete units, rather
than simply to vary continuously one of the parameters
of the signalling system in accordance with a correspondingly continuous variation in the 'meaning' of the
'messages'. As we shall see in due course, Chomsky considers that the creativity of language is one of its most
characteristic features and one that poses a particularly
challenging problem for the development of a psychological theory of language use and language acquisition.

We have now introduced a number of the more important general principles which we shall take for granted,
even when we do not draw explicitly upon them, in
the following chapters. It may be helpful if I summarize
them here. Modern linguistics claims to be more scientific
and more general than traditional grammar. It assumes
that the 'natural' medium for the expression of language
is sound (as produced by the speech organs) and that
written languages are derived from speech. The grammar of any language will comprise at least the following
three interrelated parts: syntax, semantics and phonology; and it should, among other things, account for the
ability native speakers have to produce and understand
an indefinitely large number of 'new' sentences. What has
been said in this chapter (due allowance being made for
differences of emphasis) is neutral with respect to the
theoretical differences which divide one school of linguistics from another at the present time. We now turn
to a discussion of the 'Bloomfieldian' (and 'post-Bloomfieldian' or 'neo-Bloomfieldian') school, in which, as I
have said, Chomsky received his first training in linguistics.

3 The 'Bloomfieldians'

Linguistics in the United States has been very strongly influenced in this century by the necessity of describing as many as possible of the hundreds of previously unrecorded languages existing in North America. Since the publication of the *Handbook of American Indian Languages* in 1911, almost every linguist in America has, until very recently, included some original research on one or more of the American Indian languages as part of his training; and many of the features characteristic of American linguistics can be, in part at least, explained by this fact.

First of all, the experience of working with the indigenous languages of North America has given to a good deal of American linguistic theory its practical character and its sense of urgency. Many of these languages were spoken by very few people and would soon die out. Unless they were recorded and described before this happened, they would become for ever inaccessible for investigation. In these circumstances, it is not surprising that American linguists have given considerable attention to the development of what are called 'field methods'—techniques for the recording and analysis of languages which the linguist himself could not speak and which had not previously been committed to writing. There were no doubt other relevant factors (in particular, a certain interpretation of scientific rigour and objectivity), but the fact that linguistic theory was for many American scholars no more than a source of techniques for the description of previously unrecorded languages was at least partly to blame for what Chomsky was to condemn later as its concern with 'discovery procedures'.

Franz Boas (1858–1942), who wrote the Introduction to the *Handbook of American Indian Languages* (1911) and gave there an outline of the method he had himself worked out for their systematic description, had come to the conclusion that the range of variation to be found in human languages was far greater than one might suppose if one based one's generalizations upon the grammatical descriptions of the more familiar languages of Europe. He found that earlier descriptions of the indigenous and 'exotic' languages of the North American sub-continent had been distorted by the failure of linguists to appreciate the potential diversity of languages and their attempt to impose the traditional grammatical categories of description upon languages for which they were wholly inappropriate; and he pointed out that none of these traditional categories was necessarily present in all languages. To use two of Boas's examples: The distinction between singular and plural is not obligatory in Kwakiutl, so that 'There is a house over there' and 'There are some houses over there' are not necessarily distinguished; and the distinction between present and past tense is not made in Eskimo ('The man is coming' *vs.* 'The man was coming'). Boas also gave examples of the converse situation, grammatical distinctions which were obligatory in certain American Indian languages, but which were given no place at all in traditional grammatical theory: 'Some of the Siouan languages classify nouns by means of articles, and strict distinctions are made between animate moving and animate at rest, animate long, inanimate high and inanimate collective objects.' Examples like this were used by Boas to support the view that every language has its own unique grammatical structure and that it is the task of the linguist to discover for each language the categories of description appropriate to it.

This view may be called 'structuralist' (in one of the many senses of a rather fashionable term).

It should be stressed that the 'structuralist' approach was by no means confined to Boas and his successors in America. Similar views had been expressed by Wilhelm von Humboldt (1767–1835); and they have also been expressed by European contemporaries of Boas, who were experienced, as he was, in the description of 'exotic' languages. 'Structuralism' has in fact been the rallying cry of many different twentieth-century schools of linguistics.

It would be universally agreed that the two greatest and most influential figures in American linguistics after Boas, in the period from the foundation of the Linguistic Society of America in 1924 to the beginning of the Second World War were Edward Sapir (1884–1939) and Leonard Bloomfield (1887–1949). They were very different in temperament, in the range of their interests, in philosophical persuasion and in the nature of the influence they exerted. Sapir had been trained in Germanic philology; but, while he was still a student, he came under the influence of Boas and turned to the study of American Indian languages. Like Boas, and like many American scholars down to the present day, he was an anthropologist as well as a linguist, and published widely in both fields. But Sapir's interests and professional competence extended beyond anthropology and linguistics, into literature, music and art. He published a large number of articles and reviews (dealing with very many different languages), but only one book. This was a relatively short work, called *Language*, which appeared in 1921 and was addressed to the general reader. It is strikingly different, both in content and in style, from Bloomfield's *Language*, published twelve years later.

Bloomfield, as we shall see, did more than anyone else to make linguistics autonomous and scientific (as he understood the term 'scientific'); and in the pursuit of this aim he was prepared to restrict the scope of the subject, excluding from consideration many aspects of language which, he believed, could not yet be treated with sufficient precision and rigour. Sapir, as one might expect from his other interests, takes a more 'humanistic' view of language. He lays great stress on its cultural importance, on the priority of reason over volition and emotion (emphasizing what he calls 'the prevailing cognitive character' of language) and on the fact that language is 'purely human' and 'non-instinctive'. Sapir's *Language*, though far shorter, is much more general and is easier to read (at a superficial level at least) than Bloomfield's. It is packed with brilliant analogies and suggestive comparisons, but Sapir's refusal to neglect any of the multifarious aspects of language gives to many of his theoretical statements, it must be admitted, an aura of vagueness that is absent from Bloomfield's book. Sapir's work has continued to hold the attention of linguists down to the present day. But there has never been a 'Sapirian' school in the sense in which there has been, and still is, a 'Bloomfieldian' school of linguistics in America. It is not surprising that this should be so. We shall say no more about Sapir, except to point out that many of the attitudes towards language that Sapir held are now held by Chomsky, although Chomsky's ideas have been developed in the 'Bloomfieldian' tradition of 'autonomous' linguistics.

As Bloomfield understood the term 'scientific' (and this was a fairly common interpretation at the time), it implied the deliberate rejection of all data that were not directly observable or physically measurable. J. B. Watson, founder of the so-called 'behaviourist' approach in psychology, took the same view of the aims and methodology of science. According to Watson and his followers, psychologists had no need to postulate the existence of the mind or of anything else that was not observable, in order to explain those activities and capacities of human beings that were traditionally described as 'mental' or 'rational'. The behaviour of any organism, from an amoeba to a human being, was to be described and explained in terms of the organism's *responses* to the *stimuli* presented by features of the environment. It was assumed that the organism's learning of these responses could be explained satisfactorily by means of the familiar laws of physics and chemistry, in much the same way as one might explain how a thermostat 'learns' to respond to changes in temperature and to switch a furnace on or off.[1] Speech was but one among a number of forms of overt, or directly observable, behaviour characteristic of human beings; and thought was merely inaudible speech ('talking with concealed musculature', as Watson put it). Since inaudible speech could be made audible, when necessary, thought was in principle a form of observable behaviour.

When Bloomfield came to write his monumental book *Language*, he explicitly adopted behaviourism as a framework for linguistic description. (He had no less explicitly declared his adherence to the 'mentalistic' psychology of Wundt in his earlier work, *An Introduction to the Study of Language*, published in 1914.) In the second chapter of *Language*, he went on to claim that, although we could, in principle, foretell whether a certain stimulus would cause someone to speak and, if so, exactly what he would say, in practice we could make the prediction 'only if we

1. John Marshall has informed me that it is debatable whether the early behaviourists held such an extreme view as this. He suggests that Bloomfield's behaviourism was more radical than that of many of the psychologists who influenced him because he was himself a 'convert' from mentalism. For a discussion of the historical background from this point of view the reader is referred to Marshall's review of Esper's, *Mentalism and Objectivism in Linguistics* (see Bibliography).

knew the exact structure of his body at the moment'
(p. 33). The meaning of a linguistic form was defined as
'the practical events' with which the form 'is connected'
(p. 27) and, in a later chapter, as 'the situation in which
the speaker utters it and the response which it calls forth
in the hearer' (p. 139). As an example of a simple, but
presumably typical, situation in which language might
be used, Bloomfield suggests the following: Jack and Jill
are walking down a lane; Jill sees an apple on a tree and,
being hungry, asks Jack to get it for her; he climbs the
tree and gives her the apple; and she eats it. This is the
way in which we would normally describe the events that
take place. A behaviouristic account would run somewhat differently: Jill's being hungry ('that is, some of her
muscles were contracting, and some fluids were being
secreted, especially in her stomach') and her seeing the
apple (that is, light waves reflected from the apple
reached her eyes) constitute the stimulus. The more
direct response to this stimulus would be for Jill to climb
the tree and get the apple herself. Instead, she makes a
'substitute response' in the form of a particular sequence
of noises with her speech organs; and this acts as a
'substitute stimulus' for Jack, causing him to act as he
might have done if he himself had been hungry and had
seen the apple. This behaviouristic analysis of the situation obviously leaves a lot to be explained, but we will
not stop to discuss this question at this point. Bloomfield's fable will give the reader some idea of the way in
which language was held to operate in practical situations as a substitute for other kinds of non-symbolic
behaviour; and this is sufficient for our present purpose.

Bloomfield's commitment to behaviourism had no ap-
preciable effect upon syntax or phonology in his own
work or in that of his followers (except in so far as it
fostered the development of an 'empiricist' methodology:
we shall come to this in due course). Bloomfield himself

made reference to the behaviourist point of view only when he was dealing with meaning; and what he had to say on this topic was not calculated to inspire his followers with the desire to set about the construction of a comprehensive theory of semantics. It was Bloomfield's view that the analysis of meaning was 'the weak point in language study' and that it would continue to be so 'until human knowledge advances very far beyond its present state' (p. 140). The reason for his pessimism lay in his conviction that a precise definition of the meaning of words presupposes a complete 'scientific' description of the objects, states, processes, etc., to which they refer (i.e. for which they operate as 'substitutes'). For a small number of words (the names of plants, animals, various natural substances, etc.), we were already in a position to give a reasonably precise definition by means of the technical terms of the relevant branch of science (botany, zoology, chemistry, etc.). But for the vast majority of words (Bloomfield gives examples like *love* and *hate*) this was not so. Bloomfield's attitude could not but discourage linguists from the study of meaning; and neither he nor his followers made any positive contribution whatsoever to the theory or practice of semantics. In fact, for almost thirty years after the publication of his book the study of meaning was wholly neglected by the 'Bloomfieldian' school, and was frequently defined to be outside linguistics properly so called.

The Bloomfieldian attitude towards meaning, though stultifying as far as any progress in semantics is concerned, was not wholly detrimental to the development of other branches of linguistic theory. Bloomfield himself never suggested that it was possible to describe the syntax and phonology of a language in total ignorance of the meaning of words and sentences (although there can be little doubt that he would have thought this very desirable, if it were possible). His view was that for phonological and syntactic analysis, it was necessary to know 'whether two uttered forms were "the same" or "different" ', but that for this purpose all that was necessary was a rough and ready account of the meaning of words and not a full scientific description. Semantic considerations were strictly subordinated to the task of identifying the units of phonology and syntax and were not involved at all in the specification of the rules or principles governing their permissible combinations. This part of the grammar was to be a purely *formal* study, independent of semantics.

Bloomfield's followers carried even further than he did the attempt to formulate the principles of phonological and syntactic analysis without reference to meaning. This effort reached its culmination in the work of Zellig Harris, notably in his *Methods in Structural Linguistics*, first published in 1951, though completed some years before. Harris's work also constitutes the most ambitious and the most rigorous attempt that has yet been made to establish what Chomsky was later to describe as a set of 'discovery procedures' for grammatical description.

Now Chomsky was one of Harris's pupils, and later one of his collaborators and colleagues, and his earliest publications are very similar in spirit to those of Harris. By 1957, when Chomsky's first book, *Syntactic Structures*, was published, he had already moved away, as we shall see, from the position that Harris and the other Bloomfieldians had adopted on the question of 'discovery procedures'. But he continued to maintain that the phonology and syntax of a language could, and should, be described as a purely formal system without reference to semantic considerations. Language was an instrument for the expression of meaning: it was both possible and desirable to describe this instrument, in the first instance at least, without drawing upon one's knowledge of the use to which it was put. Semantics was part of the description of the use of language; it was secondary to and dependent upon syntax, and outside linguistics proper. In recent years, Chomsky has become increasingly critical of 'Bloomfieldian' linguistics and has abandoned many of the assumptions he originally held. It is worth emphasizing therefore, not only that his earlier views were formed in the 'Bloomfieldian' school, but also that he could hardly have made the technical advances he did make in linguistics, if the ground had not been prepared for him by such scholars as Harris.[2]

2. My account of the earlier history of American linguistics, and of Chomsky's 'Bloomfieldian' background, has been criticized in reviews of the first edition of this book. I have responded to this criticism by adding a short Appendix, which I draw to the reader's attention at this point.

4   The Goals of Linguistic Theory

Before we move on to consider Chomsky's more technical contributions to linguistics, it will be as well to
introduce and explain the motives and methodological
assumptions which underlie his work. We shall concentrate mainly in this chapter upon the account that
Chomsky himself gives in his short but epoch-making
book, *Syntactic Structures*, published in 1957. As we shall
see in due course, he takes a more comprehensive view
of the scope of linguistics in his later works. Chapter 6 of
Syntactic Structures bears the title 'On the goals of linguistic theory', which I have borrowed for my own chapter.

As I have already said, Chomsky's general views on
linguistic theory as presented in *Syntactic Structures* are in
most respects the same as those held by other members of
the Bloomfieldian school, and notably by Zellig Harris.
In particular, it may be noted that there is no hint, at
this period, of the 'rationalism' that is so characteristic a
feature of Chomsky's more recent writing. His acknowledgement of the influence of the 'empiricist' philosophers, Goodman and Quine, would suggest that he
shared their views; but there is no general discussion, in
Syntactic Structures, of the philosophical and psychological
implications of grammar.

However, there are one or two points which sharply
distinguish even Chomsky's earlier work from that of
Harris and the other Bloomfieldians. In Chapter 2, I
mentioned that Chomsky lays great stress on the
creativity (or 'open-endedness') of human language and
claims that the theory of grammar should reflect the
ability that all fluent speakers of a language possess to

produce and understand sentences which they have never heard before. As Chomsky came to realize later, earlier scholars, including Wilhelm von Humboldt and Ferdinand de Saussure (1857–1913), had also insisted upon the importance of this property of creativity. Actually, it had been taken for granted, and occasionally mentioned explicitly, since the very beginnings of Western linguistic theory in the ancient world. But it had been neglected, if not denied, in Bloomfieldian formulations of the aims of linguistic theory. The reason for this seems to have been that the Bloomfieldians, in common with many other twentieth-century schools of linguistics, were very conscious of the need to distinguish clearly between *descriptive* and *prescriptive* (or *normative*) grammar: between the description of the rules that are actually followed by native speakers and the prescription of rules which, in the opinion of the grammarian, they ought to follow, in order to speak 'correctly'. There are many examples of prescriptive rules set up by grammarians which have no basis in the normal usage of native speakers of English. (One such instance is the rule which says that *It is I*, rather than the more usual *It's me*, is 'correct' English.) So concerned were the Bloomfieldians (and various other 'schools') with asserting the status of linguistics as a descriptive science that they made it a point of principle not to venture any judgements about the grammaticality, or 'correctness', of sentences, unless these sentences had been attested in the usage of native speakers and included in the corpus of material which formed the basis of the grammatical description.

Chomsky insisted that the vast majority of the sentences in any representative corpus of recorded utterances would be 'new' sentences, in the sense that they would occur once, and once only; and that this would remain true, however long we went on recording utterances made by native speakers. The English language, like all the natural languages, consists of an indefinitely large number of sentences, only a small fraction of which have ever been uttered or will ever be uttered. The grammatical description of English may be based upon a corpus of actually attested utterances, but it will describe these, and classify them as 'grammatical', only incidentally as it were, by 'projecting' them on to the indefinitely large set of sentences which constitutes the language. Using Chomsky's terminology, we will say that the grammar *generates* (and thereby defines as 'grammatical') all the sentences of the language and does not distinguish between those that have been attested and those that have not.

The distinction that Chomsky draws in *Syntactic Structures* between the sentences generated by the grammar (the *language*) and a sample of the utterances produced, in normal conditions of use, by native speakers (the *corpus*) he draws in his later writings in terms of the notions of *competence* and *performance*. This terminological change is symptomatic of the evolution in Chomsky's thought from empiricism to rationalism, which has already been mentioned and will be discussed more fully later. In his later works, though not in *Syntactic Structures*, he stresses the fact that many of the utterances produced by native speakers (samples of their 'performance') will, for various reasons, be ungrammatical. These reasons have to do with such linguistically irrelevant factors as lapses of memory or attention and malfunctions of the psychological mechanisms underlying speech. Given that this is so, it follows that the linguist cannot take the corpus of attested utterances at its face value, as part of the language to be generated by the grammar. He must *idealize* the 'raw data' to some degree and eliminate from the corpus all those utterances which the native speaker would recognize, by virtue of his 'competence,' as ungrammatical. At first sight, it might appear that Chomsky is here guilty of the confusion between description and prescription that was so common in traditional grammar. But this is not so. The view that all the utterances of a native speaker of a language are equally correct, and are proved to be so by the sole fact of their having been uttered, although it is a view that has often been maintained by linguists of an empiricist bent, is in the last resort, untenable. And Chomsky is clearly right to claim for linguistics the same right to disregard some of the 'raw data' as is accepted as normal in other sciences. There are, of course, serious problems, both practical and theoretical, involved in deciding what constitute extraneous or linguistically irrelevant factors; and it may well be that, in practice, the 'idealization' of the data advocated by Chomsky does tend to introduce some of the normative considerations that marred much of traditional grammar. But this does not affect the general principle.

A further and related difference between Chomsky's earlier and later view of the 'goals of linguistics' has to do with the role he assigns to the *intuitions*, or judgements, of native speakers. In *Syntactic Structures* he says that the sentences generated by the grammar should be 'acceptable to the native speaker' (pp. 49–50); and he considers that it is a point in favour of the kind of grammar he develops that it also accounts for the 'intuitions' of native speakers with respect to the way certain sentences are recognized as equivalent or ambiguous. But the intuitions of the native speaker are presented as independent evidence, and their explanation is regarded as being secondary to the principal task of generating the sentences of the language. In his later work, Chomsky includes the intuitions of the speakers of a language as part of the data to be accounted for by the grammar. Furthermore, he now seems to place more reliance upon the validity and reliability of these intuitions than he did earlier, when he was much concerned with the need to test them by means of satisfactory 'operational' techniques.

As we saw in the previous chapter, American linguistics in the 'Bloomfieldian' period tended to be very 'procedural' in orientation. Questions of theory were reformulated as questions of method ('How should one go about the practical task of analysing a language?'); and it was commonly assumed that it should be possible to develop a set of procedures which, when applied to a corpus of material in an unknown language (or a language treated as if it were unknown to the linguist), would yield the correct grammatical analysis of the language of which the corpus was a representative sample. One of the main points argued by Chomsky in *Syntactic Structures* is that this is an unnecessary, and indeed harmful, assumption: 'a linguistic theory should not be identified with a manual of useful procedures, nor should it be expected to provide mechanical procedures for the discovery of grammars' (p. 55, fn. 6). The means by which a linguist arrives, in practice, at one analysis rather than another might include 'intuition, guess work, all sorts of partial methodological hints, reliance on past experience, etc.' (p. 56). What counts is the result; and this can be presented and justified without reference to the procedures that have been followed to achieve it. This does not mean that there is no point in trying to develop heuristic techniques for the description of languages, but simply—to put it crudely—that the proof of the pudding is in the eating. Just as the proof of a mathematical theorem can be checked without taking account of the way in which the person constructing the proof happened to hit upon the relevant intermediate propositions, so it should be with respect to grammatical analysis. As Chomsky says, the point would be granted immediately in the physical sciences, and there is no need for linguistics to set its sights higher than they do; especially as no linguist has yet come anywhere near formulating any satisfactory *discovery procedures*.

Linguistic theory should be concerned then with the justification of grammars. Chomsky goes on to consider the possibility of formulating criteria for deciding whether a particular grammar is the best one possible for the data. He concludes that even this goal—the formulation of a *decision procedure*—is too ambitious. The most that can be expected is that linguistic theory should provide criteria (an *evaluation procedure*) for choosing between alternative grammars. In other words, we cannot hope to say whether a particular description of the data is correct, in any absolute sense, but only that it is more correct than some alternative description of the same data.

Chomsky's distinction between decision procedures and evaluation procedures has caused a lot of misunderstanding and unnecessary controversy. After all no physicist would say that Einstein's Theory of Relativity, for example, gives the best possible explanation of the data it covers, but only that it is better than the alternative theory, based on Newtonian physics, which it supplanted. Once again, why should linguistics set its sights higher than other sciences do? It is sometimes said that Chomsky's formulation of the goals of linguistic theory in terms of the comparison of alternative grammars glosses over the fact that for many languages we do not possess even a partial grammar and for no language do we have a grammar that is anywhere near being complete. This is indeed a fact. But the conclusion, that it is premature in these circumstances to talk of comparing grammars does not follow. The construction of a set of grammatical rules involves the linguist in making decisions to handle the data in one way rather than another. Even if the rules describe only some small part of the data, there must be, whether explicit or implicit, a comparison of alternatives. It is the task of linguistic theory, says Chomsky, to make the alternatives explicit and to formulate general principles for deciding between them.

One further point should be made. Although Chomsky is, in one sense, proposing that linguistic theory should, in renouncing the 'Bloomfieldian' quest for 'discovery procedures', set itself a more modest goal than previously, there is a sense also in which his theoretical proposals are incomparably more ambitious than those of his predecessors. Some years before the publication of *Syntactic Structures*, in his little-known paper on 'Systems of syntactic analysis', Chomsky had tried to formulate with mathematical precision some of the procedures of grammatical analysis outlined in Harris's *Methods in Structural Linguistics*. He was convinced by this experience, and by his examination of other 'careful proposals for the development of linguistic theory', that the works in question, though apparently concerned with the specification of discovery procedures, in fact yielded 'no more than evaluation procedures for grammars' (*Syntactic Structures*, p. 52). Chomsky's most original, and probably his most enduring, contribution to linguistics is the mathematical rigour and precision with which he formalized the properties of alternative systems of grammatical description. A fuller consideration of this topic must wait for the following chapters. Here we will mention only one or two more general points.

At the very beginning of *Syntactic Structures*, Chomsky talks of a grammar as 'a device of some sort for producing the sentences of the language under analysis'. Chomsky's use of words like 'device' and 'produce' in this context has misled many readers into thinking that he conceives of the grammar of a language in terms of some electronic or mechanical model—some piece of 'hardware'—which replicates the behaviour of the speaker of a language when he utters a sentence. It should be emphasized that he employed these terms because the particular branch of mathematics that he drew upon in his formalization of grammar also uses such terms as 'device', or even 'machine', in a perfectly abstract way without reference to the physical properties of any actual model that might implement the abstract 'device'. This point will be come clearer in the next chapter.

It is unfortunate, however, that Chomsky used the word 'produce' in the passage just cited. It almost inevitably suggests that the grammatical structure of the language is being described from the point of view of the speaker rather than the listener; that the grammar describes the production, and not the reception, of speech. There is a sense, as we shall see, in which a grammar of the kind developed by Chomsky does 'produce' sentences by the application of a sequence of rules. But Chomsky has continually warned us against identifying the 'production' of sentences within the grammar with the production of sentences by the speaker of a language. The grammar is intended to be neutral as between production and reception, to a certain extent explaining both, but no more biased towards one than it is towards the other. Chomsky does not usually talk of the grammar as 'producing' sentences. The term he customarily employs is 'generate'; and this is the term that we used earlier in this chapter. But what exactly is meant by the word 'generate' in this context?

We have already seen that a *generative* grammar is one that 'projects' any given set of sentences upon the larger, and possibly infinite, set of sentences that constitute the language being described, and that it is this property of the grammar that reflects the creative aspect of human language. But 'generative' for Chomsky has a second and equally important, if not more important, sense. This second sense, in which 'generative' may be glossed as 'explicit', implies that the rules of the grammar and the conditions under which they operate must be precisely specified. We can perhaps best illustrate what is meant by 'generative' in this sense by means of a simple mathematical analogy (and Chomsky's use of the term 'generate' does in fact derive from mathematical usage). Consider the following algebraic expression, or function: $2x + 3y - z$. Given that the variables x, y and z can each take as their values one of the integers, the expression will generate (in terms of the usual arithmetical operations) an infinite set of resultant values. For example, with $x = 3, y = 2$ and $z = 5$, the result is 7; with $x = 1$, $y = 3$ and $z = 21$, the result is -10; and so on. We can say therefore that 7, -10, etc., are in the set of values generated by the function in question. If someone else applies the rules of arithmetic and obtains a different result, we say that he has made a mistake. We do not say that the rules are indeterminate and leave room for doubt at any point as to how they should be applied. Chomsky's conception of the rules of grammar is similar. They should be as precisely specified—*formalized* is the technical term—as the rules of arithmetic are. If we go on to identify the rules of the grammar with the native speaker's linguistic *competence*, as Chomsky does in his later work, we can account for the occurrence of ungrammatical sentences, and also for the occasional inability of listeners to analyse perfectly grammatical sentences, in much the same way as we can account for differences obtained in the evaluation of a mathematical function. We say that they are due to errors of *performance*—errors made in the application of the rules.

According to Chomsky, the grammar of a language should generate 'all and only' the sentences of the language. If the reader is puzzled by the addition of 'and only' (which is a relatively trivial instance of the kind of precision that is encouraged by formalization), he need only reflect that, by setting up the grammar in such a

way that it generates every combination of English words
(and this would be a very simple grammar), one would
be sure of generating all the sentences of the language.
But most of the combinations would not be sentences.
The addition of 'and only' is therefore an important
qualification.

The generation of all and only the sentences of English,
or any other language, might seem to be impossibly
ambitious. It must be remembered, however, that this
represents an ideal, which, even if it is impossible of
fulfilment, is a goal towards which the grammarian of
any language should continually work; and one grammar can be evaluated as better than another if, all other
things being equal, it approximates more closely to this
ideal. It should also be stressed, although this may appear
somewhat paradoxical, that one is not committed by the
adoption of Chomsky's ideal of generating all and only
the sentences of the language to the view that the distinction between grammatical and ungrammatical sequences of words is invariably clearcut, so that it is
always possible to decide whether a given sequence
should or should not be generated by the grammar.
Chomsky points out in *Syntactic Structures* that it is a
commonplace of the philosophy of science that, if a theory
is formulated in such a way that it covers the clear
cases, the theory itself can be used to decide the unclear
cases. He advocates the same approach in linguistics;
and for Chomsky a generative grammar is a scientific
theory. To take a simple example (it is not one of
Chomsky's): there are many speakers of English who
would reject the putative sentence *The house will have been
being built* and others who would accept it as quite normal. Since the judgements of native speakers do not
seem to vary systematically with the dialects they speak,
let us grant that, for English as a whole, the status of
putative sentences like this is indeterminate (by contrast

with the definitely acceptable *The house will have been built, The house is being built, They will have been building the house*, etc., and the definitely unacceptable **The house can will be built*, etc.). Since we do not know in advance whether *The house will have been being built* is a grammatical sentence or not, we can formulate the rules of the grammar to include all the definitely acceptable sequences and to exclude all the definitely unacceptable sequences and then see whether these rules exclude or include such sentences as *The house will have been being built*. (Sentences of this kind are in fact generated, and thereby defined as grammatical, by the rules given for English in *Syntactic Structures*.)

In this chapter we have confined our attention, for the most part, to Chomsky's earlier views on the aims and methodology of linguistics; and I have suggested that, except for his emphasis on the importance of creativity and his rejection of discovery procedures, when he wrote *Syntactic Structures*, he was still very much a 'Bloomfieldian'. I have said that the most important and original part of Chomsky's earlier work lies in his formalization of various systems of generative grammar; and the next three chapters will be devoted to an account of this topic. We will then take up the discussion of his more recent contributions to the psychology and philosophy of language.

5   Generative Grammar: a Simple Model

Our discussion of the more technical part of Chomsky's work will be relatively informal, and will not presuppose any special training in, or aptitude for, mathematics. However, a sufficient number of terms and concepts will be introduced to give the reader some idea of the flavour of generative grammar and to make it possible for him to appreciate its significance. It should be pointed out that Chomsky's own treatment of generative grammar in *Syntactic Structures*, and indeed in most of his more accessible publications, is also fairly informal. But it rests upon a considerable amount of highly technical research which he carried out in the years preceding the publication of *Syntactic Structures*. Much of this was described, in 1955, in a lengthy mimeographed monograph, 'The logical structure of linguistic theory', which was made available to interested scholars and university libraries but has only just been published (see Appendix).

In this chapter we shall be dealing with a very simple formal system, the first of the 'three models for the description of language' discussed by Chomsky in *Syntactic Structures* and elsewhere—one which he very quickly proved was insufficiently powerful for the syntactic analysis of English and other natural languages. We will first introduce a number of terms and concepts that will be required, not only here, but also for the discussion of the more complex models of grammar in the next two chapters. Throughout these three chapters we will assume an intuitive knowledge of at least some of the sentences of English that we should definitely wish to regard as well-formed, or *grammatical*, and of at least some of the sequences of words that we should definitely wish to classify as ill-formed, or *ungrammatical*. How we have come by this knowledge and how we might go about putting it to the test are important questions, but they are irrelevant to the formalization of linguistic description, which is our present concern.

We may begin by defining the *language* that is described by a particular grammar as the set of all the sentences it generates. The set of sentences may be, in principle, either finite or infinite in number. But English (and as far as we know all other natural languages) comprises an infinite (i.e. indefinitely large) number of sentences, because there are sentences and phrases in the language that can be extended indefinitely and will yet be accepted as perfectly normal by native speakers. Obvious examples are sentences like *This is the man that married the girl that* . . . (sentences of the 'House-that-Jack-built' type) and phrases like *large, black, three-cornered* . . . *hat*, which can be expanded to any desired length by making appropriate insertions in place of the three dots. Obviously, there are certain practical limitations upon the length of any sentence that has ever been, or will ever be, uttered by native speakers of English. But the point is that no *definite* limit can be set to the length of English sentences. We must, therefore, accept that, in theory, the number of grammatical sentences in the language is infinite.

But the number of words in the vocabulary of English is, we will assume, finite. There is a considerable variation in the words known to different native speakers, and there may well be some difference between the 'active' and the 'passive' vocabulary of every individual (i.e. between the words he will himself use as a speaker and the words he will recognize and understand if someone else uses them). Indeed, neither the 'active' nor the 'passive' vocabulary of any native speaker of English is fixed and static even for relatively short periods of time. We will, however, discount these facts in our discussion of the grammar of English and assume, for simplicity, that the vocabulary of the language is both determinate and invariable, and of course finite.

We will also assume that the number of distinct operations that are involved in the generation of English sentences is finite in number. There is no reason to believe that this is an implausible assumption; and if they were not, this would mean that the sentences of English could not be generated by means of a specifiable set of rules. Now, if the grammar is to consist of a finite set of rules operating upon a finite vocabulary and is to be capable of generating an infinite set of sentences, it follows that at least some of the rules must be applicable more than once in the generation of the same sentence. Such rules, and the structures they generate, are called *recursive*. Once again, there is nothing implausible in the suggestion that the grammar of English should include a certain number of recursive rules. It is intuitively clear that in expanding the sentence *This is the man that married the girl* by adding to it the clause *that wrote the book*, it is a clause of the same type as *that married the girl* that we are adding to the original sentence.

Sentences can be represented, as we saw in Chapter 2, at two *levels*: at the syntactic level as sequences of words, and at the phonological level as sequences of phonemes. It would be possible, in principle, to consider the syntactic structure of sentences as something which is totally or partially independent of the order in which the words occur relative to one another; and certain languages, with what is described as 'free word order', have been traditionally described from this point of view. However, following Chomsky, we will make it a matter of definition that every different sequence of words (if it is well-formed) is a different sentence. Under this definition, not only are *The dog bit the man* and *The man bit the dog* different sentences, but so also are *I had an idea on my way home* and *On my way home I had an idea.*

From the purely syntactic point of view, the phonological structure of words is irrelevant; and we could represent them in any one of a variety of ways. For instance, we could list all the words in the vocabulary in some arbitrary order, number them according to their place on the list and then use these numbers to denote particular words in the syntactic description of sentences. It is the usual practice, however, to represent words as sequences of phonemes (or letters) even at the syntactic level; and we will follow this practice. We will in fact cite words and syntactic units in their normal orthographic form, but the reader should bear in mind that the spelling or pronunciation of words is, in principle, independent of their identity as syntactic units. It is generally accepted that two different words may be written or pronounced in the same way and that there can be alternative ways of spelling or pronouncing the same word.

We will now introduce a distinction between 'terminal and 'auxiliary' elements. *Terminal elements* are those which actually occur in sentences: words at the syntactic level and phonemes at the phonological level. All other terms or symbols that are employed in the formulation of grammatical rules may be described as *auxiliary elements*. In particular, it should be noted that the terms or symbols used to denote the 'parts of speech' are auxiliary elements in generative grammars of the kind we shall be considering. We will use familiar traditional terms for word classes, or 'parts of speech', as Chomsky does, and abbreviate them symbolically; N = Noun, V = Verb, etc. Other auxiliary elements will be introduced later. One point that should be stressed here is that in a generative grammar the fact that a particular word belongs to a particular class—that it is a member of the class N, let us say—must be made perfectly explicit within the grammar. In effect this means, in grammars of the type formalized by Chomsky, that every word in the vocabulary must be assigned to the syntactic class, or classes, to which it belongs: it will not be sufficient to draw up a set of definitions like 'A noun is the name of any person, place or thing' and then to leave it to the person referring to the grammar to decide whether a particular word satisfies the definition or not.

The simplest grammars discussed by Chomsky that are capable of generating an infinite set of sentences by means of a finite number of recursive rules operating upon a finite vocabulary are what he calls *finite state grammars*. These are based on the view that sentences are generated by means of a series of choices made 'from left to right': that is to say, after the first, or leftmost, element has been selected, every subsequent choice is determined by the immediately preceding elements. According to this conception of syntactic structure, a sentence like *This man has brought some bread* might be generated as follows. The word *this* would be selected for the first position from a list of all the words capable of occurring at the beginning of English sentences. Then *man* would be selected as one of the words possible after *this*; *has* as one of the words that can occur after *this* and *man*; and so on. If we had selected *that*, instead of *this*, for the first position, the subsequent choices would have been unaffected: *That man has brought some bread* is an equally acceptable sentence. On the other hand, if we had first selected *those* or *these*, we should then have to select words like *men* for the second position, followed by words like *have* for the third position—the possibilities for the fourth and subsequent positions being as before. And if we had selected *the* initially, we could continue with either *man* and *has* or *men* and *have*. One way of representing graphically what has just been said in words is by means of the 'state diagram' shown in Figure 1. (I have deliberately used a slightly more complicated example than the one Chomsky gives on p. 19 of *Syntactic Structures*.)

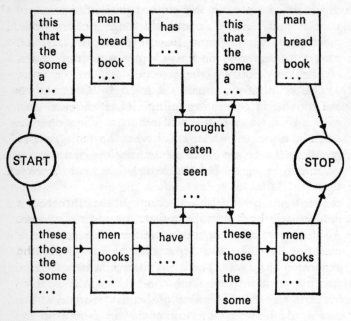

Fig. 1

The diagram may be interpreted as follows. We can think of the grammar as a machine, or device (in the abstract sense explained in the previous chapter), which moves through a finite number of internal 'states' as it passes from the *initial state* ('start') to the *final state* ('stop') in the generation of sentences. When it has produced (let us say 'printed out' or 'emitted') a word (from the set of words given as possible for that 'state') the grammar then 'switches' to a new state as determined by the arrows. Any sequence of words that can be generated in this way is thereby defined to be grammatical (in terms of the grammar represented by the diagram).

The grammar illustrated in Figure 1 will generate of course only a finite number of sentences. It can be extended, however, by allowing the device to 'loop' back to the same or some previous state at particular points of choice. For example, we could add 'loops' between {*this, that, the, some, a, . . .*} and {*man, bread, book, . . .*} and between {*these, those, the, some, . . .*} and {*men, books, . . .*}, making possible the selection of one or more elements from the set {*awful, fat, big, . . .*}, and thus the generation of sentences beginning *That awful man, That big fat man, Some big fat awful men*, etc. The grammar could also be extended in an obvious way to allow for the generation of compound sentences like *That man has brought us some bread and this beautiful girl has eaten the cheese.*

These sentences are still very simple in structure; and it would clearly be a complicated matter, even if it were possible, to construct a finite state grammar capable of generating a large and representative sample of the sentences of English. It will be observed, for example, that we have had to put *the* both with *this, that*, etc. and with *these, those*, etc. We should also have to put [*awful, fat, big*, etc.] in several different places, because *this awful man* and *these awful men*, but not **these awful man* and **this awful men*, are acceptable. Problems of this kind would multiply very quickly if we seriously set about the task of writing a finite state grammar for English; and the conception of syntactic structure that underlies this model of description has little to recommend it other than its formal simplicity. But Chomsky proved that our rejection of finite state grammar as a satisfactory model for the description of natural language is more solidly based than it would be if it rested solely upon considerations of practical complexity and our intuitions as to how certain grammatical phenomena ought to be described. He demonstrated the inadequacy of finite state grammars by pointing out that there are certain regular processes of sentence formation in English that cannot be accounted for at all, no matter how clumsy or counterintuitive an analysis we were prepared to tolerate, within the framework of finite state grammar.

Chomsky's proof of the inadequacy of finite state grammar can found in *Syntactic Structures* (pp. 21-4). It rests upon the fact that there may be dependencies holding between non-adjacent words and that these interdependent words may themselves be separated by a phrase or clause containing another pair of non-adjacent interdependent words. For example, in a sentence like *Anyone who says that is lying* there is a dependency between the words *anyone* and *is lying*. They are separated by the simple clause *who says that* (in which there is a dependency between *who* and *says*). We can easily construct more complex examples: e.g. *Anyone who says that people who deny that . . . are wrong is foolish*. Here we have dependencies between *anyone* and *is foolish*, and between *people* and *are wrong*; and we can go on to insert between *that* and *are* a clause which itself contains non-adjacent interdependent words. The result is a sentence with 'mirror image properties' that is to say a sentence of the form $a + b + c . . . x + y + z$, where there is a relationship of compatibility or dependency between the outermost constituents (a and z), between the next outermost (b and y) and so on. Any language that contains an indefinitely large number of sentences with 'mirror image properties' like this is beyond the scope of finite state grammar.

As I have said, the generation of sentences by means of a series of choices made 'from left to right' has little to recommend it other than the formal simplicity of the model. The reason why Chomsky paid any attention at all to finite state grammar is that language had been considered from this point of view in connexion with the design of efficient channels of communication during the Second World War; and the highly sophisticated mathematical theory of communication that resulted ('information theory') was extended to many fields, including psychology and linguistics, after the war. Chomsky did not prove, or claim to prove, that 'information theory' as such, was irrelevant to the investigation of language, but merely that, if it were applied on the assumption of 'word-by-word' and 'left to right' generation, it could not handle some of the constructions in English.

6 Phrase Structure Grammar

In the previous chapter we made the tacit assumption that the syntactic structure of a sentence could be fully accounted for by specifying the words of which the sentence was composed and the order in which they occurred. We saw that a finite state grammar, based on this assumption, was incapable of generating certain sentences of English. The second of Chomsky's 'three models for the description of language', phrase structure grammar, is much more satisfactory from this point of view. Any set of sentences that can be generated by a finite state grammar can be generated by a phrase structure grammar. But the converse does not hold: there are sets of sentences that can be generated by a phrase structure grammar, but not by a finite state grammar. This was one of the theorems that Chomsky proved in the more technical work that preceded the publication of *Syntactic Structures*. Let us express the relationship between phrase structure grammars and finite state grammars by saying that phrase structure grammars are intrinsically more *powerful* than finite state grammars (they can do everything that finite state grammars can do—and more).

Consider the following English sentence (I have here taken one of Chomsky's own examples): *The man hit the ball*. It is made up of five words arranged in a particular order. We shall refer to the words out of which the sentence is composed as its *ultimate constituents* (implying that these elements are not further analysable at the syntactic level). The order in which the ultimate constituents occur relative to one another may be described as the *linear structure* of the sentence. Now, linguists have generally claimed that sentences have another kind of syntactic structure in addition to, or independent of, their linear structure. A traditionally-minded grammarian might say, of our simple model sentence, that (like all simple sentences) it has a *subject* and a *predicate*; that the subject is a *noun phrase* (NP), which consists of the *definite article* (T) and a *noun* (N); and that the predicate is a *verb phrase* (VP), which consists of a *verb* (V) with its *object*, which, like the subject, is a noun phrase consisting of the definite article and a noun. Essentially the same kind of description would have been given by 'Bloomfieldian' linguists in terms of the notions of *immediate constituent analysis*: the 'immediate constituents' of the sentence (the two phrases into which it can be analysed at the first stage) are the noun phrase *the man* (which has the role, or *function* of subject), and the verb phrase *hit the ball* (which has the function of predicate); that the immediate constituents of *the man* are the article *the* and the noun *man*; that the immediate constituents of *hit the ball* are the verb *hit* and the noun phrase *the ball* (which has the function of object); and that the immediate constituents of *the ball* are the article *the* and the noun *ball*.

The notion of constituent structure, or *phrase structure* (to use Chomsky's term), is comparable with the notion of 'bracketing' in mathematics or symbolic logic. If we have an expression of the form $x \times (y + z)$, we know that the operation of addition must be carried out first and the operation of multiplication afterwards. By contrast, $x \times y + z$ is interpreted (by means of the general convention that, in the absence of brackets, multiplication takes precedence over addition) as being equivalent to $(x \times y) + z$. Generally speaking, the order in which the operations are carried out will make a difference to the result. For instance, with $x = 2$, $y = 3$ and $z = 5$: $x \times (y + z) = 16$, whereas $(x \times y) + z = 11$. There are many sequences of words in English and other languages that are ambiguous in much the same way that $x \times y + z$ would be ambiguous if it were not for the prior adoption by mathematicians of the general convention that multiplication takes precedence over addition. A classic example is the phrase *old men and women* (and more generally *A N and N*) which may be interpreted either as (*old men*) *and women*—cf. $(xy) + z$—or *old* (*men and women*)—cf. $x(y + z)$. Under the first interpretation the adjective *old* applies only to *men*; under the second interpretation it applies both to *men* and to *women*. With the phrase structure indicated, by means of brackets, as *old* (*men and women*) the string of words we are discussing is semantically equivalent to (*old men*) *and* (*old women*)—cf. $x(y + z) = (xy) + (xz)$. We will not pursue the mathematical analogy beyond this point. For our present purpose, it is sufficient to note that two strings of elements may have the same linear structure, but differ with respect to their phrase structure; and that the difference in their phrase structure may be semantically relevant.

The theoretical importance of this phenomenon, which we may refer to as *structural ambiguity* (Chomsky's term in *Syntactic Structures* is 'constructional homonymity'), lies in the fact that the ambiguity of such strings as *old men and women* cannot be accounted for by appealing to a difference in the meaning of any of the ultimate constituents or to a difference of linear structure.

The theory of immediate constituent analysis had been much discussed by Chomsky's predecessors. Chomsky's major contribution with respect to this model of syntactic structure was first of all to show how it could be formalized by means of a system of generative rules and then to demonstrate that, although phrase structure grammar was more powerful and more satisfactory for the description of natural languages than finite state grammar, it had certain limitations. Chomsky's formalization of phrase structure grammar may be illustrated by means of the following rules (which, with minor modifications, are identical with those given in *Syntactic Structures*):

  (i) *Sentence* → *NP* + *VP*
 (ii) *NP* → *T* + *N*
(iii) *VP* → *Verb* + *NP*
(iv) *T* → *the*
 (v) *N* → {*man, ball, . . .*}
(vi) *Verb* → {*hit, took, . . .*}

This set of rules (which will generate only a small fraction of the sentences of English) is a simple phrase structure grammar.

Each of these rules is of the form $X \to Y$, where X is a single element and Y is a *string* consisting of one or more elements. The arrow is to be interpreted as an instruction to replace the element that occurs to its left with the string of elements that occur to its right ('rewrite X as Y'). Rules (v) and (vi) employ brace brackets to list a set of elements any one of which, but only one of which, may be selected. (In each case only two members of the set have been given: the dots can be read as 'etc.'.) The rules are to be applied as follows. We start with the element *Sentence* and apply rule (i): this yields the *string* (i.e. the sequence of symbols: 'string' is a technical term) $NP + VP$. We inspect this string and see whether any of the elements occurring in it can be rewritten by means of the rules (i)–(vi). It will be seen that either (ii) or (iii) can be applied at this point: it does not matter which we select. Applying (iii), we get the string $NP + Verb + NP$. We can now apply (ii) twice, followed by (iv) and (v) twice, and (vi) once (in any order except that (ii) must precede (iv) and (v), as (iii) must precede (vi) and one of the applications of (ii)). The *terminal string* generated by the rules (assuming that *man, hit* and *ball* are selected at the appropriate points) is *the + man + hit + the + ball*; and it takes nine steps to generate this string of words. The set of nine strings, including the initial string, the terminal string and seven intermediary strings constitute a *derivation* of the sentence *The man hit the ball* in terms of this particular phrase structure grammar. (The reader may wish to check his understanding of the rules by constructing a sample derivation himself.)

But how does this system assign to sentences the appropriate phrase structure? The answer to this question is given by a convention associated with the operation of 'rewriting'. Whenever we apply a rule we put brackets, as it were, around the string of elements that is introduced by the rule and we label the string within the brackets as an instance of the element that has been rewritten by the rule. For example, the string *NP + VP* derived by rule (i) is bracketed and labelled as *Sentence (NP + VP)*. The labelled bracketing assigned to *NP + Verb + NP* is *Sentence (NP + VP (Verb + NP))*; and so on. An alternative, and equivalent, means of representing the labelled bracketing assigned to strings of elements generated by a phrase structure grammar is a *tree diagram*, as illustrated for our model sentence in Figure 2.

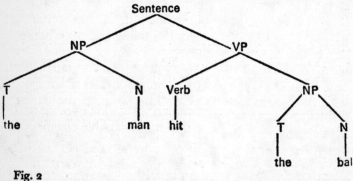

Fig. 2

Since tree diagrams are visually clearer than sequences of symbols and brackets, they are more commonly used in the literature, and we shall employ them (except for very simple instances) in what follows. The labelled bracketing, associated with a terminal string generated by a phrase structure is called a *phrase marker*.

It will be obvious that the phrase marker given in Figure 2 conveys directly the following information: the string of terminal elements *the + man + hit + the + ball* is a *Sentence* which consists of two constituents *NP* (*the man*) and *VP* (*hit the ball*); the *NP* which occurs to the left of *VP* consists of two constituents *T* (*the*) and *N* (*man*); *VP* consists of two constituents *Verb* (*hit*) and *NP* (*the ball*); and the *NP* that occurs to the right of *Verb* consists of two constituents *T* (*the*) and *N* (*ball*). It thus represents all that we said earlier might have been considered relevant in an immediate constituent analysis of the sentence, except for the fact that *the man* is the subject, *hit the ball* is the predicate, and *the ball* is the object. But these notions, and in particular the distinction between the subject and the object, can also be defined, as Chomsky suggests in *Syntactic Structures* (p. 30) and makes explicit later (notably in *Aspects of the Theory of Syntax*, p. 71), in terms of the associated phrase marker. The *subject* is that *NP*, which is directly dominated by *Sentence* and the object is that *NP* which is directly dominated by *VP*. What is meant by 'domination' should be clear, without formal definition, from the tree diagrams. We shall need to appeal to this notion in our discussion of transformational grammar in the following chapter.

There are all sorts of different ways in which the small phrase structure grammar with which we started out could be extended and thus made capable of generating more and more sentences of English. The question is whether a grammar of this general type is, in principle, adequate for the description of all the sentences that we should wish to regard as well-formed, or grammatical. Chomsky was not able to prove that there are sentences of English that cannot be generated by a phrase structure grammar (although it has now been demonstrated that there do exist certain constructions in other languages, if not in English, which are beyond the scope of phrase structure grammar in this sense). What Chomsky claimed, in *Syntactic Structures* and elsewhere, was that there are sentences of English which can be described only 'clumsily' within the framework of phrase structure grammar—that is to say, in a way that is 'extremely complex, *ad hoc*, and "unrevealing" '.

The important point to note is that Chomsky here allows for the possibility that, although two grammars may be equivalent in the sense that they each generate the same set of sentences (we will refer to this as *weak equivalence*), there may yet be good reasons for considering one grammar to be preferable to the other. In *Syntactic Structures* Chomsky claims that one of the main reasons for preferring a transformational grammar to a phrase structure grammar is that the former is, in a certain sense, simpler than the latter. It has proved very difficult, however, to make formally precise the sense in which the term 'simplicity' is being employed here. How do we decide, for example, that a grammar which requires relatively few rules, some of which however are quite complex, for the generation of a given set of sentences is, as a whole, more or less 'simple' than a second, weakly-equivalent, grammar which requires far more rules, none of which however is particularly complex, to generate the same set of sentences? There is no obvious way of balancing one kind of simplicity against another.

In his later publications, Chomsky attaches far less importance to the notion of 'simplicity', and gives correspondingly more weight to the argument that transformational grammar reflects better the 'intuitions' of the native speaker and is semantically more 'revealing' than phrase structure grammar.[1] We can illustrate the deficiencies of phrase structure grammar from this point of view with reference to the generation of corresponding active and passive sentences in English: e.g. *The man hit the ball* and *The ball was hit by the man*. We have already seen how active sentences might be generated in a phrase structure grammar, and we could easily add further rules to the system in order to generate passive sentences. What we cannot represent within the framework of a phrase structure grammar, however, is the fact (and let us grant that it is a fact) that pairs of sentences like *The man hit the ball* and *The ball was hit by the man* are 'felt' by native speakers to be related, or to 'belong' together in some way, and have the same, or a very similar meaning. As we shall see in the following chapter, this relationship between corresponding active and passive sentences, as well as many other 'intuitive' and semantic relationships, *can* be accounted for in a transformational grammar.

All the phrase structure rules introduced in this chapter so far have been *context-free*: that is to say, they have all been of the form $X \rightarrow Y$, where X is a single element and Y is a string of one or more elements, no reference being

1. Chomsky tells me that he is not himself aware of any change in his attitude over the years with respect to the role of simplicity measures and intuition. He thinks that some confusion may have been caused by the fact that *Syntactic Structures* was 'a rather watered-down version of earlier work (at that time unpublishable)' and that, for this reason, it 'emphasized weak rather than strong generative capacity'. I am sure that most linguists who read *Syntactic Structures* when it was first published in 1957 interpreted Chomsky's general views on linguistic theory in the way that I have represented them in Chapter 4. One can only wonder whether Chomsky's work would have had the effect that it did have within linguistics if *Syntactic Structures* had not been 'watered down'. (But see now Appendix 2.)

made to the context in which X is to be rewritten as Y. Consider, by contrast, a rule of the following form: $X \to Y/W — V$ (to be read as 'X is to be rewritten as Y in the context of W to the left and V to the right'—there are various ways in which the contextual restrictions may be indicated). It is by means of a *context-sensitive* rule, cast in this form, that we might wish to account for the 'agreement', or concord, that holds between the subject and the verb in English sentences (cf. *The boy runs*, but *The boys run*) and for similar phenomena in other languages; and we shall make use of context-sensitive rules in the next chapter. Here we may simply note that, from the formal point of view, context free grammars can be regarded as a special subclass of context-sensitive grammars, this subclass being defined by the property that in each of the rules $X \to Y/W — V$ the contextual variables W and V are left 'empty'. It may be added that any set of sentences that can be generated by a context-free grammar can be generated by a context-sensitive grammar; the converse, however, is not true.

The statement that has just been made, which implies that context-sensitive grammars are intrinsically more powerful than context-free grammars (as context-free phrase structure grammars are intrinsically more powerful than finite state grammars), illustrates again a very important, but highly technical, aspect of Chomsky's work which we can do no more than mention in a book of this kind. The study of the formal properties and generative capacity of various types of grammar exists as a branch of mathematics or logic, independently of its relevance for the description of natural languages. The revolutionary step that Chomsky took, as far as linguistics is concerned, was to draw upon this branch of mathematics (finite automata theory and recursive function theory) and to apply it to natural languages, like English, rather than to the artificial languages constructed by logicians and computer scientists. But he did more than simply take over and adapt for the use of linguists an existing system of formalization and a set of theorems proved by others. He made an independent and original contribution to the study of formal systems from a purely mathematical point of view. The mathematical investigation of phrase structure grammars, and more particularly of context-free phrase-structure grammar, is now well advanced; and various degrees of equivalence have been proved between phrase structure grammar and other kinds of grammar which also formalize the notion of 'bracketing', or immediate constituent structure. So far the mathematical investigation of transformational grammar, which was initiated by Chomsky, has made relatively little progress. But transformational grammar, as we shall see in the next chapter, is a far more complex system than phrase structure grammar (although it may well be the case, as Chomsky claimed in *Syntactic Structures*, that it yields a 'simpler' description of certain sentences).[2]

2. For a rather more formal treatment of the basic concepts of generative grammar, reference may be made to Appendix 1.

7 Transformational Grammar

We shall not go into a great deal of detail in our discussion of transformational grammar. However, it is impossible to understand Chomsky's more general views on the philosophy of language and mind unless one has some knowledge of the principal characteristics of the system of grammatical description which he founded some fifteen years ago, and which has been under more or less continuous development since that time.

The first point that must be made is terminological. Whereas a phrase structure grammar is one which consists solely of phrase structure rules, a transformational grammar (as originally conceived by Chomsky) does not consist only of transformational rules. It includes a set of phrase structure rules as well. The transformational rules depend upon the previous application of the phrase structure rules and have the effect, not only of converting one string of elements into another, but, in principle, of changing the associated phrase-marker. Furthermore, they are formally more heterogeneous and more complex than phrase structure rules. We give some examples of transformational rules presently. But we first need to introduce an appropriate set of phrase structure rules.

We will use those given by Chomsky in *Syntactic Structures* (p. 111)—with one or two minor changes—as follows:

(1) *Sentence* → *NP* + *VP*
(2) *VP* → *Verb* + *NP*
(3) $NP \rightarrow \begin{Bmatrix} NP_{sing} \\ NP_{pl} \end{Bmatrix}$

(4) $NP_{sing} \rightarrow T + N$

(5) $NP_{pl} \rightarrow T + N + s$

(6) $T \rightarrow the$

(7) $N \rightarrow \{man, ball, door, dog, book, \ldots\}$

(8) $Verb \rightarrow Aux + V$

(9) $V \rightarrow \{hit, take, bite, eat, walk, open, \ldots\}$

(10) $Aux \rightarrow Tense\ (+M)\ (+have + en)\ (+ be + ing)$

(11) $Tense \rightarrow \begin{cases} Present \\ Past \end{cases}$

(12) $M \rightarrow \{will, can, may, shall, must\}$

It will be observed that this set of rules allows for a wider range of choices than those given in the previous chapter. Both singular and plural noun phrases are accounted for, by rule (3); and a large number of tenses and moods are introduced (instead of just the simple past tense of *The man hit the ball*) by means of the element *Aux* and its subsequent development. Rule (10) implies that every string generated by it must contain the element *Tense* and may contain, in addition, one or more of the other strings of elements in brackets. (Elements like *s* in rule (5) and *en* or *ing* in rule (10) are morphemes rather than words. In fact, *have, be, the* and all the elements listed on the right hand side of rules (7), (9) and (12) may also be regarded as morphemes. But we need not dwell here upon the difference between a 'word' and a 'morpheme' in linguistic theory.)

Assuming that the lists given in rules (7) and (9) are considerably extended, this system of phrase structure rules will generate a large (but finite) number of what we may call *underlying strings*. It should be emphasized that an underlying string (as indeed will be evident from the above rules) is not a sentence. The transformational rules have yet to be applied. One of the strings generated by these rules is *the + man + Present + may + have + en + open + the + door* (which, given the transformational rules of *Syntactic Structures,* underlies both the active sentence *The man may have opened the door* and the corresponding passive *The door may have been opened by the man*). The reader may wish to verify that this string is indeed generated by the rules and to construct the associated phrase marker.

Chomsky derived passive sentences from underlying strings in *Syntactic Structures* by means of an optional rule which we may give, rather informally, as follows:

$$(13)\ NP_1 + Aux + V + NP_2 \rightarrow NP_2 + Aux + be + en + V + by + NP_1.$$

This rule differs in various respects from the phrase structure rules. Not just one element, but a string of four elements, appears to the left of the arrow; and the operation that is carried out by the rule is quite complex —involving the permutation of the two *NP*s (this is indicated by the subscripts) and the insertion of the elements *be, en* and *by* at particular points.

There is, however, an even more important difference between the phrase structure rules (1)–(12) and the transformational rule (13); and this has to do with the way in which we interpret the symbols which occur in the rules. In a phrase structure rule a single symbol designates one and only one element in the string to which the rule applies. But in a transformational rule a single symbol may refer to a string of more than one element, provided that the string in question is *dominated* by (i.e. derived from: see p. 61) this symbol in the associated phrase marker. It is in this sense that transformational rules are said to operate upon phrase markers rather than simply upon strings of elements.

We will first of all illustrate what is meant by this statement with reference to a purely abstract example. Given that the string $a + d + e + b + f + c + g + h$ has been generated by a set of phrase structure rules which assign to it the phrase marker illustrated in Figure 3 (the reader can easily reconstruct these rules

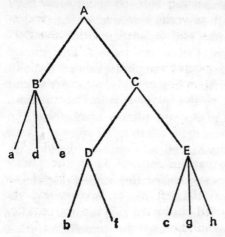

Fig. 3

for himself), this string will be converted by means of the transformational rule $B + D + E \rightarrow E + B$ into the string $c + g + h + a + d + e$ with the associated phrase

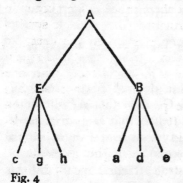

Fig. 4

marker shown in Figure 4. In other words, since the string of terminal symbols itself constitutes part of the phrase marker, we can say that the rule converts one phrase marker into another; and this is the defining property of transformational rules. The rule we have just given has the effect of deleting everything dominated by D (including D itself) and permuting B and E, keeping their internal structure intact. The phrase marker given in Figure 3 and the phrase marker given in Figure 4 may be described, respectively, as *underlying* and *derived*, with respect to the transformation in question. (In deciding that the derived phrase marker has the particular form I have attributed to it in Figure 4, I have begged an important theoretical question, to which we will return briefly in a moment.)

If we now look at our illustrative underlying string (*the* + *man* + *Present* + *may* + *have* + *en* + *open* + *the* + *door*) and at the associated phrase marker (which I have left the reader to construct for himself), we shall see that *the* + *man* is wholly dominated by *NP*, *Present* + *may* + *have* + *en* by *Aux*, the single element *open* by *V* and *the* + *door* by *NP*. This means that the transformational rule (13) is applicable and, if applied (for it is an optional rule), will convert the underlying string into (13a) with the appropriate derived phrase marker:

(13a) *the* + *door* + *Present* + *may* + *have* + *en* + *be* + *en* + *open* + *by* + *the* + *man.*

But what is the appropriate derived phrase marker? This is a difficult question. Granted that NP_2 becomes the subject of the passive sentence, that *be* + *en* becomes part of *Aux* in the same way that *have* + *en* or *may* is (this, as we shall see, is necessary for the operation of subsequent rules) and that *by* is attached to NP_1 to form a phrase, there are still a number of points about the structure of the derived phrase marker that remain unclear. Two possible phrase markers are given in

Figures 5 and 6. It will be observed that they differ in that one takes *by* + NP_1 to be a part of the verb phrase whereas the other treats it as an immediate constituent of the sentence, equivalent in 'status', as it were, to NP_2

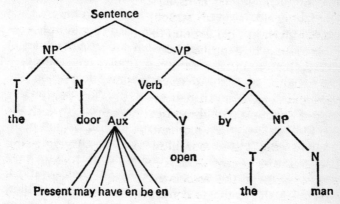

Fig. 5

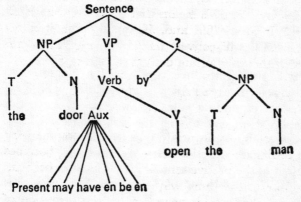

Fig. 6

and *VP*. (It will also be noticed that I have put a question mark where the label for the bracketed phrase *by* + NP_1 should be.)

We have touched here, on an important theoretical problem. The derived string produced by one transformational rule may serve as the underlying string for the operation of a subsequent transformational rule, and will therefore need to have associated with it the appropriate derived phrase marker. Chomsky and his followers have worked on this problem and have tried to establish a set of conventions according to which a particular kind of formal operation (e.g. deletion, permutation or substitution) is defined to have a particular effect upon the topology of the phrase marker it transforms; and we followed these conventions when we decided that the effect of the rule $B + D + E \rightarrow E + B$ operating upon the underlying phrase marker shown in Figure 3 was the derived phrase marker in Figure 4. But this was a very simple example from the point of view of the operations involved and the shape of the phrase marker to which they applied; and furthermore it was a purely abstract example unaffected by any empirical considerations. The reader will appreciate that the situation is very different when it comes to formulating a set of transformational rules for the description of English or some other natural language.

We will now introduce, and briefly discuss, two further transformational rules (slightly different in form from the corresponding rules in *Syntactic Structures*, but based upon them and having the same general effect). The first is the obligatory 'number transformation':

$$(14) \quad Present \rightarrow \begin{cases} s/NP_{sing}\text{\_\_\_\_} \\ O/\text{elsewhere} \end{cases}$$

This is a context-sensitive rule, which says that *Present* is to be rewritten as s if and only if it is immediately preceded in the underlying string by a sequence of one or more elements dominated by NP_{sing} in the associated phrase marker, but is to be rewritten in all other contexts as 'zero' (i.e. as the absence of a suffix). It is this rule which accounts for the 'agreement' between subject and verb manifest in such sentences as *The man goes* vs. *The man go or *The man is* . . . vs *The man are . . . . If it is applied to (13a) it yields:

(14a) *the + door + s + may + have + en + be + en + open + by + the + man.*

It will be observed that what we might call the 'abstract' verbal suffix *s* is here introduced *in front of* the element to which it is subsequently attached (in the same way that *en* and *ing* are introduced by phrase structure rule (10) in front of the element to which they are later attached). We have called these 'abstract' suffixes because, as we shall see, they assume a variety of forms, including 'zero', in various contexts.

The rule by which these 'abstract' suffixes are placed after the appropriate stems (the 'auxiliary transformation') may be given as follows:

$$(15) \begin{Bmatrix} Tense \\ en \\ ing \end{Bmatrix} + \begin{Bmatrix} M \\ have \\ be \\ V \end{Bmatrix} \rightarrow \begin{Bmatrix} M \\ have \\ be \\ V \end{Bmatrix} + \begin{Bmatrix} Tense \\ en \\ ing \end{Bmatrix}$$

This rule says that any pair of elements the first of which is *Tense*, *en* or *ing* and the second of which is *M*, *have*, *be* or *V* are to be (obligatorily) permuted, the rest of the string to the left and the rest of the string to the right remaining unchanged. If the rule is applied to (14a) it will permute *s + may* (i.e. *Tense + M*), *en + be* and *en + open* (*en + V*), successively from left to right, yielding:

(15a) *the + door + may + s + have + be + en + open + en + by + the + man*

One more transformational rule has yet to apply, which puts a word-boundary symbol (we shall use a space) between every pair of elements the second of which is not *Tense*, *en* or *ing* and the first of which is not *M*, *have*, *be* or *V*. Applied to (15a), this yields:

(16a) *the door may + s have be + en open + en by the man*

And this is the form that our illustrative string would have after all the relevant transformational rules have operated.

Finally, in a grammar of the kind outlined by Chomsky in *Syntactic Structures*, there is a set of 'morphophonemic' rules, which will convert the string of words and morphemes into a string of phonemes. These would re-write *may + s* as the phonemic representation of what is spelled *may*, *open + en* as what is spelled *opened* (*be + s* as what is spelled *is*, *run + en* as what is spelled *run*, and so on). We end up therefore, as we should, with the phonemic representation of *The door may have been opened by the man*.

Those readers who were previously unfamiliar with Chomsky's system of transformational grammar may have found it rather tedious working through this step-by-step derivation of a single sentence. But they will now have acquired a sufficient understanding of the way the grammar is designed and operates for them to appreciate the significance of some of the more general points made in this and later chapters. At this stage in our discussion of transformational grammar, it may be helpful to introduce a diagram showing how the grammar outlined in *Syntactic Structures* was organized (see Figure 7). The input

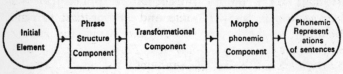

Fig. 7

to the grammar is the initial element (as explained in the previous chapter) which generates a set of underlying strings by means of the phrase structure rules in the first 'box' of the diagram. The second 'box' comprises the transformational rules, of which some are optional and others obligatory. These rules take, as their 'input', single underlying strings, or pairs of underlying strings (we shall come back to this point), and by successively modifying these strings and their associated phrase markers, generate as their 'output' all and only the sentences of the language, represented as strings of words and morphemes, and assign to each sentence its derived constituent structure. The third 'box' of rules then converts each of these sentences from its syntactic representation as a string of words and morphemes to its phonological representation as a string of phonemes (and in this way relates the two levels of analysis that were referred to in Chapter 2 under the term 'duality' of structure).

According to this model of generative grammar different types of simple sentences are accounted for by means of *optional* transformational rules. For example, all the following sentences are related in that they derive from the same underlying string: (i) *The man opened the door*, (ii) *The man did not open the door*, (iii) *Did the man open the door?* (iv) *Didn't the man open the door?* (v) *The door was opened by the man*, (vi) *The door was not opened by the man*, (vii) *Was the door opened by the man?* (viii) *Wasn't the door opened by the man?* They differ in that: (i) has had no optional transformation applied to the underlying string; (ii) has had the *Negative* transformation applied; (iii) the *Interrogative*; (iv) the *Negative* and *Interrogative*; (v) the *Passive*; (vi) the *Passive* and *Negative*; (vii) the *Passive* and *Interrogative*; and (viii) the *Passive*, *Negative* and *Interrogative*. Of these eight sentences, the first (a simple, active, declarative sentence) is defined by Chomsky, in

Syntactic Structures, as a *kernel sentence*. It should be emphasized (and this is clear from our detailed consideration of the derivation of a passive sentence above) that non-kernel sentences, such as (ii)–(viii), are not derived from kernel sentences, such as (i), but from a common underlying string. That is to say, there are no sentences generated without the application of at least a small number of *obligatory* transformations, including rules comparable in effect with rules (14) and (15) above.

Compound sentences, in which two clauses are *co-ordinated* (e.g. *The man opened the door and switched on the light*) and complex sentences, in which one clause is *subordinated* to another (e.g. *The man who opened the door switched on the light*), are generated by means of *conjoining* and *embedding* transformations, respectively, which take as 'input' a pair of underlying strings (e.g. *the + man + Past + open + the + door* and *the + man + Past + switch + on + the + light*) and combine them in various ways. Conjoining and embedding transformations constitute the class of *generalized* transformations in *Syntactic Structures*; and it is the repeated application of these rules which accounts for the existence of such recursive structures as *This is the . . . that lived in the house that Jack built* or *. . . a big, black, three-foot long, . . . , wooden box* (see p. 48). All the generalized transformations are of course optional.

So much, then, by way of a general summary of the earlier version of transformational grammar, presented in *Syntactic Structures*. Chomsky claimed that one of the advantages of this system, the third and most powerful of his 'models for the description of language', was that it could account more satisfactorily than phrase structure grammar for certain types of structural ambiguity. To take one of Chomsky's famous examples: a sentence like *Flying planes can be dangerous* is ambiguous (cf. *To fly planes can be dangerous* and *Planes which are flying can be dangerous*);

and yet, under both interpretations, the immediate constituent analysis is, presumably, $(((\textit{flying}) (\textit{planes}))$ $(((\textit{can}) (\textit{be})) (\textit{dangerous})))$. This is a different kind of structural ambiguity from that manifest in a phrase like *old men and women* discussed in the previous chapter. It would be possible to generate a sentence like *Flying planes can be dangerous* within a phrase structure grammar and to assign to it two different phrase markers—differing with respect to the labels assigned to the node dominating *flying*. But this would not be an intuitively satisfying account of the ambiguity; and it would fail to relate the phrase *flying planes*, on the one hand, to *planes which are flying*, and, on the other, to *someone flies planes*. The transformational analysis accounts for the ambiguity by relating two different underlying strings (let us say *plane + s + be + ing + fly* and *someone + fly + plane + s*) to the same derived string. Many other examples could be given of structurally ambiguous sentences which can be accounted for rather nicely in terms of transformational grammar: *I don't like eating apples* ('... apples for eating' *vs.* '... to eat apples'), *I disapprove of his drinking* ('... the fact that he drinks' *vs.* '... the way in which he drinks': cf. Chomsky, *Language and Mind*, p. 27), etc.

This transformational explanation of structural ambiguity depends upon the application of *optional* rules; and is in accord with the more general principle (which may be taken as axiomatic in the study of any system of communication) that meaning implies *choice*. This principle, it should be observed, states that the possibility of selecting one alternative rather than another is a *necessary*, but not a *sufficient*, condition for the expression of a difference of meaning. The most obvious application of the principle is when one word rather than another is selected from the set of words that could occur in a given position (cf. *The man opened the window* vs. *The man opened the door*). Here we are concerned with the 'choice' of a different set of rules (or a difference in the order in which the same set of rules is applied) in the generation of two or more sentences from the same underlying string. I have said that 'choice', in this sense, is not a *sufficient* condition for there being a difference of meaning in the resultant sentences. For example, *John looked the word up in the dictionary* and *John looked up the word in the dictionary* differ (according to *Syntactic Structures*) in that an additional optional transformation has been applied in the generation of the former sentence. The two sentences are not, however, different in meaning; and the transformational rule in question (which has the effect of converting *Past + look + up + the + word* to *Past + look + the + word + up* at a particular point in the derivation) may be described as *stylistic*.

In 1965, in *Aspects of the Theory of Syntax*, Chomsky put forward a more comprehensive theory of transformational grammar, which differed from the earlier theory in a number of important respects. For our purpose, it will be sufficient to mention only the most general differences between the *Syntactic Structures* grammar and what we may call an *Aspects*-type grammar. Once again, a diagram may be helpful (cf. Figure 8).

The most striking difference between the two grammars, as represented in Figures 7 and 8, is the additional 'box' of rules in the *Aspects*-type grammar labelled 'Semantic Component'. In *Syntactic Structures* it was argued that, although semantic considerations are not directly relevant to the syntactic description of sentences, there are 'striking correspondences between the structures and elements that are discovered in formal, grammatical analysis and specific semantic functions' (p. 101) and that, 'having determined the syntactic structure of the language, we can study the way in which this syntactic structure is put to use in the actual functioning of the language' (p. 102). In the years that followed the publication of *Syntactic Structures*, Chomsky and his collaborators came to the conclusion that the meaning of sentences could, and should, be submitted to the same

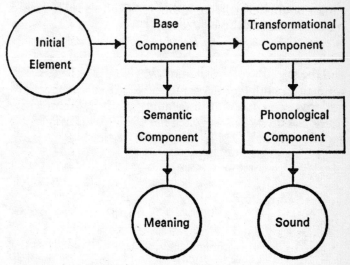

Fig. 8

kind of precise, formal analysis as their syntactic structure, and that semantics should be included as an integral part of the grammatical analysis of languages. The grammar of a language is now seen by Chomsky as a system of rules relating the meaning (or meanings), of each sentence it generates to the physical manifestation of the sentence in the medium of sound.

In *Aspects*, as in *Syntactic Structures*, the syntax falls into two parts. But the two syntactic components operate somewhat differently. It is now the *base* of the grammar (which is roughly comparable with the phrase structure part of the earlier system) rather than the transformational component, that accounts for the semantically relevant options, including the possibility of forming recursive constructions. The difference between a declarative and an interrogative sentence, or between an active and a passive sentence, is no longer described in terms of optional transformations, but in terms of a choice made in the base rules. For example, there might be a base rule of the following form:

(2a) $VP \rightarrow Verb + NP \,(+ \, Agentive)$

and the selection of the element *Agentive* would distinguish the strings underlying passive sentences from the strings underlying the corresponding active sentences. There would then be an *obligatory* transformational rule, corresponding to rule (13) above, operating if and only if the 'input' string contained the element *Agentive*. This proposal (which corresponds with Chomsky's in spirit, rather than in detail) has the advantage that, if we formulate the transformational rule correctly, it gives us a label for the node dominating $by + NP_1$ in the derived phrase markers associated with passive sentences (see p. 71).

The base rules generate an indefinitely large set of underlying phrase markers (which represent the *deep structure* of all the sentences characterized by the system); and these are converted into derived phrase markers (which represent the *surface structure* of the sentences) by the transformational rules, most of which (apart from 'stylistic' rules) are now obligatory. The meaning of each sentence is derived, mainly if not wholly, from its deep structure, by means of the rules of semantic interpretation; and the phonetic interpretation of each sentence— its physical description as an acoustic 'signal'—is derived from its surface structure by means of the phonological rules.

We need not go into the more technical details which distinguish an *Aspects*-type grammar from the conceptually simpler system of *Syntactic Structures*. All that remains to be added to this account of the general characteristics of the 1965 version of transformational grammar is that various semantically relevant grammatical notions are now explicitly defined in terms of deep structure relations. (This was merely hinted at in *Syntactic Structures*.) We may note, in particular, the distinction between the 'logical' (deep structure) and 'grammatical' (surface structure) subject of a sentence. The 'logical' subject is that *NP* which is immediately dominated by *S* (= *Sentence*) in the deep structure; the 'grammatical' subject is the leftmost *NP* which is immediately dominated by (the topmost) *S* in the surface structure. For example, in a sentence like *John was persuaded by Harry to take up golf*, the grammatical subject is *John* (it is this notion of 'subject' which is relevant to the statement of the agreement holding between the subject and the verb in English: *John was persuaded* vs. *They were persuaded*, etc.). But the deep structure of this

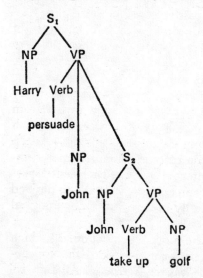

Fig. 9

sentence consists of one sentence (S_2) embedded within another (S_1); and each sentence has its own logical subject. We can represent the deep structure of this sentence, informally and omitting all but the essential information, as it is given in Figure 9. It will be seen that the logical subject of S_1 (the *matrix* sentence) is *Harry*, and that of S_2 (the *embedded* sentence) it is *John*. Furthermore, the deep structure subject of S_2 is identical with the deep structure object of S_1 (that *NP* which is immediately dominated by *VP*). As Chomsky points out, it is these deep structure relations that are essential for the correct semantic interpretation of the sentence.

8   Post-*Aspects* Developments in Chomskyan Linguistics

In this chapter, we shall look at some of the developments that have taken place in linguistics since 1965, when, as we have just seen, Chomsky put forward a far more comprehensive theory of transformational grammar than he did in his earlier work. Chomsky himself now refers to his 1965 theory as *the standard theory* of transformational grammar. We will use the same term, though it has been thought by some of Chomsky's critics to be unfairly loaded in favour of the system of transformational grammar outlined in *Aspects of the Theory of Syntax*.

The standard theory of *Aspects* is to be contrasted, on the one hand, with Chomsky's own *extended standard theory* and, on the other, with what may be regarded, from Chomsky's point of view at least, as non-standard theories—of which there is now an almost bewildering variety competing for acceptance. Many of these might also be described from a more neutral vantage-point as extensions of the standard theory. To avoid confusion, however, we will reserve the term 'extended standard theory' for Chomsky's own modifications of the 1965 version of transformational grammar. Before we embark upon the task of comparing the best-known and more important of the non-standard theories with the standard theory, and subsequently with Chomsky's extended standard theory, I must explain what I mean by 'Chomskyan' and 'post-Chomskyan' in the title of this chapter. It might well be objected that they are as misleading in their way as 'standard' and 'extended standard' are.

As I pointed out in the Introduction, the 'Chomskyan' school of linguistics is not just one among many. If it was true when the first edition of this book was published, in 1970, it is even more obviously the case now (in 1977) that every school of linguistics tends to define its position on major theoretical issues in relation to Chomsky's own pronouncements on the same issues. There is a sense therefore in which all the theories that we are going to consider are Chomskyan—and it is for that reason that we are concerned with them here. Some of them, however, are also post-Chomskyan in the rather special sense that they are deliberately presented by their authors as replacing, or supplanting, the standard theory of transformational grammar. Of course, the extended standard theory might also be described as post-Chomskyan in this sense; but I will reserve the term 'Chomskyan' for developments in the theory of transformational grammar initiated or approved by Chomsky himself. It is an indication of Chomsky's stature in the field that so much of what is intended to be post-Chomskyan—an antithesis to one or other of his theses— should also be, in other respects, very obviously Chomskyan. Indeed the history of the past ten years can be summed up, as far as Chomskyan and post-Chomskyan developments are concerned, as thesis, antithesis—and counter-thesis!—but so far no synthesis!

The most immediate distinctively post-Chomskyan challenge to the standard theory has come from *case-grammar*. As we saw at the end of the preceding chapter, Chomsky drew a distinction in *Aspects* between the deep-structure subject or object and the surface-structure subject or object of a sentence and claimed that it was the deep-structure functions that were semantically relevant. Many linguists, however, have taken the view that notions like 'subject' and 'object' are relatively superficial, that their definition varies from language to language and that they play no part in determining the meaning of the sentence as such. In an influential paper published in 1968, 'The case for case', C. J. Fillmore argued that the most satisfactory grammatical analysis of a sentence was one in which the constituents of each clause, at the deepest level of syntactic analysis, were what he called *cases*: e.g. Agent, Instrument and Place.

This use of the term 'case' is a generalization of the more traditional usage, according to which, in certain languages, different forms of the same noun are said to differ in case (Nominative, Accusative, Genitive, Dative, etc.) and verbs (and prepositions) are said to govern their objects, or complements, in such-and-such a case. For example, in Latin the object of the verb *videre* ('to see') must be in the Accusative case (e.g. *hominem*: 'a/the man'), the object of *meminisse* ('to remember') in the Genitive (e.g. *hominis*: 'a/the man'); the object of *imperare* ('to order') in the Dative (e.g. *homini*: 'a/the man'); and so on. The subject of all these verbs, as generally in Latin, is in the Nominative (e.g. *homo*: 'a/the man'); and the subject is not traditionally regarded as being governed by the verb in the way that the object is. In Latin, as in many languages (Russian, German, etc.), nouns are inflected for case: *homo*, *hominem*, *hominis* and *homini* are all forms of the same noun (conventionally referred to by means of the Nominative form, *homo*). In English, (as in French, Italian or Spanish —not to mention Chinese, Malay and a vast number of other languages) nouns are not inflected for case, such inflectional variation as there is in English being restricted to pronouns: cf. *he* vs *him*, *I* vs *me*, *they* vs *them*, etc. From a more general point of view, however, prepositions or postpositions can be thought of as having the same kind of semantic and syntactic function as the cases have in a case-inflected language. (The difference between prepositions, e.g. *to*, *by*, or *from* in English, and postpositions is that, whereas prepositions come before the noun phrase with which they are associated, postpositions come after. Many languages, e.g. Turkish, Japanese, Hindi, have postpositions. For convenience, we will use the more familiar term 'preposition', in what follows, to cover both prepositions and postpositions.)

Up to a point, it is possible to assign particular meanings to what would be traditionally called cases in the grammatical analysis of languages like Latin— meanings having to do with agency, location and the source or goal of movement, etc.—and, in terms of these meanings, to put the case-inflected noun-phrases (with or without prepositions) of Latin and other such languages into functional correspondence with noun-phrases and adverbial phrases in languages that do not have case in the traditional sense of the term. Indeed, it has long been common practice to make use of the notions of agency, location and the source or goal of movement in the grammatical analysis of languages of strikingly different grammatical structure. What is distinctive about case-grammar (though it has its precursors, in pre-Chomskyan linguistics, in the work of scholars like Hjelmslev and, more especially, Tesnière) is the identification of case as a deep-structure category. There are several versions of case-grammar, of which Fillmore's is the best known.

In case-grammar, the verb occupies a central, or pivotal, position in the sentence; and each verb governs (in a recognizably extended sense of this traditional term) a set of obligatory and/or optional deep-structure cases, which are filled, as it were, by expressions that may occur as subjects, objects or prepositional phrases at a more superficial level. For example, the verb 'open' might be classified in the lexicon associated with a case-grammar of English as one which governs an Agent, an Entity and, optionally, an Instrument. (The term 'Entity' is not Fillmore's: it refers to the most neutral, semantically undifferentiated, deep-structure case which is labelled differently by different authors.) Such sentences as (i) *The jailer opened the door (with a key)*, (ii) *The door was opened (by the jailer)(with a key)*, (iii) *The door opened*, (iv) *The key opened the door*, etc., would all be derived, in Fillmore's version of case-grammar, from an underlying structure in which *(by) the jailer* has the case-role of Agent, *the door* has the case-role of Entity and *(with) the key* has the case-role of Instrument. The Agent-expression (i.e. the expression that is in the Agent case or has the case role of Agent in the deep-structure specification) is the subject in (i), but an omissible adverbial modifier in (ii)—cf. Figures 6 and 7 and Rule (2a) of Chapter 7; the Entity-expression is the object in (i), but the subject in (ii); the Instrument-expression is an omissible adverbial modifier in (i) and (ii), but the subject in (iv). Sentences (i)-(iv), and others, are transformationally related in case-grammar by virtue of their being derived from a common deep structure (due allowance being made for the distinction of obligatory and optional cases).

It is not difficult to see the attractions of case-grammar. Notions having to do with agency and causation, location and locomotion, acting on behalf of or to the advantage (or disadvantage) of someone, and similar notions that have been invoked in works on case-grammar, are of more obvious semantic relevance than are the grammatical relations associated with the distinction between subject and predicate or subject and object; they are readily identifiable across languages (in at least the most typical situations in which each such notion is invoked); and they have been recognized by a number of psychologists as playing an important part in the acquisition of language by children. Despite these attractions, case-grammar is no longer seen by the majority of linguists working within the general framework of transformational-generative grammar as a viable alternative to the standard theory. The reason is that when it comes to classifying the totality of the verbs in a language in terms of the deep-structure cases that they govern, the semantic criteria which define these cases are all too often unclear or in conflict.

Neither Chomsky nor his followers have been paying much attention recently to case-grammar as such. But Fillmore's 'The case for case' has had its effect upon the development of the extended standard theory. Chomsky now attaches more importance than he did in *Aspects* to what he, rather misleadingly, refers to, in his most recent publications, as 'thematic relations'—misleadingly, because the terms 'theme' and 'thematic' are well established in linguistics in a quite different sense (and one that is closer to their everyday, non-technical sense). But Fillmore's version of case-grammar, though it is the best-known and so far the most influential, is but one version of what may be more generally, and more satisfactorily, described as *valency-grammar*; and it would be unwise to rule out the possibility of some kind of valency-grammar being developed as a successful rival to the standard and the extended standard theory.

Valency-grammars are normally formalized (in so far as they have been formalized) as *dependency-grammars*, which (like *categorial grammars*) are weakly, and perhaps strongly, equivalent to phrase-structure grammars (see Appendix 1). They directly reflect the view that within the sentence (or its propositional nucleus) there is a single governing element—the verb—and a set of dependent expressions whose number and semantic, or logical, type is determined by the *valency* of the verb. This notion of valency (the term 'valency' being borrowed from chemistry) was introduced into linguistics by the French scholar Tesnière, whose work lacked the mathematical precision of that of Chomsky or Harris, but can be seen in certain respects as foreshadowing the development of transformational grammar. The notion of valency clearly derives from, but extends, the traditional distinction of transitive and intransitive verbs; and it can be related to the classification of predicates, in formal logic, in terms of the number of expressions with which they can be combined in well-formed formulae. It is undoubtedly true, for many languages at least, that the selection of a particular verb determines to a considerable degree the grammatical structure of the sentence (or its propositional nucleus). So far the notion of valency has been more extensively discussed and applied in Germany and the Soviet Union than it has been elsewhere. But certain of the central ideas of valency-grammar are also to be found in some of the more obviously post-Chomskyan work that is now being published.

For example, one of the most recent developments in post-Chomskyan syntax is the emergence of what its adherents call *relational grammar*. Unlike some of the other proposed alternatives to the standard theory, relational grammar attaches considerable importance to the grammatical relations of being subject, object or indirect object of the sentence. It operates (as Tesnière did) with a hierarchical ordering of subject, object and indirect object; and it uses this hierarchical ordering to determine what position in a phrase-marker will be occupied by which expression when one phrase-marker is converted into another by means of a transformational rule. In this respect, relational grammar can claim to be more traditional than the standard theory is, for good or ill, in the way in which it establishes a transformational correspondence between active and passive sentences. The effect of switching from the active to the passive is to reduce the valency of the verb by eliminating the subject-expression or demoting it to the status of an optional, and structurally dispensible, part of the propositional nucleus. But in English, and many other languages, every sentence must have a grammatical subject. So—to make the point informally and in deliberately traditional terms—the object of the active becomes the subject of the passive. The converse process is seen, in many languages, in the formation of causative constructions: e.g. in the formation of a sentence meaning 'John got Bill to kill Harry' from the structure underlying a sentence meaning 'Bill killed Harry'. Here, the valency of the two-place (i.e. transitive) verb meaning 'kill' is augmented. The resultant three-place causative verb meaning 'cause-to-kill' takes as its subject, not the subject or object of the inner transitive verb, but the additional expression referring, characteristically, to the causal agent; and this, in many languages, involves the demotion of the subject of the inner verb to the status of indirect object in the three-place structure (the position of direct object being filled already). It is important not to exaggerate the similarities between valency-grammar and relational grammar—the more so as relational grammar has not yet been widely exemplified in the published literature. But there are certain discernible similarities of the kind mentioned in this paragraph.

What is generally regarded as a more serious challenge to the standard theory comes from *generative semantics*. Though it is now firmly entrenched in current discussions of linguistic theory, the term 'generative semantics' is misleading in several respects. Generative semantics is not merely, or even primarily, a theory of semantics. Still less is 'generative' in contrast with 'non-generative', in this context, as it is when one talks about the difference between generative grammar and pre-Chomskyan, non-generative grammar. The term 'generative semantics' refers to an alternative version of transformational-generative grammar—one which differs from the standard version of *Aspects* in that the rules of the semantic component are said to be 'generative', rather than 'interpretive'.

According to the standard theory, every sentence has two identifiable levels of syntactic structure: *deep structure* and *surface structure*. Deep structures are phrase-markers (containing lexical items) that are generated by the rules of the base-component. They are converted into surface structures by the application of an ordered set of transformational rules, some of which apply cyclically (see Appendix 1). The deep structures serve as input to the semantic component and the surface structures as input to the phonological component (see Figure 8). Both the semantic rules and the phonological rules are purely *interpretive*: the function of the semantic rules is to interpret the output of the base-component by assigning to each sentence a *semantic representation* (or several semantic representations in the case of ambiguous sentences) as the function of the phonological rules is to assign to each sentence a phonetic representation. The term 'interpret', it should be noted, is here being used in a technical sense. The semantic interpretation associated with a sentence by the grammar is not its meaning, but a formal representation of its meaning (in what is, strictly speaking, a formal meta-language: see Appendix 1) in terms of a set of symbols each of which denotes a universal atomic concept; and the phonetic interpretation of a sentence is not its pronunciation, but a formal representation of its pronunciation in terms of a set of symbols each of which denotes some universal phonetic feature. These symbols are the elements, or *primes*, of the semantic and the phonetic levels of representation, respectively; and the notion 'level of representation' is rigorously defined within Chomsky's formalization of the theory of grammar.

But the standard theory is formulated within the framework of certain more general Chomskyan beliefs about the nature of language and linguistic competence. In particular, it is Chomsky's belief that every speaker of any natural language (by virtue of his possession of the specifically human capacity to acquire language) knows, in some sense, what counts as a humanly possible speech-sound and what counts as a humanly possible concept (or conceptual distinction); and that he also knows some of the conditions that determine the well-formed combinations of sounds and meanings that are brought together in the words and sentences of particular languages. We will come back to this part of Chomsky's thought in Chapters 9 and 10. It suffices for the present to emphasize the fact that when Chomsky says that the grammar of a particular language (a *language-particular grammar*) is a system of rules and principles that links sound with meaning, he is taking for granted the native speaker's ability to perform another kind of interpretation, by means of which the phonetic representations are converted into sound and the semantic representations into meaning. The missing links are supplied, in intent at least, by the more general theory of grammar, which Chomsky refers to as *universal grammar*. It is by virtue of his knowledge of universal grammar that the speaker of a natural language is held to be able to interpret the phonetic and semantic representations (or, more precisely, the mental schemata that are their psychological correlates in language-performance).

Generative semantics is far from being as radical an alternative to the standard theory as it has sometimes seemed to be, both to its proponents and to some of its opponents. Like Chomsky, the generative semanticists take the view that language-particular grammars are generative devices whose function it is to relate semantic representations and phonetic representations; they operate with the same kind of semantic and phonetic primes; they make essentially the same assumptions as Chomsky does about the native speaker's ability to interpret these primes (or their cognitive correlates) by virtue of his knowledge of universal grammar; and, finally, the kind of grammatical model to which they appeal is not merely generative, but transformational. What then is the difference between generative semantics and the standard theory?

At first sight, the difference is clear enough: the standard theory model is syntactically-based and the generative-semantics model is semantically-based. That is to say, whereas the standard theory puts all the generative capacity of the grammar in the syntax (and more particularly in the base-component), generative semantics puts all the generative capacity of the grammar in the rules of semantic well-formedness. It is this conception of the difference between generative semantics and the standard theory which accounts for the use of the term 'generative semantics' in the first place. But now, after some years of involved and at times acrimonious argument, it is accepted by both the proponents and the opponents of generative semantics that its difference from the standard theory cannot be characterized simply in terms of the directionality of the relation that holds between syntax and semantics. Much of the initial plausibility of generative semantics disappears when this point is appreciated. It is only too easy to think of a generative grammar as a model of the language-user's production and comprehension of actual utterances (cf. Chapter 4). Looked at from this point of view, the generative-semantics model can be seen as one which more directly reflects the conversion of meaning to sound in production and of sound to meaning in comprehension. But neither the standard theory model nor the generative-semantics model is intended to be a model of language performance. Furthermore, it is hardly more realistic to think of the production of utterances as a process in which the speaker first of all forms in his mind a sentence-sized idea, as it were, and only then selects a syntactic structure and words with which to express this idea than it is to conceive

93

of it as a process in which the speaker first decides upon some syntactic structure and then chooses words to fit it. What then is the difference between the standard theory and generative semantics when they are both regarded as models of competence rather than performance?

The principal difference is that, whereas the standard theory draws a distinction between the deep structure of a sentence and its semantic interpretation (the latter being derived from the former by the purely interpretive projection rules of the semantic component), the generative-semantics theory draws no such distinction. According to the generative-semantics hypothesis the deep structure of a sentence *is* its semantic representation; and this is converted into a surface structure, in much the same way as an *Aspects*-type deep structure is converted into a surface structure, by means of the application, in sequence, of a set of transformational rules. Since Chomskyan transformational rules, by definition, convert phrase markers into phrase-markers, it follows that, for the generative semanticist, the semantic representation of a sentence is a phrase-marker (i.e. a labelled bracketting). However, it differs from an *Aspects*-type deep structure (which, as we have seen, is also a labelled bracketting) in that its terminal elements are not words, like *kill* or *man* in English, but semantic primes like CAUSE, COME ABOUT, NOT and EXISTENT or MALE, ADULT and HUMAN.

The generative semanticists have justified their rejection of an independent, syntactically-motivated level of deep structure by observing that pairs of sentences which differ in terms of their syntactic structure and the words that they contain may be semantically equivalent (or at least semantically related to one another) in much the same way as pairs of sentences that are held to be transformationally related in an *Aspects*-type grammar: cf. *John used the key to open the door* and *John opened the door with the key,* or *John bought the car from Harry* and *Harry sold the car to John.* Whether such pairs of sentences have exactly the same meaning or not is debatable. But they will serve their present purpose. Granted that *John bought the car from Harry* and *Harry sold the car to John* are derived from a common underlying semantic representation, the words 'sell' and 'buy' would be inserted into the phrase markers by a transformational rule of substitution operating upon different syntactically structured complexes of semantic primes. These rules of *lexicalization* (unlike the very different rules of lexicalization in the standard theory) would not apply at a distinct and identifiable level of syntactic representation (the level of deep structure), but would be scattered, as it were, throughout the other transformational rules.

Generative semantics is best regarded perhaps as the culmination and consolidation of several tendencies, all of which are present elsewhere in post-Chomskyan linguistics. The most obvious of these is the tendency to motivate syntactic rules by means of semantic evidence. As we saw in Chapter 3, Chomsky took a characteristically 'Bloomfieldian' view of the relation between syntax and semantics in his earliest work (without, however, accepting Bloomfield's behaviouristic notion of meaning). However, it has always been evident, both to Chomsky and to Harris, that (as Harris made the point in 1957) 'some major element of meaning remains constant under transformation'. By the mid-1960s many linguists (notably J. J. Katz and P. M. Postal, whose work was particularly influential) were prepared to drop the qualification implicit in the phrase 'some major element', saying, forcefully and programmatically: 'Transformations do not change meaning'. This slogan expresses a point of view which Chomsky accepted, at least tentatively, at the time that he was writing *Aspects*. In terms of the standard theory (all the 'non-stylistic' transformational rules being obligatory), identity of deep structure

95

is a sufficient condition of identity of meaning. The generative semanticist goes further: he makes identity of meaning a sufficient condition for postulating transformational relatedness and identity of deep structure. In doing so, he is carrying to an extreme the practice of using semantic data as evidence for syntactic relatedness. But this practice was common in almost all the transformational work, both Chomskyan and post-Chomskyan, that was published in the decade following the appearance of *Aspects*: it is partly a cause and partly a consequence of the greatly increased attention that linguists have been paying to semantics in recent years.

Another general tendency of much post-Chomskyan linguistics is the acceptance of a point of view that can be summed up in the slogans 'Deep structures are universal' and 'All languages have the same deep structure'. The second of these is, strictly speaking, uninterpretable in terms of the Chomskyan notion of deep structure: languages do not have a deep structure (or a surface structure), but each sentence of a language does. Translated into Chomskyan terms, the second slogan (which is not uncommon, in the form in which I have just given it, in the non-linguistic literature) might read as follows: 'All natural languages have (i.e. are generated by) the same base component (excluding the lexicon)'. Interpreted in this way, the second slogan expresses what has come to be called the universal base hypothesis, and more will be said about this presently. Neither the generative semantics theory nor the standard theory commits its adherents to the universal base hypothesis. (It is worth pointing out, in passing, that Chomsky himself has never subscribed to it, though what he has said about formal and substantive universals has often been misunderstood as implying that he does: see Chapter 10.) But many transformational grammarians, from both the 'generativist' and the 'interpretivist' camps, have been attracted by the universal base hypothesis; and they have seen as evidence for it a kind of convergence in the increasingly 'deep', or more 'abstract', analyses that linguists have been providing for 'superficially' dissimilar structures in different languages.

The reader will note that I deliberately slipped into the last sentence the words 'deep', 'superficial' and 'abstract', signalling the fact that I was using them loosely, not to say equivocally, by putting them between quotation-marks. It is quite possible to define a notion of transformational depth (in terms of the number of rules applying in the generation of the phrase-marker, or otherwise). It is arguable, however, that the universal base hypothesis has gained some of its support from the very looseness with which such evocative, and potentially equivocal, words as 'deep', 'abstract' and 'superficial' have been used in its formulation. However that may be, it is undeniable that it has seemed to be an attractive hypothesis, not just to the generative semanticists, but to many linguists who would disagree with them on other issues.

There is of course an important difference between a 'generativist' and an 'interpretivist' version of the universal base hypothesis. There is no *Aspects*-type base-component in a generative-semantics model. Instead, there are formation-rules whose function it is to generate a set of well-formed semantic representations. It is the formation-rules, therefore, that are held to be universal by the generative semanticist. In contrast, an 'interpretivist' who subscribes to the universal base hypothesis is committed to the very different (and, at first sight at least, far more interesting) proposition that the purely syntactic rules of an *Aspects*-type base-component are universal. We will come back to this point.

A third general tendency of much of the most recent Chomskyan and post-Chomskyan linguistics is the increasing employment of the conceptual and termino-logical apparatus of modern formal logic and formal semantics. Both 'generativists' and 'interpretivists' have concentrated their attention, in the last few years, on a range of topics (negation, quantification, presuppo-sition, etc.) whose clarification and analysis owes much to the work of logicians and philosophers. Generative semanticists, in particular, have been inclined to identify the deep structure of a sentence (i.e. its semantic representation) with what the philosopher would refer to as its *logical form*. For example, a sentence like *Everyone loves someone* is ambiguous with respect to its logical form. And its ambiguity is accounted for, in standard systems of formal logic, by the relative order of the quantifiers (the formal correlates of *everyone* and *someone*) in the formulae which represent the two different propositions expressed by the sentence. The generative semanticist would give exactly the same account of the ambiguity; saying that the sentence in question is derived, by transformational rules, from two different semantic representations, the one having *someone* at a higher level than *everyone* in the underlying phrase-marker and the other having *everyone* higher than *someone*. In this respect, the generative semanticist's conception of underlying structure closely matches the philosopher's conception of logical form. Indeed, the semantic representations with which generative semanticists operate are almost identical with the formulae of standard first-order logic.

Reference has just been made to the branch of logic known as formal semantics; and this brings us to the last of the alternatives to the standard theory, other than the Chomskyan extended standard theory, that will be dealt with here. In origin, formal semantics is the study of the semantics of the propositional calculus, the predicate calculus and other formal languages constructed by logi-cians. (For some discussion of the grammar of formal languages, see Appendix 1.) Usually, the meaning of a sentence in a formal language is defined to be its *truth-conditions*: i.e. the conditions which must be met in any world, or state of affairs, that the sentence purports to describe in order for the sentence to be true. Many formal languages are such that it is possible to construct a finite or infinite set of complex sentences out of a finite set of simple sentences. If a formal language has this syntactic property together with the more particular semantic property that the meaning of every complex sentence is a function of the meanings of the simple sentences of which the complex sentence is composed, the task of providing a semantic analysis of the language (i.e. an interpretation of each sentence in terms of its truth-conditions) can be split into two parts: (i) that of assigning an interpretation to each of the simple sentences; (ii) that of specifying for every distinct means of combining sentences that the syntactic rules of the language permit the principle, or function (in the mathematical sense), which determines the meaning of the resultant combination. The second of these two parts of the semantic analysis will be facilitated if it is the syntactic structure itself which determines the meaning of the successively more complex combinations of sentences. Several formal languages have been constructed that have this property. But formal languages are under the control of their designers and, within limits, they can be provided with whatever properties their designers think fit to provide them with. What about natural languages?

One scholar who took the view that the semantic structure of natural languages could, and should, be analysed like the semantic structure of formal languages (under a standard truth-conditional interpretation) was the American logician Richard Montague (who died in 1971). He was not alone in taking this view. But what has come to be called *Montague-grammar* appears to have won more support so far than other systems that are strongly influenced by work within the field of formal semantics. There is no need for us to go into the technicalities of Montague-grammar. It is sufficient to point out that Montague's system differs, not only from the *Aspects*-system, but from all the other Chomskyan and post-Chomskyan alternatives considered in this section, in several respects. The most important has to do with the close correspondence that Montague establishes between the syntax and the semantics; and he does this by adopting a particular kind of *categorial grammar* (see Appendix 1). Another important difference between Montague-grammar and other kinds of Chomskyan and post-Chomskyan generative grammar is that, when it comes to excluding certain strings of words as ill-formed, Montague throws much more weight on the semantics than he does on the syntax. This is more a matter of his pre-theoretical attitude towards the notion of grammaticality. But it is arguable, and has been argued, that in *Aspects* Chomsky went too far in the other direction, excluding (by means of the device of *selection restrictions*) sentences which, if they are ill-formed (e.g. *Sincerity admires John*), are semantically, not syntactically, ill-formed. It is too early to say what effect Montague-grammar will have upon linguistics in the next few years. It has been mentioned here because it has a number of powerful advocates among linguists. Though Montague-grammar was not strongly influenced by the work of Chomsky, as far as Montague's own development of the system was concerned, it has been suggested recently (notably by Barbara H. Partee) that a more powerful type of Montague-grammar might be constructed—a grammar with a categorial base-component and a transformational extension to it—and that a Montague-grammar of this kind would be more appropriate than any currently available alternative version of transformational grammar, for relating the semantic interpret-ations of natural-language sentences to their syntactic structure.

Having looked at the most important post-Chomskyan alternatives to the standard theory, we may turn now to the so-called *extended standard theory* of Chomsky and his more immediate associates. The extended standard theory has been in a state of more or less continuous development for the last ten years. It differs from generative semantics in that, like the standard theory of *Aspects*, it is an 'interpretivist' theory within which sentences are assigned a deep-structure representation distinct from their semantic representation, and the transformational rules apply after the insertion of words from the lexicon in the underlying phrase-markers. It differs from the standard theory, however, in that it has abandoned the principle that only the deep structure of a sentence is relevant to the determination of its semantic representation. Indeed, the development of the extended standard theory from its earliest version of 1970 ('Deep structure, surface structure and semantic interpretation') to its most recent 1976 version (*Reflections on Language*) can be described, in a very general way, as the pro-gressive devaluation, for the process of semantic inter-pretation, of the notion of deep structure. In the earlier version, the semantic interpretation of a sentence (in the specialized Chomskyan sense of 'interpretation') is determined jointly by its deep structure and its surface structure. But more recently Chomsky has come to believe 'that a suitably enriched notion of surface struc-ture suffices to determine the meaning of sentences under interpretive rules' (*Reflections on Language*, Chapter 3). What this enrichment of the notion of surface structure consists in is something that cannot be discussed here. It is sufficient for our purposes that it should be seen as involving what I have referred to as a corresponding devaluation of the notion of deep structure.

It is important to realize, however, that, as far as Chomsky is concerned, the notion of deep structure still plays much the same role in syntax as it always has done in his formalization of transformational grammar. (In saying this, I am deliberately glossing over the fact that, for technical reasons, complex sentences did not have unitary deep structures in the 1957 version of transformational grammar. For present purposes, at least, the term 'deep structure' can be taken to cover, retrospectively, the underlying phrase-markers of *Syntactic Structures*. One of the few innovations in the *Aspects*-system that can be described, without reservation, as an improvement is the introduction of the notion of generalized phrase-markers. Another is the strict separation of the syntax and lexicon, together with a technique for cross-classifying words in terms of sets of syntactic properties.) In the passage from which the quotation in the previous paragraph is drawn, Chomsky makes it quite clear that the notion of deep structures is, in principle, no more closely bound up with the principle of semantic interpretation than the notion of surface structure is.

He also insists—and this is a very important point for anyone who wishes to understand Chomsky's thought—that there is no correlation between depth, in the technical sense of being transformationally less complex, and either universality or importance: 'There is a widespread feeling that semantics is that part of language that is really deep and important, and that the study of language is interesting primarily insofar as it contributes to some understanding of these questions of real profundity.' He allows that 'there is some merit to this view'. But, comparing physics with linguistics, and, within linguistics, comparing semantics with phonology, he argues that 'physics is significant, applications aside, because of its intellectual depth, and if it were to turn out that the principles of phonology are considerably more sophisticated and intricate than those of semantics, that they enter into non-trivial arguments to explain surprising facts, that they give us much more insight into the nature of the organism, then phonology will be a far deeper theory than semantics, despite the more limited intrinsic interest of the phenomena with which it deals'. As we have already seen (and, having pointed this out himself, Chomsky deliberately uses the term 'deep' both technically and non-technically in the passage from which I have just quoted), the several senses in which the word 'deep' can be used has led to considerable confusion. This point must be borne constantly in mind when we look at the psychological and philosophical implications of transformational grammar in Chapters 9 and 10.

We have now almost concluded our general comparative account of the most notable Chomskyan and post-Chomskyan alternatives to the standard theory of 1965. It is no part of my purpose to predict which, if any, of these alternatives will triumph. Nor can there be any question, in a book of this nature, of going into the technical details of the various systems. There is one point of a more technical character, however, that must be made; and this has to do with the relative *power* of different transformational grammars.

As we saw in the preceding three chapters, Chomsky's earliest work in generative grammar was directed towards showing that of the 'three models for the description of language' (to quote the title of his 1956 paper) whose formal properties he had investigated— finite-state grammar, phrase-structure grammar and transformational grammar—the first was definitely not powerful enough for the purpose and the second, though perhaps capable in principle of generating all and only the sentences of any natural language, was not capable of assigning to them structural descriptions that would reveal their formal interrelations. Transformational grammars are intrinsically more powerful than phrase-structure grammars. It is arguable, however, that they are too powerful.

The suggestion that a grammar, or a theory, might be condemned on the grounds of its excessive power frequently causes difficulty. The word 'powerful', like the word 'deep', has various non-technical or semi-technical senses, in addition to the technical sense in which it is being used here. In one of these semi-technical senses a powerful theory is one that accounts for a large body of data and does so with maximum simplicity and elegance; and, in this sense of 'powerful', the more powerful a theory is, the better it is. But suppose we think of some proposed model of universal grammar (in the sense in which universal grammar is opposed to language-particular grammars) as a theory whose aim it is to distinguish natural languages, actual and potential, from other systems which (whether they are used for communication or not) might be thought to resemble natural languages in terms of their formal properties. Looked at from this point of view, our model would be too powerful if it generated, in addition to all actual and potential natural languages, systems that we have reason to believe are neither actual nor potential languages. What we are after, therefore, is not the most powerful kind of generative grammar, but a generative grammar that is just powerful enough to do what it is required to do.

It has long been suspected that, unless they are restricted in some way, transformational grammars are far too powerful; and this has now been proved to be the case in connection with the universal base hypothesis, to which reference was made earlier in this chapter. In a series of important papers, P. S. Peters and R. W. Ritchie have shown that any natural language (not to mention systems that are neither actual nor potential natural languages) can be generated by a transformational grammar that contains any one of an infinite number of base-components. There is a trivial sense, therefore, in which every natural language can be said to have the same base-component. In order to give empirical content to the universal base hypothesis (within the framework of transformational grammar), more specific restrictions must be imposed upon the base-component or the transformational component than are imposed by the standard theory. Indeed, it is now generally accepted that, whether one wishes to defend some version of the universal base hypothesis or not (and Chomsky, as we have seen, does not), transformational grammar, in any of its Chomskyan or post-Chomskyan forms, is far too powerful for the description of natural languages, unless it is restricted in some way. Much of the most interesting theoretical work that is currently being done, by Chomsky and others, in the field of transformational grammar has as its goal that of imposing upon either the base-component or the transformational component (or both) conditions that are (as Chomsky puts it in one of his most recent papers) 'explicit and as restrictive as possible'. The reason is clear: 'We want universal grammar to make as strong a statement as possible about the nature of language and thus to be subject to critical tests and to provide explanations for the phenomena attested in descriptive study.'

Basic research of this kind is very much in the spirit of Chomsky's earliest work on what he referred to, at that time, as 'the logical structure of linguistic theory'. It is my contention, throughout this book, that Chomsky's most original contribution to linguistics lies in his having promoted such research and having made clear its significance.

Twenty years after the publication of *Syntactic Structures*, the status of transformational grammar is still a matter of controversy among linguists; and, as we have seen in this chapter, there are now several alternative Chomskyan and post-Chomskyan versions of transformational grammar. It should be added that, although we have not dealt with it here, Zellig Harris's system of transformational grammar, very different from Chomsky's, has also been modified and extended by its author, since it was first developed in the mid-1950s. Several other kinds of generative grammar also have been, and are being, proposed: *applicational grammar* (S. K. Shaumjan), *systemic grammar* (M. A. K. Halliday, R. A. Hudson, etc.), *stratificational grammar* (S. M. Lamb). It is difficult to compare these and other comprehensive models of linguistic description in terms of their power with the more obviously Chomskyan and post-Chomskyan versions of transformational grammar. Any such comparison presupposes that the grammars in question have been formalized within a common framework: and this is not the case. We have naturally restricted our attention in this chapter to what has just been described as the 'more obviously Chomskyan and post-Chomskyan versions of transformational grammar'. But any reader who looks further into this question can readily verify for himself the statement that I made in the Introduction and repeated at the beginning of this chapter. All current work in theoretical linguistics carries, to a greater or less degree, the mark of Chomsky's influence.

9 The Psychological Implications of Generative Grammar

As I emphasized in Chapter 4, the earlier works of Chomsky were written within the tradition of 'autonomous' linguistics. It is only later, in *Aspects of the Theory of Syntax*, *Cartesian Linguistics* and *Language and Mind*, that he began to refer to linguistics as a branch of cognitive psychology and to insist upon the importance of generative grammar for the investigation of the structure and predispositions of the human mind. However, as I said in the Introduction, it is for these later views, rather than for his more technical contributions to linguistics as an independent discipline, that Chomsky is now best known. We shall therefore devote the next two chapters to an exposition of Chomsky's current views on these psychological and philosophical issues, dividing the material, somewhat arbitrarily as it will appear, between the two headings of 'psychology' and 'philosophy'.

Although Chomsky's general position in *Syntactic Structures* is, as far as he reveals it, indistinguishable from that of the 'Bloomfieldians' and other empiricists, there is one point on which he disagreed with Bloomfield and many of his followers from very early on. (I am not now referring to Chomsky's rejection of 'discovery' in favour of 'evaluation'. This issue, which we discussed in a previous chapter, though important in the post-war development of linguistics, is in principle independent of the empiricist position.) Bloomfield, as we have seen, was a behaviourist (at the time that he wrote *Language*), and many of his followers shared his belief that a 'mechanistic' account of language in terms of 'stimulus-and-response' was more objective and more scientific than the traditional 'mentalistic' description of language as a vehicle for the 'expression of thought'. In the year that *Syntactic Structures* was published, B. F. Skinner's *Verbal Behavior* also appeared; and it was reviewed in due course by Chomsky. Skinner (who is Professor of Psychology at Harvard University) is one of the most eminent and most influential advocates of behaviourist psychology alive at the present time; and his book constitutes the most detailed attempt that has yet been made to account for the acquisition of language within the framework of behaviouristic 'learning theory'. Chomsky's review is now a classic, in which he not only subjects Skinner's book to a penetrating examination, but at the same time reveals his own mastery of the relevant psychological literature.

Chomsky has since repeated his arguments against behaviourism on many occasions. Briefly, they amount to the following. One of the most striking facts about language is its 'creativity'—the fact that by the age of five or six children are able to produce and understand an indefinitely large number of utterances that they have not previously encountered—and the behaviourist's 'learning theory', however successful it might be in accounting for the way in which certain networks of 'habits' and 'associations' are built up in the 'behaviour-patterns' of animals and human beings, is totally incapable of explaining 'creativity'—an aspect of human 'behaviour' manifest most clearly (though perhaps not exclusively) in language. Chomsky further claims that the terminology of behaviourism ('stimulus', 'response', 'habit', 'conditioning', 'reinforcement', etc.), though it can be made precise (and has been made precise in its application to more restricted domains), as actually applied to language, is so loose that it could cover anything and is thus completely devoid of empirical content. In the absence of any overt 'response', the behaviourist takes refuge in an unobserved and unobservable 'disposition to respond'; and having accounted, in principle, for the association of words (as 'responses') with objects (as 'stimuli') and for the learning of a limited set of sentences in the same way, he either says nothing at all about the formation of new sentences or at this point appeals to some undefined notion of 'analogy'.

Chomsky's criticisms of behaviourism are undoubtedly valid. It does not follow of course (and as far as I know Chomsky has never claimed that it does) that no aspects of language, or the use of language, can be reasonably described in terms a 'stimulus-and-response' model. There can be little doubt, however, that the behaviourist account of the acquisition of language, as formulated at present, fails to come to grips with, let alone solve, the problem posed by what Chomsky calls 'creativity'.

Neither the earlier nor the later versions of transformational grammar are presented by Chomsky as psychological models of the way people construct and understand utterances. The grammar of a language, as conceived by Chomsky, is an idealized description of the linguistic *competence* of native speakers of that language (see p. 44). Any psychological model of the way this competence is put to use in actual *performance* will have to take into account a number of additional facts which the linguist deliberately ignores in his definition of the notion of *grammaticality*. These psychologically relevant facts include the limitations of human memory and attention, the time it takes for neural 'signals' to pass from the brain to the muscles that are involved in speech, the interference of one physiological or psychological process with another, and so on. Many of the sentences which the linguist regards as grammatical (well-formed in terms of the rules set up to describe the competence of the 'ideal' native speaker) would never in fact occur 'naturally'; and, if constructed deliberately for the purpose of some linguistic experiment, will be difficult, and perhaps impossible, for actual native speakers to understand, because they cannot be 'processed' without 'overloading' the various psychological mechanisms involved in the reception and comprehension of speech. This is one way in which the utterances actually produced by speakers of a language might differ significantly, for psychologically explicable reasons, from the sentences described as 'grammatical' by the linguist. Another difference, and one which Chomsky has more frequently stressed, is that the utterances produced will contain a variety of mistakes and distortions (mispronunciations, unfinished sentences, hesitations, changes of construction in the middle of a sentence, etc.) due to the malfunctioning of the psychological mechanisms involved or to their inherent limitations. These deviations from the grammatical norm are a valuable part of the psychologist's data and, when properly analysed, may give him some insight into the structure and operation of the mechanisms underlying the use of language.

Although linguistics and psychology take a different point of view with respect to the investigation of language, Chomsky has always maintained that there are important connexions between the two disciplines. In fact, the change that one can discern between his earlier and later view of the relationship between psychology and linguistics (to which I have already referred) is largely a matter of emphasis. If Chomsky now describes linguistics as a branch of psychology rather than as an independent discipline, he is not suggesting that the linguist should turn from the investigation of language to the investigation of the use of language, from linguistic competence to linguistic performance. What he is saying is that the most important reason for being interested in the scientific study of language, and more especially in generative grammar, is that it has a contribution to make to our understanding of mental processes. Linguistics is incorporated in psychology, therefore, not by virtue of any substantial change in subject matter or method, but for the ultimate significance of its results.

Even Chomsky's appeal to 'intuition', which is more prominent in his later work (and which has frequently been misunderstood), can be interpreted in this light. According to Chomsky, two grammars may be *observationally* adequate (and weakly equivalent) in that they both generate the same set of sentences. But one will be *descriptively* more adequate than the other if it is in accord with the 'intuitions' of native speakers, with respect to such questions as 'structural ambiguity' and the equivalence or non-equivalence of certain types of sentences. This is the terminology used in *Aspects of the Theory of Syntax* and in other recent works. The terminological distinction is revealing. It shows that for Chomsky the 'intuitions' of the speaker (that is to say, his mental representation of the grammar of the language), rather than the sentences themselves, are the true object of description. As we saw in Chapter 4, Chomsky had previously laid more stress on 'simplicity' as a criterion for the evaluation of weakly equivalent grammars; and, when he did talk of the speaker's judgements with respect to such questions as 'structural ambiguities', it was never suggested that these judgements, or 'intuitions', were of primary concern: they testified to the informant's apprehension of the structure of his language, but they did not themselves constitute the subject matter of linguistics. It is sometimes thought that Chomsky's appeal to the 'intuitions' of the native speaker (including the 'intuitions' of the linguist as a speaker of his own native language) implies some relaxation of the standards of rigour and objectivity characteristic of Bloomfieldian linguistics and other modern approaches. This is not so. Chomsky does not claim that the speaker's 'intuitions' are immediately accessible; nor does he say that they are all equally reliable. It is arguable that some of the work inspired by Chomsky's formulation of the goals of linguistics rests on a too ready acceptance of a particular linguist's 'intuitions'. In principle, however, whether a given sentence is acceptable, whether it is equivalent to some other sentence or not, and what its implications are —all these and similar questions which fall within the scope of the native speaker's 'intuition', as Chomsky uses this term, are subject to empirical verification.

As early as 1958 Chomsky collaborated with the psychologist George Miller in writing a paper entitled 'Finite State Languages' and in 1963 they contributed two chapters to the *Handbook of Mathematical Psychology* (there is also a further chapter written by Chomsky alone). One of these chapters by Miller and Chomsky, 'Finitary models of language users', draws in some detail the implications of generative grammar for the investigation of the psychological mechanisms underlying linguistic performance.

It follows immediately from Chomsky's proof that finite state grammars are incapable of generating some of the sentences to be found in English and other languages, that no performance model which is based on the same principle of 'left-to-right' derivation is worthy of serious consideration. We can therefore exclude all those theories of the production and reception of speech which assume that the probability of occurrence of a given word in a particular position in an utterance is determined solely by the words that have been selected for the preceding positions. It may not seem very plausible that anyone should seek to account for the production of an utterance like *We have just been running* by saying that the speaker first selects *we* from the set of words permissible at the beginning of English sentences and then, having made this choice, selects *have*, as one of the words which has a certain probability of occurrence after *we*; then, having chosen *we* and *have*, selects *just*, by virtue of its probability of occurrence after *we have*; and so on. Plausible or not (and common sense 'plausibility' is after all not always reliable), this conception of the production of the speech has inspired a considerable amount of psychological research (including, it might be added, some of George Miller's earlier work). Chomsky proved that this approach is misguided, despite the sophistication of the statistical theory it draws upon.

The second of Chomsky's 'models for the description of language' was phrase structure grammar; and, as we saw in Chapter 6, various kinds of phrase structure grammars can be constructed according to the restrictions imposed upon the format or mode of operation of the rules. It is an interesting fact, as proved by Chomsky, that context free phrase structure grammars are equivalent in generative capacity to what are called *push-down storage* devices in *automata theory*. We cannot go into this highly technical question in any detail, but it may be mentioned briefly, in order to give the reader some idea of the kind of hypotheses about performance models that can be suggested by a study of the formal properties of language and the generative capacity of particular types of grammar.

The human memory, as we have said, has presumably only a finite (though perhaps very large) amount of storage at its disposal, and it may operate, to some extent at least, on the 'push-down' principle of 'last in, first out', so that, other things being equal, we recall most easily and most quickly what we have 'stored' in memory most recently. It is reasonable to suppose that the *long-term*, or permanent, memory contains a good deal of information, including the rules of the grammar, to which access is made during the 'processing' of utterances. But we are concerned here with what psychologists call the *short-term* memory, which we use, for example, when we commit to memory (without learning or repetition) a list of unconnected items (e.g. nonsense syllables or digits). There are very severe limits upon the capacity of short-term memory, the number of items that we can 'store' there being of the order of seven ('seven plus or minus two', as Miller put it in the title of a famous paper). So much is background information relevant to the hypothesis we are about to discuss.

This is the so-called 'depth hypothesis', developed in the early 1960s by Victor Yngve, who was at that time working on the problems of syntactic analysis by computer. Let us begin by giving a purely abstract example of a phrase structure grammar, which includes a number of recursive rules:

(1) $A \rightarrow B + C$	(6) $D \rightarrow \{d, \ldots\}$
(2) $B \rightarrow (B) + D$	(7) $E \rightarrow \{e, \ldots\}$
(3) $B \rightarrow E + (B)$	(8) $F \rightarrow \{f, \ldots\}$
(4) $B \rightarrow F + (B) + G$	(9) $G \rightarrow \{g, \ldots\}$
(5) $C \rightarrow \{c, \ldots\}$	

(I have followed a common convention in using capitals for auxiliary elements and lower case letters for terminal elements.) It will be observed that rules (2), (3) and (4) are recursive, but in different ways. Rule (2) is *left recursive*; rule (3) is *right recursive*; and rule (4) is *self-embedding*. Figures 10, 11 and 12 illustrate what is meant by these terms.

Now, Yngve's hypothesis was that left-recursive structures add to the 'depth' or psychological complexity, of a sentence, because recursion to the left, unlike recursion to the right, increases the amount of 'space' taken up in the short-term memory during the processing of the sentence. When the 'depth' of a sentence goes beyond the critical limit (this limit being determined by the capacity of the short-term memory) its continuation becomes unmanageable. And one of the reasons why there are transformations in language, Yngve suggested, is to enable the speaker to avoid excessive 'depth' by using equivalent right-branching constructions, rather than left-branching constructions, at certain points in the production of sentences. This hypothesis predicts, therefore, that a phrase like *John's friend's wife's father's*

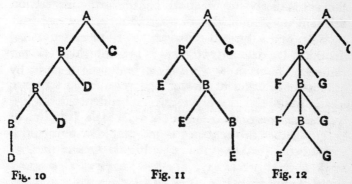

Fig. 10   Fig. 11   Fig. 12

gardener's daughter's cat should be more difficult to 'process' than the equivalent right-branching version, *The cat belonging to the daughter of the gardener of the father of the wife of the friend of John.*

The 'depth hypothesis', as formulated by Yngve, is almost certainly incorrect, since it rests on the assumption that sentences are 'processed' by human beings in the way that they were generated by his computer program. Moreover, it is not clear that left-branching structures are as difficult for human beings to 'process' as they should be according to the hypothesis. English has a variety both of left-recursive and right-recursive constructions; and there may well be a general tendency, as Yngve claimed, to avoid excessive 'depth' by taking advantage of this fact. But there are other languages, including Turkish and Japanese, where the recursive constructions are predominantly left-branching.

Furthermore, as Chomsky has pointed out in his discussion of Yngve's hypothesis, it is *self-embedding* constructions (as exemplified in Figure 12) that seem to cause the greatest difficulty; and this cannot be explained in terms of the notion of 'depth'. As a simple example of self-embedding, consider a sentence like *The book the man left is on the table.* Here we have one sentence *The man left the book* (strictly speaking, the string underlying this sentence) embedded in the middle of *The book is on the table* (and subjected to a variety of other operations, including the deletion of *the book* in the embedded relative clause). The resultant complex sentence is perfectly acceptable. But let us now embed yet another sentence in the middle of the previously embedded clause: *The book the man the gardener saw left is on the table.* It is a moot point whether this sentence is acceptable or not. And if we embed a further sentence within *the gardener saw (the man)* to yield, let us say, *The book the man the gardener I employed yesterday saw left is on the table,* we will surely say that the 'output' is unacceptable. Such sentences, despite the formal simplicity of the process of self-embedding, are undeniably difficult to 'process' in both the production and the reception of speech. The explanation, as Chomsky says, cannot be simply that there are severe limitations on the capacity of the short-term memory (although this is no doubt one of the factors involved), because *self*-embedding constructions are significantly more difficult to 'process' than other constructions derived by the embedding of one element in the middle, rather than at the left or right of a string. In other words, all structures generated by means of a rule of the form $X \rightarrow V + (Y) + W$ (where V and W are strings of one or more elements) involve the temporary 'storage of' W while Y is being 'processed'. Self-embedding occurs when a rule has the more specific property that X and Y take the same 'value' (as in rule (4) above). The identity of

X and *Y* appears to introduce additional complexity from the point of view of production and comprehension. Chomsky and Miller suggested, as a hypothesis capable in principle of explaining this fact, that the underlying psychological mechanism is of such a kind that it cannot, or can only with difficulty, execute a particular operation if it is already in the midst of executing the same operation.

More recent research would tend to suggest that neither Yngve's 'depth' hypothesis nor Chomsky's hypothesis about self-embedding is of itself sufficient to explain the phenomena. The important point, for present purposes, is that the investigation of the formal properties of language, in terms of notions which derive from generative grammar, has implications for the study of the psychological 'mechanisms' and processes underlying linguistic performance. Psychologists were not slow to perceive these implications. George Miller's collaboration with Chomsky in the late 1950s has already been mentioned; and Miller's authority and reputation as a psychologist was such that his colleagues could not but take seriously what was, for most of them, a radically novel way of looking at language.

By the early 1960s the whole new sub-discipline of *psycholinguistics* had come into being. It has been gathering strength ever since. The term 'psycholinguistics' antedates by about a decade the birth of what I have just referred to as a whole new sub-discipline. Psychologists had long been interested in language; and 'Bloomfieldian' linguistics, as we have seen, had been strongly influenced by behaviourist psychology. When the term 'psycholinguistics' was first used, it referred to a rather loose inter-disciplinary synthesis of current psychology and linguistics—a synthesis in which, for a short while, 'information-theory' looked like having a strong catalyzing effect (see Chapter 5). Psycholinguistics is something very different nowadays. Whether it is more properly regarded as a sub-discipline of psychology or of linguistics, or alternatively as a hybrid which is part equally of both, is a question of secondary importance. What distinguishes the new psycholinguistics from the old is the very intimacy of the association between psychology and linguistics in what can rightly be described as the new sub-discipline of psycholinguistics. It was the revolutionary impact of Chomsky's ideas, more than anything else, that created this new sub-discipline. Not surprisingly, some of the earliest of the distinctively new psycholinguistic work was designed to establish the psychological validity of transformational rules.

As we saw in Chapter 7, the way in which Chomsky accounted for the relationship between corresponding active and passive sentences, corresponding affirmative and negative sentences, corresponding declarative and interrogative sentences, and so on, was by means of a set of optional transformational rules (one of which, the passive transformation, we have studied in some detail). Under this analysis, kernel sentences (simple, affirmative, active, declarative sentences like *John was reading a book*) were simpler in terms of the number of rules applied than non-kernel sentences. It was tempting to postulate that kernel sentences were not only linguistically simpler (i.e. in terms of a particular model of competence), but also psychologically simpler, and, assuming a close correspondence between competence and performance, to set up experiments designed to test the psychological validity of transformational processes.

The results of some of the earlier experiments were very encouraging. It was shown, for example, that active sentences could be remembered more easily than passive sentences, and affirmative sentences more easily than negative sentences. Even more strikingly, it was demonstrated in an experiment based on the time taken to respond to different types of sentences, not only that the latencies, or reaction times, were longer for passive sentences and negative sentences, but that the difference between the latency for corresponding affirmative active sentences and negative passive sentences was equal to the sum of the differences for affirmative active and affirmative passive sentences, on the one hand, and for affirmative active and negative active sentences, on the other. This could be interpreted as a confirmation of the hypothesis that the 'processing' of sentences included a set of transformational operations, each of which took a certain fixed amount of time to carry out.

These experiments were, in fact, vitiated by a failure to take into account a number of relevant factors. However we describe the difference between active and passive sentences in English, it is quite clear that the greater 'naturalness' of one rather than the other depends upon the kind of noun phrase or nouns that occur as the underlying subject and object, whether they are definite or indefinite, whether they refer to human beings or things, etc. For instance, *John was reading a book* is more 'natural' than *A book was being read by John*; but the passive sentence *John was hit by a car* is more 'natural' than the corresponding active sentence *A car hit John.* Unless the corresponding active and passive sentences in an experiment of the kind referred to above are equally 'natural', one cannot be sure what is the source of the additonal psychological complexity that is being measured by the difference in the latencies. A further potentially relevant factor is the difference in the length of corresponding active and passive sentences. Any experiment that is designed to test the psychological validity of a particular grammatical model must evidently control for all the relevant, or potentially relevant, performance variables, as far as these can be determined. By the mid-1960s psychologists whose research was directly inspired by generative grammar had become more aware of this problem.

Meanwhile, the earliest version of Chomskyan transformational grammar had given way to the *Aspects*-system, which had obvious advantages for psycholinguistics. It was more comprehensive and more clearly articulated; and, most important of all, it gave explicit recognition to the process of semantic interpretation. Even if theoretical linguistics could get along well enough by treating languages as purely formal systems, psycholinguistics could not. It had become evident during the earlier period of psycholinguistic research, not only that there was no direct correspondence between transformational complexity and psychological complexity (in so far as this could be determined by controlled experiment), but also that it is difficult, if not impossible, to separate syntactic processing from semantic processing. Even if there is a distinction to be drawn between two kinds of psychological processing—which is, to say the least, debatable—there is no reason to suppose that the comprehension of an utterance involves going through a full-scale syntactic analysis. It is more plausible to hypothesize that the hearer operates with various perceptual 'strategies' and surface-structure 'cues' as he extracts from the acoustic signal the message that it contains: i.e., in terms of the standard theory of *Aspects*, as he determines the deep structure of the sentence that is uttered.

What we may think of as the second period of Chomskyan psycholinguistic research is characterized, then, by its greater interest in semantics and by its recognition of the importance of taking into account all the information, contextual and acoustic, that the hearer can bring to bear upon the task of interpreting an utterance. The fact that both the production and the comprehension of utterances is a temporally ordered process, subject to modification at various stages before completion, was seen once more as a fact of crucial significance, as it had been ten or fifteen years earlier in the hey-day of 'information-theory'. It was no longer possible, however, to suppose that either production or comprehension could be accounted for in terms of a finite-state processor operating 'from-left-to-right', and word-by-word, and making reference to no more than the transitional probabilities of occurrence (see Chapter 5). A complete syntactic analysis of the incoming signal might not be necessary. But it was by now clear that the heuristic 'strategies' with which the 'on-line' processor operates must be able to draw, at times at least, upon a knowledge of syntactic interdependencies which a transformational grammar of the *Aspects*-type would handle at the level of deep structure. Such experiments as were carried out during this second period of Chomskyan psycholinguistic research with the aim of demonstrating the psychological reality or unreality of standard-theory deep structures were inconclusive. So too were experiments of various kinds designed to test the psychological validity of the standard-theory formalization of the meaning of words in terms of sets of allegedly universal features.

We are now in the midst of what we may think of, in the present context, as the third period of Chomskyan—and post-Chomskyan—psycholinguistic research. As we saw in the preceding chapter, there are now a considerable number of competing models of generative grammar for psycholinguistics to choose from. But none of them has yet been developed in sufficient detail for it to be made the basis of precisely formulated general psycholinguistic hypotheses. Indeed, it is probably true to say that most psycholinguists have now realized that the definitive generative model of linguistic competence is something which, if it is ever to be constructed, will not be constructed in the near future. They can be much more eclectic, therefore, in their attitude to what is currently exciting the interest and imagination of theoretical linguists. And that is all to the good! Chomsky, for one, has always stressed the complexity of the relationship between grammatical competence and language-performance.

One of the most productive areas of Chomskyan and post-Chomskyan psycholinguistic research in the last fifteen years or so has been the study of child language-acquisition. It would be impossible even to summarize here either the results of this research or the various theoretical controversies by which it has been influenced. But one general point can, and must, be made, in view of the philosophical issue of the nativism that we shall be discussing in the following chapter. All the clearly interpretable evidence that has been collected and studied by workers in the field of child language-acquisition is consistent with Chomsky's nativism. But it cannot be said to give particularly strong positive support to it. All children, it would appear, pass through roughly comparable stages in the process of learning (or as many specialists prefer to say, acquiring) their native language: the babbling stage, the one-word ('holophrastic') stage, the two-word stage, and so on. This is in itself hardly surprising; and it is consistent with almost every conceivable hypothesis about the determinants of language-acquisition. What is more interesting is the fact that at each of the discernibly distinct stages in the process of language-acquisition all children (regardless of the cultural and socio-economic environment in which they are being brought up and independently of the language that they hear about them) produce utterances of similar structure at the same stage of development. It might be tempting to see this fact as evidence for the hypothesis that children are born with a language-acquisition device (LAD), which includes the genetically-transmitted knowledge of what Chomsky refers to as *formal* and *substantive universals* (see Chapter 10). But there are alternative explanations.

One of these is that, although there is no language-acquisition device as such (i.e. no device that is restricted to the acquisition of language and is species-specific, in the biologist's sense of being both common to all members of the species and unique to that species), the child is born with a set of species-specific problem-solving 'strategies', and with biologically-determined limitations on the maturation of these 'strategies' and on the development of the psychological 'equipment' (memory, etc.) involved in language-processing. This is still a 'nativist' hypothesis. But, as we shall see, it is not Chomsky's. Perhaps the fairest evaluation of the situation is to say that such results as have been obtained so far in the investigation of child language-acquisition speak neither for nor against the existence of a genetically-transmitted language-acquisition device of the kind that Chomsky postulates in *Aspects* and elsewhere.

One final point should be made in this connexion. As we saw in Chapter 8, Chomsky has never committed himself to the universal base hypothesis. Passages can be quoted from his writings which suggest that, for a time at least, he flirted with it; but he has always rested his case for nativism on a rather different, and less traditional, conception of universal grammar. We shall be looking at this in the following chapter. What needs to be said here is that, in so far as Chomsky's case for nativism rests, empirically, upon the speed with which the child accomplishes the task of language-acquisition on the basis of partly degenerate data, it is now generally taken to be weaker than it seemed to be, to many psycholinguists, when he first put forward his views on this question in the mid-1960s. The process of language-acquisition lasts several years; and the utterances that the child hears around him may not contain as many instances of ungrammatical strings of words as Chomsky has been taken to be suggesting. Rightly or wrongly, many psycholinguists feel that this makes language-acquisition essentially less mysterious and more amenable to explanation, at least in principle, in terms of the maturation of more general cognitive abilities.

Chomsky's influence upon the investigation of the acquisition of language is not as strong now, or as direct, as it was in the second period of psycholinguistic research. Far less attention is now being paid to the acquisition of purely grammatical competence, and correspondingly more attention to the acquisition of all that is systematic and of communicative value in what Chomsky described, in *Aspects*, as performance. However, if Chomsky's influence upon the course of psycholinguistic research is, in this respect and in general, less evident than it once was, this is only because psycholinguists have, for the most part, conceded the main point that Chomsky was making when he first attacked the behaviourist's approach to the psychology of language for its pseudo-scientific bias and its failure to come to grips with any of the real problems.

10 The Philosophy of Language and Mind

We now turn from the psychological to the more philosophical implications of generative grammar. It should be remembered, however, that this distinction I am drawing is, as I said at the beginning of the previous chapter, somewhat arbitrary. For it is part of Chomsky's case that linguistics, psychology and philosophy are no longer to be regarded as separate and autonomous disciplines.

Chomsky believes that linguistics can make an important contribution to the study of the human mind and that, even now, it provides evidence in favour of one position rather than the other in the long-standing philosophical dispute between *rationalists* and *empiricists*. The difference between these two doctrines, at its most extreme, is as follows: the rationalist claims that the mind (or 'reason'—hence the term 'rationalism') is the sole source of human knowledge, the empiricist that all knowledge derives from experience ('empiricism' comes from the Greek word for 'experience'). But there are of course less extreme formulations of the difference; and in the long history of Western philosophy the debate between representatives of the two camps has taken a variety of forms.

In the seventeenth and eighteenth century, and in a good deal of European and American philosophy since then, one of the main points at issue has been the relationship between the mind (if there is such a thing, as many empiricists would deny) and our perception of the external world. Is this simply a matter of the passive registration of sense-impressions and their subsequent combination in terms of laws of 'association', as the British empiricists, Locke, Berkeley and Hume, claimed was the case? Or should we say rather, with such philosophers as Descartes, that our perception and understanding of the external world rests upon a number of 'ideas' (that is, the knowledge of certain propositions and certain principles of interpretation) and that these 'ideas' are 'innate', and not derived from experience? The empiricist doctrine has been very influential in the development of modern psychology; and, combined with *physicalism* and *determinism*, it has been responsible for the view held by many psychologists, that human knowledge and human behaviour are wholly determined by the environment, there being no radical difference in this respect between human beings and other animals, or indeed between animals and machines. (By 'physicalism' is meant, in this context, the philosophical system according to which all statements made about a person's thoughts, emotions and sensations can be reformulated as statements about his bodily condition and observable behaviour, and can thus be brought within the scope of 'physical' laws; by 'determinism' is meant the doctrine that all physical events and phenomena, including those actions and decisions of human beings that we might describe as resulting from 'choice' or 'freewill', are determined by earlier events and phenomena and are subject to the laws of cause-and-effect, so that our impression of freedom of choice is totally illusory. Behaviourism, to which reference was made in the discussion of Bloomfield's theory of language in Chapter 3, is therefore a particular version of physicalism and determinism.) Chomsky's view of man is very different: he believes that we are endowed with a number of specific faculties (to which we give the name 'mind') which play a crucial role in our acquisition of knowledge and enable us to act as free agents, undetermined (though not necessarily unaffected) by external stimuli in the environment. These are the issues that Chomsky deals with in his philosophical writings, most notably in *Cartesian Linguistics*, *Language and Mind* and *Problems of Knowledge and Freedom*. Before plunging into these deep and turbulent waters, it will be as well to discuss the linguistic evidence that Chomsky appeals to as a support for his rationalist philosophy.

As we have seen, 'Bloomfieldian' linguistics was remarkably, and at times almost ostentatiously, un-interested in general theoretical questions. Most American linguists (and many linguists in other parts of the world too, it must be admitted), if they had been asked twenty-five years ago what was the main purpose of linguistics, would probably have said that it was 'to describe languages'; and they might well have referred to the practical advantages of a training in the subject for anthropologists, missionaries and others whose business it was to communicate with peoples speaking a language for which grammars had not yet been written. They would have left the matter at that. Very few of them, if any, would have given the kind of answer that Sapir had suggested to this question in his book *Language* published a generation before: that language is worth studying because it is unique to man and indispensable for thought. Indeed, they might well have challenged the propriety of using the word 'language' in the singular in the way that I have just done, since this tends to imply that all languages have something in common, and the 'Bloomfieldians', as we have seen, were rather sceptical on this point. Bloomfield himself had said, in a much-quoted passage, that 'the only useful generalizations about language are inductive generalizations' and that 'features which we think ought to be universal may be absent from the very next language that becomes access-ible'.

Chomsky's attitude, in this respect (as in others), is radically opposed to Bloomfield's. He holds that it is the central purpose of linguistics to construct a deductive theory of the structure of human language which is at once sufficiently general to apply to all languages (and not only all known languages, but also all possible languages— we will come back to this) and at the same time not so general that it would also be applicable to other systems of communication or anything else that we should not wish to call languages. In other words, linguistics should determine the universal and essential properties of human language. In fact, Chomsky's position on this point is similar, as he acknowledges, to that of the Russian linguist, Roman Jakobson, who has been resident in the United States for a number of years and has long been one of the most outspoken critics of the 'Bloomfieldian' tradition.

Like Jakobson, Chomsky believes that there are certain phonological, syntactic and semantic units that are *universal*, not in the sense that they are necessarily present in all languages, but in the somewhat different, and perhaps less usual, sense of the term 'universal', that they can be defined independently of their occurrence in any particular language and can be identified, when they do occur in particular languages, on the basis of their definition within the general theory. For example, it is held that there is a fixed set of up to twenty *distinctive features* of phonology (e.g. the feature of *voicing* that distinguishes *p* from *b* or *t* from *d* in the pronunciation of the English words *pin* and *bin* or *ten* and *den*, or the feature of *nasality* that distinguishes *b* from *m* or *d* from *n* in *bad* and *mad* or *pad* and *pan*). Not all of these will be found in the phonemes of all languages; but from their various possible combinations every language will, as it were, make its own selection. Similarly at the level of syntax and semantics. Such syntactic categories as Noun or

Verb or Past Tense, and such components of the meaning of words as 'male' or 'physical object', belong to fixed sets of elements, in terms of which it is possible to describe the syntactic and semantic structure of all languages, although no particular language will necessarily manifest all the elements recognized as 'universal' in the general theory. These phonological, syntactic and semantic elements are what Chomsky calls the *substantive universals* of linguistic theory.

Far more characteristic of Chomsky's thought, and more original, is his emphasis on what he refers to as *formal universals*; that is, the general principles which determine the form of the rules and the manner of their operation in the grammars of particular languages. For example, the transformations which relate various sentences and constructions, Chomsky claims, 'are invariably *structure-dependent* in the sense that they apply to a string of words by virtue of the organization of these words into phrases' (*Language and Mind*, p. 51). All the transformations that we discussed in Chapter 7 (and notably the passive transformation) satisfy this condition, since, as we saw, their applicability was determined by the analysability of the 'input' string with reference to the associated phrase marker (and this is what Chomsky means by 'structure-dependency'). It is an important fact about language, says Chomsky, that it does not make use of structure-independent operations in order to relate one sentence type, let us say, to another. For example, the relationship between the declarative sentence *John was here yesterday* and the corresponding interrogative *Was John here yesterday?* might seem at first sight to be describable in terms of a simple operation permuting the first and second words (with an accompanying change of intonation, which we will neglect here). This operation would be structure-independent, if it were specified by means of a rule which made no reference to the syntactic function of *John* and *was*. Consideration of a wider class of examples (such as *His elder brother was here yesterday* and *Was his elder brother here yesterday? The blast off took place on time* and *Did the blast-off take place on time?*) shows us that the rule must be expressed somewhat as follows (to put it informally): 'Permute the whole of the subject noun phrase with the first auxiliary verb, introducing the auxiliary verb *do* for the purpose, when there is no other.' It thus turns out that those sentences like *John was here yesterday* and *Was John here yesterday?*, that can be related by means of a rule of the form 'Permute the first two words' also fall within the scope of the more general structure-dependent rule: it just happens to be that the subject noun phrase is a single word and occupies the first position of the declarative sentence and the second word is an auxiliary verb. According to Chomsky, it will always prove to be the case that what appear to be valid structure-independent operations are special instances of more general structure-dependent operations.

Chomsky and his associates have tentatively proposed a number of more specific universal constraints upon the operation of grammatical rules. Limitations of space prevent us from mentioning more than one of these. We will take what Chomsky calls the 'A-over-A' principle (which is one of the three constraints he discusses in *Language and Mind*). This means that, if a transformational rule makes reference to a phrase of type A and the string of elements to which the rule applies contains two such phrases, one being included within the other, the rule will operate only upon the larger phrase. (In the associated phrase marker the larger phrase of type A dominates the phrase of type A that it includes.) Obvious examples of strings of elements that come within the scope of this principle are noun phrases which contain noun phrases. For instance, *the book on the desk* is a noun phrase, and *the desk*, which is included within it, is also a noun phrase. According to the 'A-over-A' principle, any rule that moves, deletes or otherwise operates upon noun phrases could apply to the whole phrase *the book on the desk*, but not to *the desk*. There are a number of facts in the grammar of English and other languages that appear to be satisfactorily explained in terms of this general principle. On the other hand, as Chomsky points out, there are certain rules that violate the principle, although they appear to be otherwise well motivated; and in the present state of research it is not clear whether the 'A-over-A' principle should just be abandoned or whether it is possible to modify it in such a way that it will cover the exceptions also. And this seems to hold for all the more specific constraints that have been proposed so far: they are only partially satisfactory, since they explain only some of the relevant data. Although the 'A-over-A' principle, as it is at present formulated, is, by Chomsky's own admission, probably not valid, it will serve as an illustration of the kind of constraints upon the application of grammatical rules that Chomsky has in mind when he talks of the formal universals of linguistic theory.

It may be worth pointing out that, as far as substantive universals are concerned, Chomsky's view is not necessarily in conflict with Bloomfield's, since he accepts that any one of his allegedly universal features might be absent, not only 'from the very next language that becomes accessible', but also from very many quite familiar languages. It is for this reason I referred earlier to the difference between Chomsky's view of 'universals' and the 'Bloomfieldian' view as one of 'attitude'. Bloomfield and his 'structuralist' disciples, for reasons that were explained in Chapter 3, followed Boas in stressing the diversity of human languages, Chomsky emphasizes their similarities. Clearly, one must give due recognition to the differences of grammatical structure that are found throughout the languages of the world. But there can be little doubt that the Bloomfieldians, as well as many other schools of linguists, in their anxiety to avoid the bias of traditional grammar, have tended to exaggerate these differences and have given undue emphasis to the principle that every language is a law unto itself. The grammatical similarities that exist between widely separated and historically unrelated languages are at least as striking as their differences. Moreover, recent work in the syntactic analysis of a number of languages lends support to the view that the similarities are deeper and the differences more superficial.

As we saw in Chapter 9, Chomsky himself has been more cautious than some of his followers in accepting that languages are more similar in their deep structure than they are in their surface structure. He attaches far more importance to the fact (and let us grant, provisionally, that it is a fact) that different languages make use of the same formal operations in the construction of grammatical sentences. And it is upon this kind of similarity between languages, as we shall see presently, that he rests his case for a rationalist philosophy of language.

It will be recalled that finite state grammars and phrase structure grammars were criticized by Chomsky as being insufficiently powerful for the description of natural languages. One of the most obvious deficiences of current versions of transformational grammar, as Chomsky has pointed out, is that they are *too* powerful (see Chapter 8 and Appendix 1). There is an extremely important principle involved here; and it is essential to an understanding of Chomsky's notion of 'universal grammar'. When we discussed 'the goals of linguistic theory' in Chapter 4, we saw that the linguist, in writing a generative grammar of a particular language, sets himself the task of characterizing 'all and only' the sentences of that language. (This is of course an ideal, at present unrealized for any natural language: but this does not affect the principle.) The same point holds on the more general plane. Linguistic theory, as we have seen, should be both general enough to cover all particular languages, and yet not so general that it will apply to other systems of communication (and thereby define them implicitly as 'languages'). Transformational grammar, in its present form, allows for the possibility of a variety of operations and various ways of building up sequences of operations which, as far as we know, are not required for the description of any human language. This means that it is more general than it need be as a theory of the structure of human language. The problem is to decide whether there are any formal limitations that we can incorporate in the theory of transformational grammar such that the grammars of particular languages, written within these deliberately imposed limitations, will not only be in principle capable of accounting for all the sentences that are actually found in those languages, but will exclude as *theoretically* impossible the maximum number of non-sentences. As we have seen, Chomsky believes that there are certain very specific conditions which govern the operation of grammatical rules in all languages; and it is by means of these conditions, provided that they can be determined and formalized, that he proposes to restrict the power of transformational grammar.

We now come to the philosophical consequences of Chomsky's notion of universal grammar. If all human languages are strikingly similar in structure, it is natural to ask why this should be so. It is equally natural, or so it might appear to an empiricist philosopher, to answer this question by appealing to such obviously relevant facts as the following: all human languages make reference to the properties and objects of the physical world which, presumably, is perceived in essentially the same way by all physiologically and psychologically normal human beings; all languages, in whatever culture they might operate, are called upon to fulfil a similar range of functions (making statements, asking questions, issuing commands, etc.); all languages make use of the same physiological and psychological 'apparatus' and the very way in which this operates may be held responsible for some of the formal properties of language. Now all these facts are, as I have said, relevant; and they may well have exerted an influence upon the structure of language. But many of the universal features of language, both substantive and formal, are not readily explained in this way. The only conceivable explanation, says Chomsky, in terms of our present knowledge at least, is that human beings are genetically endowed with a highly specific 'language faculty' and that it is this 'faculty' which determines such universal features as structure dependency or the 'A-over-A' principle (to take the two examples mentioned earlier in this chapter). It is at this point that Chomsky makes contact with the rationalist tradition in philosophy.

Chomsky's conclusion is reinforced, he claims, by a consideration of the process by which children learn their native language. All the evidence available suggests that children are not born with a predisposition to learn any one language rather than any other. We may therefore assume that all children, regardless of race and parentage, are born with the same ability for learning languages; and, in normal circumstances, children will grow up as what we call 'native speakers' of that language which they hear spoken in the community in which they are born and spend their early years. But how does the child manage to develop that creative command of his native language which enables him to produce and understand sentences he has never heard before? As we have seen, Chomsky maintains that it is only by assuming that the child is born with a knowledge of the highly restrictive principles of universal grammar, and the predisposition to make use of them in analysing the utterances he hears about him, that we can make any sense of the process of language-learning. Empiricist theories of language-learning cannot bridge the gap between the relatively small number of utterances (many of them full of errors, distortions and hesitations) which the child hears about him and his ability to construct for himself on the basis of this scanty and imperfect data, in a relatively short time, the grammatical rules of the language. It is the child's inborn knowledge of the universal principles governing the structure of human language that supplies the deficiency in the empiricist account of language-acquisition. These principles are part of what we call the 'mind', being represented in some way no doubt in the structure or mode of operation of the brain, and may be compared with the 'innate ideas' of Descartes and the rationalist tradition going back to Plato.

It was pointed out towards the end of the preceding chapter that the balance of opinion seems to have shifted in the last few years towards the view that the so-called 'primary' data (i.e. the utterances to which the child is exposed) is not as degenerate as Chomsky has frequently been understood to have suggested. It is only fair to add here that Chomsky claims that he has been misrepresented and misunderstood on this matter: 'Just how degenerate is this experience? I know of no reliable evidence, but the problem appears to have been misunderstood, and some incorrect statements have been made about what has been asserted. As for the problem, suppose that a scientist were presented with data, two per cent of which are wrong (but he doesn't know which two per cent). Then he faces some serious difficulties, which would be incomparably more serious if the data were simply uncontrolled experience, rather than the result of controlled experiment, devised for its relevance to theoretical hypotheses.' ('Conditions on rules of grammar', footnote 6.) Chomsky goes on to say that he has never asserted that 'the great majority of the sentences that the child hears are ungrammatical' and that he has never given any 'quantitative estimates'.

As the quotation in the previous paragraph makes clear, Chomsky considers that, in the circumstances in which children acquire their native language, the presence of even a relatively small number of ungrammatical utterances in the 'primary' data constitutes a serious problem for any purely empiricist theory of language-acquisition. In view of the difference of opinion that exists between Chomsky and his empiricist critics on this particular question, it is worth re-emphasizing the fact that many of the psychologists working in the field of language-acquisition who disagree with Chomsky with respect to the plausibility of the hypothesis that children have an inborn knowledge of the principles of universal grammar would nonetheless agree with him when he says that purely empiricist theories of language-acquisition are incapable of explaining the facts.

Chomsky's theory of transformational grammar was originally formulated, as I have stressed throughout this book, within the framework of 'autonomous' linguistics. Such few references as there are in his earlier writings to philosophical issues would suggest that he, like most other linguists and psychologists, saw no reason to dispute the empiricist theory of knowledge and perception. This fact should be borne in mind in any assessment of his current philosophical views. Having been trained himself in the predominantly empiricist tradition of modern science, he is well aware that his notion of the genetic transmission of the principles of universal grammar will strike many philosophers and scientists as absurdly fanciful. As he pointed out in his radio discussion with Stuart Hampshire (printed in *The Listener* of 30 May 1968): 'The empiricist view is so deep-seated in our way of looking at the human mind that it almost has the character of a superstition.' After all, we do not accuse the biologist of unscientific mysticism when he postulates the genetic transmission and subsequent maturation of the quite complex 'instinctual' behaviour patterns characteristic of various species. Why should we be so ready to believe that human behaviour, which is demonstrably more complex and more flexible, *must* be accounted for without the postulation of certain highly specialized abilities and dispositions (to which we give the name 'mind') with which we are genetically endowed and which manifest themselves, in the appropriate circumstances, at a certain stage of our development?

It is of course the traditional associations of the word 'mind' that are responsible for much of the hostile reaction to Chomsky's rationalism (or 'mentalism'). Many philosophers, and most notably perhaps Descartes, have drawn a very sharp distinction between 'body' and 'mind'; and they have claimed that the physiological functions and operations of the 'body', unlike the workings of the 'mind', are subject to the same 'mechanical', or 'physical', laws as the rest of the 'material' world. Chomsky's position is, however, somewhat different. Like Descartes and other 'mentalists', he believes that human behaviour is, in part at least, undetermined by external stimuli or internal physiological states: he is thus opposed to 'mechanism' (or 'physicalism', in the usual sense). On the other hand, he differs from Descartes and most philosophers who would normally be called 'mentalist' in that he does not subscribe to the ultimate irreducibility of the distinction between 'body' and 'mind'. In the radio interview to which I have already referred, he makes the point that 'the whole issue of whether there's a physical basis for mental structures is a rather empty issue', because, in the development of modern science, 'the concept "physical" has been extended step by step to cover anything we understand', so that 'when we ultimately begin to understand the properties of mind, we shall simply . . . extend the notion "physical" to cover these properties as well'. He does not even deny that it is possible in principle to account for 'mental phenomena' in terms of 'the physiological processes and physical processes that we now understand'. It will be clear from these quotations that, although Chomsky describes himself as a 'mentalist', it is mechanistic determinism, and more particularly behaviourism, to which he is opposed and that in contrast with such philosophers as Plato or Descartes, he might equally well be described as a 'physicalist'.

11   Interim Assessment (1977)

In the previous chapters of this book I have tried to give a clear and sympathetic account of Chomsky's views on language, and I have deliberately refrained from making any kind of critical comment that might hold up or complicate the exposition. I must not leave the reader with the impression, however, that Chomsky's position is impregnable and his critics simply misguided or malevolent. In this final chapter therefore I will redress the balance somewhat by giving a more personal assessment of the significance of Chomsky's work. Although my own views are very similar to Chomsky's on most issues, there are some points on which I think he has overstated his case.

I have already said that it was Chomsky's research on the formalization of syntactic theory that constitutes his most original and probably his most enduring contribution to the scientific investigation of language; and there can be little doubt about this. He has greatly extended the scope of what is called 'mathematical linguistics' and opened up a whole field of research, which is of interest not only to linguists, but also to logicians and mathematicians. Even if it were decided eventually that none of Chomsky's work on generative grammar was of any direct relevance to the description of natural languages, it would still be judged valuable by logicians and mathematicians, who are concerned with the construction and study of formal systems independently of their empirical application. I will say no more about this point.

It is of course the fact that Chomsky's model of transformational grammar was designed for the analysis of natural languages and has been employed with considerable success for that purpose over the last ten or fifteen years that has attracted the attention of psychologists and philosophers. Chomsky himself has argued, as we have seen, that the findings of transformational grammar have certain very definite implications for psychology and philosophy. He has made a strong, and to my mind convincing, case against behaviourism (in its extreme form at least); and he has argued, again cogently, that the gap between human language and systems of animal communication is such that it cannot be bridged by any obvious extension of current psychological theories of 'learning' based on laboratory experiments with animals. This follows from the principle of 'creativity' manifest in the use of language and does not depend, it should be observed, upon the validity of any particular model of generative grammar, or indeed even upon the possibility of constructing one.

At this point, something should be said about the attempts that have been made recently to teach language to chimpanzees and the implications that the results of these experiments have for the Chomskyan version of 'nativism'. Earlier attempts had been made to teach chimpanzees spoken language; and they had failed. It now appears that the reason for their failure is that chimpanzees simply do not have the same kind of vocal apparatus that human beings have. More recent experiments, therefore, have operated with communication-systems that make use of the manual-visual, rather than the vocal-auditory, channel; and they have been remarkably successful. The experiments have been so successful, in fact, that they are now commonly believed to have disproved Chomsky's assertion (in *Language and Mind*, p. 59) that 'acquisition of even the barest rudiments of language is quite beyond the capacities of an otherwise intelligent ape'. Well, have they?

One of the chimpanzees, Washoe, was learning the American Sign Language (ASL), widely used by the deaf-and-dumb in the United States. This is a 'logographic', rather than an alphabetic, system, in the sense that it is not based on the principle of finger-spelling, but has signs each of which can be related directly, and one-by-one, to individual words (or their meanings). Not only did Washoe succeed in learning over a hundred signs before she grew too difficult to manage (at the age of six years), but she used the signs appropriately, producing them spontaneously herself and interpreting them correctly when they were produced by others. Even more impressive is the fact that she was able to produce appropriate new sequences of signs: i.e. sequences that she had never met before. Admittedly, the sequences were never very long. But they were as long as the spoken utterances of human children at an early stage of language-acquisition. It would appear, therefore, that Washoe (unlike, for example, von Frisch's honey bees: see Chapter 2) has demonstrated the ability to construct new combinations of discrete units; and this is what we have been calling 'creativity'.

Sarah, another equally famous chimpanzee, has been learning a rather different communication-system: one that, unlike ASL, is not parasitic upon pre-existing human languages, but was constructed especially for the purpose. Furthermore, unlike Washoe, who has acquired her knowledge of ASL by interacting in a more or less natural way with her trainers, Sarah has been taught by means of a systematic programme based on the 'operant-conditioning' principle of behaviourist psychology. Sarah's 'language' consists of a set of sentences whose 'words' are coloured plastic tokens. These are arranged vertically on a magnetic board according to rules established by the inventors of the system. This allows for the construction of both affirmative and negative statements, questions, conditional sentences and quantified phrases (*some apples*, *all the apples*, *no apples*). The syntax of the system is such that it has some degree of structure-dependence; and Sarah appears to have been able to cope with this.

Well, then, have Washoe and Sarah (who are but the first and most famous of what is now quite a large number of chimpanzees that have been involved in such experiments) demonstrated a capacity for language? The answer to this question is unclear. The two chimpanzees have between them shown that certain non-human primates are capable of learning systems that have some degree of rule-governed 'creativity' and some degree of structure-dependence. It is open to Chomsky to object, however, that the difference between a fully developed natural language and systems of the kind that Washoe and Sarah have been learning is qualitative, rather than quantitative. Disputes as to what is qualitative and what is quantitative are notoriously difficult to resolve; and many scientists would say that they are rather pointless.

As far as I can see, the results of the experiments with chimpanzees leave the whole question of the species-specificity of language exactly where it was before; and it is, up to a point, definitional. It has been argued that, if the chimpanzees have not succeeded in acquiring at least the 'barest rudiments' of language, children in the earlier stages of language-acquisition have not succeeded in acquiring the 'barest rudiments' of language either. But the argument, as it stands, is fallacious. For children go way beyond the stage at which, so far at least, the chimpanzees stop. According to the Chomskyan hypothesis, this is because children are operating with a species-specific maturational disposition that the chimpanzees lack; and, if this is so, despite the alleged structural similarities between young children's utterances and the utterances of Washoe and other chimpanzees learning ASL, it is legitimate to say that, whereas children are quite obviously acquiring language, the chimpanzees have not demonstrated that they are. Of course, it may yet turn out that chimpanzees, or representatives of some other non-human species, will refute the Chomskyan hypothesis by acquiring a communication-system with the same kind and the same degree of structure-dependency and rule-governed creativity that human languages have. So far they have not done so.

It is important to realize in this connection that to describe as quantitative what Chomsky might hold to be qualitative does not of itself solve the problem of accounting for the differences between human languages and other communication-systems. It should also be pointed out that there has been a good deal of rather superficial discussion, in popular treatments of the difference between language and non-language, of what have come to be called the *design-features*, or general properties, of language. Three of these have been mentioned in this book: *duality*, *creativity* and *structure-dependence*. Others that might have been mentioned are *arbitrariness* and *discreteness*. All these, apart from structure-dependence, to which, as we have seen, Chomsky attaches particular importance, appear on a well-known list of sixteen properties drawn up by C. F. Hockett about fifteen years ago. There are two general points that must be made about this list. The first is that it is very heavily weighted in favour of signalling-systems that make use of the vocal-auditory channel. It is arguable, however, that language should not be bound, by definition, to transmission in the vocal-auditory channel; and, as we have seen, any claim to the effect that Washoe and Sarah are acquiring language depends upon our acceptance of the fact that transmission in the vocal-auditory channel is not a definitional property of language.

This point is of some importance. There is some

evidence to suggest that the two hemispheres of the human brain are involved in rather different aspects of language-processing and that, whereas the left hemisphere (in most people) carries out the more characteristically linguistic processes, the right hemisphere deals with the less characteristically linguistic processes, including some of the processing of the vocal signal as such. It is at least conceivable that man's biological pre-disposition to acquire speech is to be distinguished from his biological predisposition to acquire language (on the assumption that he has both); and it is important to appreciate that evidence for the one cannot be taken as evidence for the other. The two are often confused.

The second point is even more important. Hockett's list of design-features is often taken as a check-list of properties that particular signalling-systems either have or do not have. Systems are then graded as being more or less similar to natural languages according to the number of features that they share with natural languages. It turns out, for example, that, according to this way of comparing communication-systems, the sets of signals used by such birds as thrushes and crows differ from human languages only with respect to the features of *prevarication* (the ability to lie) and *reflectiveness* (the ability to communicate about the system itself). The comparison stands condemned by the absurdity of the results that it yields. And one does not need to look for long to see what is wrong with the method of comparison. Not only does each distinguishable feature count equally in the classification, but many of the features are so loosely defined that their identification with similarly named features in natural languages must be rejected. This is arguably the case for open-endedness (i.e. 'creativity') and it is most certainly the case for semanticity, arbitrariness, discreteness and duality. Furthermore, it is the degree to which languages have these properties and the way the design-features interact with one another that makes of language-systems the flexible instruments for communication that they are. Chomsky may be right or wrong about the species-specificity of language. But one thing is clear: what his theory of generative grammar seeks to formalize —rule-governed, structure-dependent, creativity whose complexity is defined by the power of the grammar— is certainly an essential part of language.

So much may be said, then, about the vexed question of the relation between human language and animal communication-systems. It may be worth repeating that, although Chomsky has given good reason to believe that the model of 'stimulus-and-response' is incapable of accounting for *all* the facts of language behaviour, he has not shown that it cannot explain *any* of them. It might well be that some of the words referring to objects in the child's environment and certain utterances that occur frequently in the repetitive situations in which he finds himself in early life are learned by him in a way that is quite reasonably described in behaviourist terms (by saying that the words and utterances are 'responses' and the objects and situations are 'stimuli'); and it could also be true that this part of language not only can, but must, be learned and related to the external world and the world of social activity in this way. As far as I know, there is no evidence to suggest that this view is wrong or even implausible. What Chomsky has demonstrated is that the behaviourist account of language acquisition, if it is not entirely abandoned, must be supplemented with something more substantial than rather empty appeals to 'analogy'.

But what of the wider philosophical issues that he has raised in his later work? Here I think that the only verdict that can be returned, on the evidence available, is that Chomsky's case for rationalism is not quite as strong as he suggests. It rests, as we have seen, upon the alleged universality of certain formal principles of sentence construction in natural languages; and he is committed to the view 'that if an artificial language were constructed which violated some of these general principles, then it would not be learned at all, or at least not learned with the ease and efficiency with which a normal child will learn human language' (*The Listener*, 30 May 1968, p. 688). But this hypothesis, as Chomsky's critics have pointed out, is not subject to direct empirical verification. For it is obviously impracticable to bring up a child from birth with no knowledge of any natural language, exposing him only to utterances in an artificial language spoken in a full range of 'normal' situations. Nor is it at all clear how one would go about designing an acceptable psychological experiment bearing less directly upon the issues involved.

Even if we grant for the sake of argument that the formal principles to which Chomsky appeals are universal in the sense that they do indeed hold in all languages actually spoken by human beings, are we justified in maintaining that they are peculiarly congenial to the human mind, so that any *conceivable* human language *must* conform to them? Since we cannot prove, as yet, that languages violating these principles could not be learned or used by human beings, we are entitled to withhold our assent to Chomsky's hypothesis that these formal universals are innate. An alternative explanation of their universality might be that all languages have a common origin in the remote past and have preserved the formal principles of their source.[1] Whether all exist-

1. This point has been explicitly discussed by Chomsky in *Language and Mind* (pp. 74-5), where he argues that it 'involves a serious misunderstanding of the problem at issue'. It is true, as he says, that the hypothesis of common origin 'contributes nothing to explaining' how 'the grammar of a language must be discovered by the child from the data presented to him'. But this is not the problem for which the hypothesis of common origin is being proposed here as an ex-

ing languages do in fact derive from one source is not known—and, once again, we are faced with what seems to be an unverifiable hypothesis—but it is a possibility that should be allowed for.

In so far as linguistics is an empirical science, whose purpose it is to construct a theory of the structure of human language, it is of course important that linguists should incorporate within the theory all the substantive and formal universals that can be established in the investigation of particular languages. Chomsky is right, I believe, when he says that the diversity of structures found throughout the languages of the world is less striking than the 'structuralists' have claimed. On the other hand, it should be emphasized that relatively few languages have yet been described in any great detail. Syntactic research of recent years, much of it inspired directly by Chomsky's work, seems to me to lend a fair amount of support to the adherents of 'universal grammar'. But the results that have been obtained so far must be regarded as very tentative; and this fact should be borne in mind when linguistic evidence is being used in philosophical arguments.

It is in any case arguable that some of the old philosophical and psychological oppositions, like rationalism *vs.* empiricism, instinct *vs.* learning, mind *vs.* body, heredity *vs.* environment, and so on, have lost much of their force. Current work in the comparative study of animal and

---

planation. Chomsky's assumption that certain formal principles of grammar are innate is intended to account for two problems simultaneously: (i) the universality of the principles (on the assumption that they are in fact found to be universal) and (ii) the child's success in constructing the grammar of his language on the basis of the utterances he hears around him. It is the second of these questions that Chomsky regards as the more important ('the language is "re-invented" each time it is learned, and the empirical problem to be faced by the theory of learning is how this invention of grammar can take place').

human behaviour would suggest that behaviour which is normally described as 'instinctual' requires very particular environmental conditions during the period of 'maturation'. Whether one says that such behaviour is 'innate' or 'learned by experience' is a matter of emphasis: both 'instinct' and 'environment' are necessary, and neither is sufficient without the other. As we saw at the end of the last chapter, Chomsky, though he calls himself a 'mentalist', does not wish to be committed to the traditional opposition of 'body' and 'mind'. His position would seem to be consistent with the view that the 'knowledge' and 'predispositions' for language, though 'innate', require rather definite environmental conditions during the period of 'maturation'. One might go on to suggest, as an alternative to Chomsky's hypothesis, that it is not a 'knowledge' of the formal principles of language as such that is innate, but a more general 'faculty', which, given the right environmental conditions, will interact with these to produce linguistic competence.[2] This could still be called a 'rationalist' hypothesis in the sense that it contradicts the more extreme form of empiricism. But then there are probably very few extreme empiricists. Most philosophers and

2. Chomsky says that he is not convinced that this is a true 'alternative': he accepts that the proper environmental conditions are necessary for the maturation of innate structures (cf. *Aspects of the Theory of Syntax*, pp. 33-34). He believes that 'no more is at stake than a decision as to how to apply the term "knowledge" in a rather obscure area'. He further suggests that I should point out that 'even the most narrow empiricist would not regard a hypothesis as devoid of empirical content because it is not directly testable in practice', that it is generally accepted by modern empiricists 'that meaningful hypotheses, in general, must only meet the condition that some possible evidence have some bearing on them—that they not be entirely neutral with respect to all conceivable evidence'. I did not intend to give the impression in my criticism of Chomsky's hypothesis that I regard it as meaningless or vacuous, but it may be as well to make this point explicit.

psychologists would no doubt accept that some mental faculties are specific to human beings (although they might prefer not to use the words 'mental faculty') and are both biologically and environmentally determined. Once again, it must be admitted that there is no evidence to show that this alternative hypothesis (which many scholars who call themselves 'empiricists' might favour) is correct. But I am not claiming that Chomsky is wrong. What I am saying is that the evidence, so far at least, is inconclusive.

The fact that we have delivered a verdict of 'not proven' on Chomsky's particularly strong form of the rationalist thesis does not mean that it is without importance. He has shown that there is nothing inherently unscientific about the assumption, or hypothesis, that competence in speaking a language implies that the speaker has in his 'mind' (whether they are 'innate' or 'learned') a number of generative rules of a highly restricted kind and is capable of 'storing' and operating upon abstract 'mental structures' in the course of producing or analysing utterances. This in itself is a considerable achievement, given the strong prejudice that existed not long ago among psychologists and linguists, and perhaps also philosophers of science, against any theory that went beyond the observable data. Chomsky was surely right to challenge 'the belief that the mind must be simpler in its structure than any known physical organ and that the most primitive of assumptions must be adequate to explain whatever phenomena can be observed' (*Language and Mind*, p. 22).

It would be inappropriate in a book of this nature, and impossible in the space available, to give a detailed criticism of Chomsky's theory of generative grammar from a purely linguistic point of view.[3] I must be content

3. For a critical discussion of the more technical points in what is now referred to as the standard theory the reader is referred to

with two general points. The first has to do with the distinction he draws between 'competence' and 'performance', which was mentioned in Chapters 4 and 9. Although a distinction of this kind is undoubtedly both a theoretical and a methodological necessity in linguistics, it is by no means certain that Chomsky himself draws it in the right place. It can be argued that he describes as matters of 'performance' (and, therefore, as irrelevant) a number of factors that should be handled in terms of 'competence'. The second point is that, on questions of detail, any linguist's judgement of what is a more 'natural' or more 'revealing' way of describing the data will tend to be somewhat arbitrary. Furthermore, it is not always clear when the differences between two alternative descriptions of the same data are differences of substance and when they are merely differences of terminology and notation.

Both of the points that I have just made require amplification in the light of more recent developments. To take first the question of competence and performance. In a famous passage of *Aspects of the Theory of Syntax* (p. 3), Chomsky says: 'Linguistic theory is concerned primarily with an ideal speaker-listener in a completely homogenous speech-community, who knows its language [i.e. the language of the community] perfectly and is unaffected by such grammatically irrelevant conditions as memory limitations, distractions, shifts of attention and interest, and errors (random or characteristic) in applying his knowledge of the language [i.e. the language-system] in actual performance.' It has been argued by many, and I agree, that Chomsky's use of the term 'performance' to cover everything that does not fall within the scope of a deliberately idealized and theoreti-

---

P. H. Matthews's review of *Aspects of the Theory of Syntax* (see Bibliography). Many of these criticisms carry over to the extended standard theory.

cally restricted notion of linguistic competence is unfortunate. It would have been preferable, in my view, to restrict the notion of 'performance' to the production and interpretation of utterances on particular occasions of the use of language and to introduce other distinctions to account for the idealization (cf. 'in a completely homogenous speech-community') and decontextualization (cf. Chomsky's definition of a language as a set of sentences, rather than as a set of appropriately contextualized utterances).

It does not follow, however, from this essentially terminological point that Chomsky's idealization itself is illegitimate; and I do not believe that it is. Linguists can and should give full recognition to differences of dialect and style and to their social and contextual determinants; and it falls within the province of sociolinguistics, both theoretical and descriptive, to do just this. Dell Hymes, who has argued, cogently, for the extension of the notion of 'competence', makes the further point that 'a child from whom any and all of the grammatical sentences might come with equal likelihood would be . . . a social monster' (*Foundations of Sociolinguistics*, p. 75). This is true; and Chomsky would not wish to deny it. Nor would he wish to deny the fact of stylistic and dialectal variation or its positive communicative and social function. It so happens, however, that what Chomsky takes, rightly or wrongly, to be the crucial property of human language can be studied, in his opinion, without taking socially and contextually determined variation into account. As far as I know, there is no reason to dispute what he has to say on this point. Generative grammarians (though not, I think, Chomsky) may have rested their case for or against the postulation of some particular grammatical rule upon data of questionable validity; and, when challenged, they may have adopted too readily what has been aptly called the 'my-dialect-your-dialect gambit'. If so, it is their cavalier attitude to what should be standard procedures of empirical verification, not the principle of idealization as such, that is at fault.

This point has been emphasized because there has recently been a noticeable shift of interest within linguistics from the more narrowly grammatical to the social and the behavioural aspects of language. It is important to realize that, although the sociolinguistic viewpoint is, for its own purposes, valid, it does not invalidate the Chomskyan idealization. Neither viewpoint is more 'realistic' than the other; they both involve some kind of idealization (as all empirical science does); they are equally legitimate, but different.

The second point mentioned above has to do with the question of terminological and notational difference. As we saw in Chapter 8, there is now a considerable number of alternative versions of Chomskyan or post-Chomskyan generative grammar. Chomsky has claimed that some of these are no more than 'notational variants' of his own system. It is by no means clear that he is right on this issue. The problem is that, whereas the weak equivalence of two grammars is something that is clearly decidable (provided that they have both been fully formalized), the question of strong equivalence is much more complex. Two grammars are said to be strongly equivalent if they assign to the sentences that they generate the same structural descriptions (cf. Appendix 1). The problem is that scholars may disagree as to what is significant and what is not in the formal representation of the structure of a sentence. Unless the parties to any dispute that has to do with strong equivalence can come to some agreement about the significance or non-significance of terminological and notational variation, the dispute itself is fruitless; and much of the more technical arguments between Chomsky and those who favour some other form of generative grammar has had something of this character.

The comments that have just been made are intended to show that even those linguists who are generally sympathetic to Chomsky's views may differ from him on various issues. Other scholars of course have more fundamental objections to his theory of generative grammar.

Earlier in this chapter I said that we must at least envisage the possibility that Chomsky's theory of generative grammar will be dismissed one day, by the consensus of linguists, as irrelevant to the description of natural languages. I should add that I personally believe, and very many linguists will share this belief, that even if the attempt he has made to formalize the concepts employed in the analysis of languages should fail, the attempt itself will have immeasurably increased our understanding of these concepts and that in this respect the 'Chomskyan revolution' cannot but be successful.

12 The Chomskyan Revolution: a Progress Report (1991)

When I was a student in the early 1950s, I once went to a special lecture by F. J. Ayer that had been publicized by the organizers with the surprising (and crowd-drawing) title 'Second Thoughts on Existentialism'. Ayer was, of course, the principal British apologist for logical positivism in its heyday and had been publicly critical of what was then emerging as a fashionable philosophical movement, recently imported from France (just as philosophical and literary structuralism was to be imported a decade or so later). The first sentence of his lecture, as I now recall it, was: 'My second thoughts on existentialism are the same as my first thoughts.'

When I came to write this chapter, I was tempted to take a leaf out of Ayer's book: to call this chapter 'Second Thoughts on Chomsky' (or perhaps even 'Third Thoughts', since this is now the third edition of the book) and to begin by explaining that my second (or third) thoughts are, in all essentials, unchanged from my first thoughts (for some comments relevant to this point see Appendix 2). I have opted instead for 'The Chomskyan Revolution: a Progress Report (1991)'. As will soon become clear, I am still a Chomskyan, as far as linguistics is concerned, after my fashion (and in my own interpretation of 'Chomskyan'). Indeed, as far as generative grammar is concerned, I might fairly claim to be a more orthodox Chomskyan (in the original sense of this adjective) than Chomsky himself has latterly become: I might claim to be (if I may borrow the French saying) more Catholic than the Pope! I am also interested in what may be distinguished from generative grammar (properly so called) as either 'generativism' or 'the generative enterprise' (see below). As will be evident from the preceding chapter, I have been, and still am professionally sceptical or agnostic about some parts of this.

The subtitle that I have given to this chapter, I should point out, is not intended to be ironical; it is, however, ambiguous, and deliberately so. I am concerned primarily to report the progress that has been made by the (so-called) Chomskyan revolution since 1977. But I am also concerned to explain, briefly and non-technically, as I myself understand it, the role that the Chomskyan revolution has played in the advances that have been made recently in linguistics and in related disciplines.

I must first say a word about the 'Whiggist' phrase 'Chomskyan revolution'. (Chomsky himself does not like the term 'Chomskyan', because it seems to personalize what he would prefer to think of as the impersonal, or collective, advance of knowledge in the mature sciences, but I have no reason to believe that he rejects the term 'revolution'.) That there was a revolutionary change of 'paradigm' in 'mainstream' linguistics, initiated by the publication of Chomsky's *Syntactic Structures* in 1957, is widely, though not universally, accepted. What exactly was revolutionary about it; whether it really was one of 'only four major breakthroughs' in the advance of linguistics from its earliest beginnings (as C. F. Hockett, one of the leading members of the 'post-Bloomfieldian' school said, in his generous 1965 assessment of Chomsky's achievement – he was to be more critical later); just how much of what is conventionally attributed to Chomsky was truly original to him: these are all questions about which there is plenty of scope for legitimate disagreement.

I have made it clear that I share the common view that Chomsky's early work did indeed have a revolutionary impact upon both the theory and the practice of linguistics. And the first edition of this book may well have played its part in popularizing (though it did not originate) the phrase itself: 'the Chomskyan revolution'. In Chapter 4, I said: 'Chomsky's most original, and probably his most enduring, contribution to linguistics is the mathematical rigour and precision with which he formalized the properties of alternative systems of grammatical description' (p. 42). And at the end of the immediately preceding chapter, as part of what has now become the 'Interim Assessment (1977)' (unchanged in this respect from that of 1970), I said: 'even if the attempt [Chomsky] has made to formalize the concepts employed in the analysis of languages should fail, the attempt itself will have immeasurably increased our understanding of these concepts', so that 'in this respect the "Chomskyan revolution" cannot but be successful'. More recently, in an admittedly and unashamedly 'Whiggist' survey of developments in linguistics since 1950, entitled 'The Last Forty Years: Real Progress or Not?' (1990), I have reaffirmed, and to some degree I hope justified, the view 'that Chomsky's work on the theory of generative grammar and his development of particular kinds of generative grammar' did indeed constitute a 'major breakthrough' in the history of linguistics, 'which, as far as we can be sure of these things, has taken us along the path of progress'. My present thoughts on this issue, then, are the same as my first (and second) thoughts were.

Fred D'Agostino's (1986) account of Chomsky's work, written from a philosophical point of view, refers to the earlier of the two passages from this book which I have just quoted (which, as I have said, I saw no reason to change in the second, revised, edition), to Dell Hymes's reaction to the point that I make there in his (1972) review of the first edition, and also to Emmon Bach's earlier (1965) assessment of Chomsky's originality. D'Agostino notes that, whereas Bach puts the emphasis on the 'revolution of method' and I on the 'revolution of rigour', Hymes 'claims that [the Chomskyan revolution] resulted from Chomsky's demonstration of the formal inadequacy of previous modes of linguistic explanation'. Conceding that there is 'at least a grain of truth in each of these characterizations', he declares it as his own view 'that Chomsky's most revolutionary contribution to linguistics was embodied in his advocacy of a thoroughly individualistic point of view' (p. 59). He might also have referred to yet another, and among Chomskyan linguists at least a more widely accepted, assessment, that of Neil Smith and Deirdre Wilson, in their (1979) book which actually used the phrase 'the Chomskyan revolution' on its title-page: 'Chomsky was probably the first to provide detailed arguments from the nature of language to the nature of mind, rather than vice versa' (p. 10). Chomsky, it would appear is all things to all persons. In this respect, he is like that other 'modern master', Ferdinand de Saussure, his great predecessor in the orthodox, 'Whiggist', histories of 'mainstream linguistics' which appear in the standard textbooks. The fact that both Chomsky and Saussure are so widely cited, outside as well as within linguistics, and that there can be so many (not necessarily inconsistent) assessments of their originality, is itself striking evidence of that originality.

Be that as it may, the quotation from D'Agostino will serve as a peg upon which to hang one or two introductory comments which, though they address (in a preliminary way for the moment) the specific point which he makes, are also of more general import and apply to several other published accounts of 'the Chomskyan revolution' and its effect.

The first comment is that there is a distinction to be drawn between the effect of Chomsky's work on linguistics, on the one hand, and on the philosophy of language and the philosophy of linguistics, on the other. As far as I can see, there is nothing in Chomsky's theory of generative grammar of the 'classical' period which ties it to an individualistic, rather than a 'collectivistic' (or social), point of view; and similarly, there is nothing in the methods of analysis practised by Chomskyan linguists which distinguishes their analyses, in this respect, from those of non-Chomskyan linguists (see p. 150 above). For example, Chomsky's famous (and much-criticized) statement about the competence of 'the ideal speaker-listener in [an idealized] completely homogeneous speech-community' is compatible with either a 'collectivist' or an 'individualistic' view of language-systems. It is also compatible with a variety of other alternatives (including the abstract, 'Platonistic' view that has been advocated most notably by J. J. Katz). I will return to this point in some detail later.

Few linguists preface all or any of their publications with a recital of their ontological *Credo*. In fact, most practitioners of linguistics (and a good many theorists) are not particularly strong on 'ontological commitment' and, I imagine, have no views one way or another about the ontological status of languages (in the sense in which a philosopher would understand 'ontological'). In this respect, they are like most practitioners (and many theorists) in other disciplines: they just get on with the practical business of describing what they (and most other people) call languages, regardless of whether languages exist in the 'real world' or not and, if they do exist, what exactly their mode of existence is. True, there are those who do regularly pay lip-service to this or that philosophical (or metatheoretical) article of faith; but often it is no more than lip-service. As I shall be emphasizing at various points in this chapter, there is often very little connection between the philosophical stance adopted by linguists and the kind of day-to-day linguistics that they do. Chomsky is of course serious about his 'ontological commitment' and defends it with subtle and sophisticated philosophical arguments. But, as we shall see, it has very little effect on his linguistics, except in his choice of what he takes to be crucial data. He engages in argument about the data with linguists who do not share his philosophical views, and the kind of arguments that both sides accept are, usually, if not always, philosophically neutral.

My second comment, which balances the first, is that there is of course a very important philosophical dimension to 'the Chomskyan revolution' (as I made clear in Chapter 10). Moreover, for most people other than linguists, it is Chomsky's powerful advocacy of a set of philosophical doctrines associated with what has come to be called 'the generative enterprise', rather than his work on the theory of generative grammar as such, that is at the heart of 'Chomskyan revolution'. I will therefore devote at least as much space, in my 'progress report', to this philosophical (and metatheoretical) dimension as I will to the Chomskyan revolution in linguistics.

My treatment of what is, if it were dealt with fully, a large and, in places, quite difficult body of material is necessarily selective and personal. Others might include topics that I have omitted and would have dealt differently with what I have chosen to include. But I have concentrated, I think, on what are generally agreed to be the major general themes. Most of these, as we shall see, develop naturally enough out of Chomsky's earlier work.

I will organize what I have to say under a number of headings, which should help readers with diverse backgrounds, and more or less knowledge of linguistics, to relate the interconnected topics to what they know already or find in other accounts of Chomsky's thought.

Chomsky's linguistics and Chomskyan linguistics.

Over the last fifteen years or so, it as become even more necessary than it was in 1977 to draw a distinction between Chomsky's ideas and Chomskyan ideas: between Chomsky's own ideas and those of the many linguists, philosophers, psychologists and others who have been influenced by him. (As has been noted already, Chomsky himself has objected to the use of the term 'Chomskyan', on the grounds that it personalizes what should be impersonal in properly scientific work, but the term is convenient, and widely used; and not everyone shares Chomsky's view of the impersonality of science.) Any theory, idea or system of grammar that has been influenced by Chomsky's own work – whether directly or indirectly, and to whatever degree – I will now call 'Chomskyan'. In what follows, therefore, the term 'Chomskyan' is being used very broadly and subsumes what was distinguished as 'post-Chomskyan' in Chapter 8 (p. 84).

Chomskyan linguistics, thus defined, is a very broad church indeed. It has within it many sects and denominations, not all of which can be mentioned here. I will concentrate rather upon Chomsky's own views, as these have developed from the mid-1970s, and upon the quite radical changes that he has made during this period to his system of generative grammar. Indeed, I shall do little more than mention a few of the other currently competing systems.

My presentation of Chomsky's views will be as fair and as clear as I can make it, but it will also be appropriately critical and, I hope, responsible. As will be evident from the later chapters of the second edition of this work (which have been left unchanged: see the Preface to the present edition), I am out of sympathy with some, though not all, of Chomsky's views on language and linguistics. Nevertheless, I am – like many, perhaps most, linguists with an informed interest in theoretical issues – to some considerable degree Chomskyan. My commitment to Chomskyan linguistics, however, has always been more eclectic than that of many. This will be evident from earlier chapters and from the immediately preceding section.

Generative grammar and 'the generative enterprise'.

Somewhat similar to the distinction between Chomsky's linguistics and Chomskyan linguistics (but not to be identified with it) is the distinction that I will draw between generative grammar as such and what has been called 'the generative enterprise' (which I have elsewhere referred to as 'generativism', in a sense different from the sense in which this term was used, in contrast with 'interpretivism', in Chapter 8). Regrettably, this distinction is not clearly drawn in most textbooks of linguistics (or indeed in several of Chomsky's own publications), where the term 'generative grammar' is used for both. And the situation is further confused for non-specialists by the fact that the term 'generative grammar' is also employed both by Chomsky and others (including me in earlier chapters of this book and in Appendix 1), to refer to the theory of generative grammars. Generally speaking, the context in which the expression 'generative grammar' is used will make it clear in which of these two senses it has to be understood.

A generative grammar, as we have seen, in the preceding chapters is a mathematically precise (formalized) set, or system, of rules which, operating upon (or in association with) a vocabulary, generates the sentences of a language and assigns to each a structural analysis. (Strictly speaking, the definition that I have just given defines a particular subclass of generative grammars: sentence-generating grammars. But this is the only such subclass of generative grammars with which Chomsky and most linguists have been concerned.) There are many different kinds of (sentence-generating) generative grammars, Chomskyan and non-Chomskyan. In this book we have concentrated upon Chomskyan generative grammars, and more particularly upon transformational grammars of the kind that Chomsky himself has promoted (and has been revising and modifying) since the mid-1950s.

There is no need to say any more about generative grammars or the theory of generative grammars for the moment. I will mention some of the major differences between earlier and more recent versions of Chomsky's own system of transformational grammar in later sections. Here I want to insist upon two points. The first is that, as I have already implied, it is important not to confuse an interest in the theory of generative grammars with a commitment to 'the generative enterprise'. The second is that it is equally important to realize that generative grammars as formalized by Chomsky are not the only kinds of generative grammars. Moreover, they may not be the best for linguistics: there are many experienced and knowledgeable linguists who think that they are not. But even if Chomsky's critics are ultimately proved right on this score, this will not reduce by one jot or tittle the magnitude of Chomsky's achievement. For a rather more technical account of what may be described, broadly, as Chomskyan generative grammars reference may be made to Appendix 1.

If generative grammar (and the theory of generative grammar) is not to be confused with what I have elsewhere called 'generativism' and, in the heading for this section, am calling 'the generative enterprise', what is 'generativism' (in this sense)? By 'generativism', or 'the generative enterprise', I mean commitment to a set of philosophical beliefs, including rationalism (in contrast with empiricism) and nativism, to a particular view of universal grammar, and to the incorporation of linguistics, in principle at least, within cognitive psychology. It is, of course, Chomsky's generativism, rather than his work on the theory of generative grammar, which has had the widest appeal outside, and even inside, linguistics. We shall begin, therefore, by considering some of the recent developments in Chomsky's (and Chomskyan) generativism.

'Plato's problem' – and Chomsky's solution: genetic anamnesis

Chomsky, as I said in Chapter 10, now stands firmly in 'the rationalist tradition going back [through Descartes, Leibniz, Kant and others] to Plato' (p. 135). He has done so publicly and consciously since the early 1960s; and there is no reason to doubt that he subscribed to a publicly undeclared version of rationalism long before that time (even though his earliest published work shows no sign of this and is consistent with either rationalism or empiricism: see Appendix 2). What may be referred to as 'The Cartesian connection' – the connection between Descartes' theory of 'innate ideas' and Chomsky's views on the acquisition of language – has been proclaimed by Chomsky himself from the outset (i.e., from when he first went public, as it were, on rationalism) and has been defended by him against a variety of criticisms ever since. He has also referred, in the past, to the similarity between his own view of inborn knowledge, or 'innate ideas', and Plato's doctrine of anamnesis, or recollection. It is only recently, however, that he has been using the expression 'Plato's problem' in what is fast becoming a quasi-technical (and contextually restricted) sense.

'Plato's problem', in its most general form, may be expressed as follows: how can human beings come to know as much as they do when, apparently, they are born in ignorance and the evidence available to them in life for what they know (or belief) is so limited? Plato solved this problem – or rather, dissolved it – by denying that the human mind is empty of knowledge at birth. Some knowledge, he said, is innate by virtue of the mind's (or soul's) prior existence; and what we call learning, in such cases, is a matter of the remembrance or recollection ('anamnesis' in Greek) of what was known previously. Recollection could be prompted by experience, including appropriately conducive questioning (as Socrates prompted the slave boy's 'recollection' of his mathematical knowledge by appropriate leading questions in the famous passage in Plato's *Meno*).

Plato did not apply his doctrine of *anamnesis* to the specific problem of (what is customarily referred to as) the acquisition, or learning, of language. It is this very problem, however, with which Chomsky has been primarily concerned in all his work. Indeed, it is a very considerable part of his achievement to have demonstrated that it was a problem; and, moreover, that it was a problem which could not be solved, even in principle, within the arbitrary constraints of empiricist – and, more particularly, behaviourist – theories of learning. As we have seen, Chomsky's solution is (and has been from the early 1960s at least) that language-acquisition is inexplicable unless we assume that children are born with a knowledge of what he calls universal grammar: i.e., of 'the universal principles governing the structure of human language' (p. 135). Chomsky's theory of universal grammar, like any other scientific theory, is subject to continuous modification: we shall be looking at some of the more recent modifications presently. What is to be emphasized here, as Chomsky himself has been emphasizing in his most recent publications, is that his solution is essentially Platonic.

It is however a thoroughly modern – and purely secular, non-dualist – version of Platonic rationalism, in which genetic transmission and environmentally triggered, organic, processes of growth and maturation replace Plato's postulates of pre-existence and recollection. It is a theory of what might well be called *genetic anamnesis*.

That Chomsky's appeal to the Platonic notion of 'anamnesis' no longer seems as scandalously unscientific and mystical as it did to many when he first referred to it some years ago is in itself a very considerable educative achievement on his part. As he has pointed out (without always making explicit reference to 'anamnesis'), there is good evidence, accepted by all biologists, for the genetic transmission of various kinds of skill and knowledge in other species. It would be surprising, therefore, if similar biological mechanisms were not operative in human beings. The question, of course, is how much genetically-transmitted knowledge there is and whether it is specific to the acquisition (or 'growth') of linguistic competence (see p. 148). I think it is fair to say that, although Chomsky has successfully rehabilitated and dymystified a traditional rationalist and 'nativist' position, converting it in principle into an empirically testable hypothesis, the actual empirical evidence in favour of the hypothesis of what I am now calling genetic anamnesis – it is not Chomsky's term – is perhaps slightly, but no more than slightly, stronger than it was in 1977.

Chomsky is inclined to exaggerate the progress that has been made in the empirical confirmation of his own theory of grammar in recent years when, for example, he presents as a matter of attested fact, supportive of the hypothesis of genetic anamnesis, such things as the child's allegedly innate knowledge of 'the existence of empty categories' and the child's similarly inborn 'precise knowledge of their properties' (*Language and Problems of Knowledge and Freedom*, 1988, p. 90). 'Empty categories' are hypothetical constructs within a particular theory, which, as I have mentioned already, is rejected by many, and perhaps most, linguists who practise Chomskyan, if not Chomsky's, linguistics. Their ontological status is questionable, and it is at the very least premature to say, as Chomsky does in the passage to which I have just referred, that their 'discovery . . . may be compared with the discovery of waves, particles, genes, valence, and so on . . . in the physical sciences'. We shall come back to the comparison that Chomsky makes, here and elsewhere, between linguistics and the physical sciences, towards the end of this chapter. Meanwhile, let us note that the hypothesis of genetic anamnesis, though so far not strongly confirmed in the form in which Chomsky has developed it, is none the less a perfectly respectable scientific hypothesis.

I-language and E-language; competence and performance; languages and grammars.

As we have seen in Chapters 4 and 9, in *Aspects of the Theory of Syntax* (1965) Chomsky drew a crucial theoretical distinction between competence and performance: between 'the speaker-hearer's knowledge of his language' and 'the actual use of language in concrete situations'. He noted at the time that his own competence/performance distinction was related to Saussure's (1916) distinction between *langue* and *parole*. This is a distinction which had long been familiar to European structuralists and had been accepted by most of them. But it had been rejected by the Bloomfieldian school of American structuralists, whose views, on this and on other issues, Chomsky strongly criticized (see Chapter 3 and Appendix 2). It had also been rejected, incidentally, by the so-called 'London School', headed by J. R. Firth, which was otherwise as strongly critical of the Bloomfieldians as Chomsky was, and for partly similar reasons.

More recently, Chomsky has been drawing a comparable distinction between what he calls I-language and E-language. The letters 'I' and 'E' stand for, or can be associated mnemonically with, the terms 'internal(ized)' and 'external(ized)' (see especially, Chomsky, *Knowledge of Language*, 1986, Chapter 2). It should perhaps be mentioned here, however, in advance of what will be explained below and to avoid confusion on what is a crucial point, that, in the context of Chomsky's present views 'internalized' (as distinct from 'internal') hardly makes sense. It is a throwback to an earlier period and, arguably, to a quasi-empiricist notion of language-acquisition. There is no longer any question of making internal (i.e., mental) what was previously external (i.e., outside the 'internalizing' organism). In fact, as we shall see, the term 'acquisition' is no longer applicable to the process during which the child proceeds from an 'initial state' of non-competence, or partial competence, to a (more or less) final 'steady state' of (more or less) full competence in a particular 'native' language.

In addition to the I-language/E-language distinction, Chomsky has also been drawing a related, and initially puzzling, distinction between grammars and languages. In so far as it is possible to explain these more recent notions in the space available to me here, I will do so. But I will also criticize Chomsky's presentation of them, which seems to me to be unnecessarily confusing and in certain respects misguided.

I have already pointed out that Chomsky's original distinction between 'competence' and 'performance' was made to do too many different jobs: that he described as matters of 'performance' (and, therefore, as irrelevant) a number of factors that should be handled in terms of [different kinds of] 'competence' (p. 150). A similar point may now be made about Chomsky's current distinction between I-language and E-language. The term 'E-language' is unclearly defined and serves mainly, as 'performance' did in *Aspects*, to label, somewhat dismissively, a variety of things which Chomsky (for quite good reasons) does not wish to be concerned with. But let us first deal with the new term 'I-language'. We can approach this by looking again at the 'competence'/'performance' distinction in relation to the Saussurean and post-Saussurean distinction of *langue* and *parole*.

Saussure's distinction has been subject to a considerable amount of misunderstanding. Part of this is due to the fact that the French terms he used have been wrongly translated into English as 'language' and 'speech'. But there are also well-known inconsistencies in the French text of the *Cours* (1916) itself, which are attributable to the circumstances of its posthumous compilation and publication. It is therefore difficult to relate Chomsky's 'competence'/'performance' distinction to the Saussurean *langue/parole* distinction on every dimension.

The task is further complicated by the fact that, although we have in each case two partly coincident dichotomies, there are really three things to be kept apart, not two. We have first of all the language (English, French, etc.) considered as a system of rules operating upon a vocabulary; and this can be identified without much difficulty either with Saussure's *langue* or, for the moment at least, with Chomsky's 'competence'. Let us refer to this, technically, as the *language-system*. Then we have, on the one hand, the use of the language-system (in particular situations) and, on the other, the product or products of the use of the language-system. Unfortunately the English word 'utterance' (like the word 'speech', but unlike the word 'language') covers both the use of a language (acts of utterance) and the products of that use (the stretches of spoken or written language that are produced). Chomsky's term 'performance' is appropriate enough for 'the use of [a] language in concrete situations', as he defined it in *Aspects* (p. 4), but it would not normally be understood to refer to the products of language-use. Saussure's *parole*, in contrast, is more appropriate for the products of use, or performance, than it is for language-performance itself; and, as we have noted, it is restricted in normal usage (and in many passages of the *Cours*) to the products of speech ('the spoken word'). Let us keep Chomsky's term 'performance' (as he originally defined it) for the activity of utterance (generalizing 'utterance' to cover both speech and writing); and let us introduce 'text' for the products of the activity of utterance (whether written or spoken). These three terms – 'language-system', 'performance' and 'text' – will enable us to explain the distinction between I-language and E-language and, at the same time, to distinguish what Chomsky groups together under the term E-langage.

The principal difference between Chomsky's 'competence' and Saussure's *langue* is that 'competence' definitely refers to something psychological or mental (i.e. something in an individual's mind or brain), whereas Saussure's *langue*, in some passages at least, refers to the language-system as something social and supra-individual ('a social fact'). Some versions of post-Saussurean European structuralism, however, have adopted other, including 'autonomous' or abstract, views of language-systems, considering them from neither an individualistic nor a social point of view. I will argue later that there are, in fact, several equally legitimate ways of defining the language-system, for different purposes and in different branches of linguistics, and that there is no reason to link language-systems as exclusively as Chomsky does to linguistic competence (regardless of whether competence is defined to be located in the individual or in society).

I pointed out in the opening section of this chapter (in relation to D'Agostino's remarks about Chomsky's individualism) that the famous passage in *Aspects* about the competence of the 'ideal speaker-listener' would not necessarily commit Chomsky to an individualistic view of competence (though it became clear shortly afterwards that he did in fact take this view). There is no doubt, however, that Chomsky's new term 'I-language', as it is defined, does so commit him. In fact, there is a further convenient (but fortuitous) mnemonic connection, not only between the 'I' of 'I-language' and 'internal', but also between the 'I' and both 'individual' and 'idiolect'. An I-language is, quite simply, the language-system that is stored internally (i.e., in the mind or brain) of the individual: that is to say, it is what is referred to in the more or less standard terminology of modern linguistics as someone's *idiolect* (i.e., a particular person's individual language-system).

All this is straightforward enough. It is the term 'E-language' that causes trouble. I do not propose to go into this question in detail here. It will suffice for the moment to note that Chomsky uses the term 'E-language' to refer, not only to both performance and to text, but also to languages (i.e. language-systems) considered as social entities. Indeed, 'E-language' is the term that he would use for English, French, or whatever, as such languages are normally conceived (as well as for texts in English, French, etc.). I will pick up this point later.

But in concluding this section, I should note that, in certain publications, Chomsky treats the opposition between grammars and languages as comparable with, if not identical to, the opposition that he has established between I-languages and E-languages. Grammars, we are told, are 'real' in that they exist in the world (i.e., in the minds or brains of individuals), whereas languages (in the normal sense of this term) do not exist 'in the world', are more or less indeterminate in structure and are of uncertain ontological status. This point too I will pick up later.

Deep structure and universal grammar.

Few technical distinctions of modern theoretical linguistics have been so widely adopted outside linguistics as Chomsky's distinction between deep structure and surface structure, which he first drew in *Aspects* (1965); few, too, have been so widely misinterpreted or misunderstood. Part of the misunderstanding derives undoubtedly from the metaphorical resonances and collocational associations of the adjective 'deep'. These together with the connection between deep structures and meaning in the standard theory of transformational grammar, on the one hand, and the assumed universality of deep structures, on the other, have encouraged many writers to link Chomsky's deep structures with, for example, Wittgenstein's 'deep grammar' or Jungian 'depth psychology'. Chomsky himself has long been aware of these unfortunate and misleading associations (see above p. 102), and for the last few years he has preferred to talk of D-structure and S-structure. This terminological change is accompanied, as we shall see, by a radical change in the original technical conception of deep structure, so that current D-structures and S-structures cannot be simply identified with the classical deep structures and surface structures of the standard theory.

Not all of the misunderstanding to which I have just referred, some of it shared by linguists, was due, however, to the metaphorical associations of the adjective 'deep' (see pp. 96 ff.). As far as the common association of deep structure with universality is concerned, I noted in Chapter 8 that Chomsky himself has explicitly argued against the view that all languages have the same deep structure and has pointed out that the thesis which this view embodies is, strictly speaking, nonsensical in terms of the technical definition of 'deep structure' given in *Aspects*. At the same time, linguists and others can be forgiven for having drawn from Chomsky's earlier statements about universal grammar a conclusion that can be formulated, loosely, in terms of the distinction between the deep structure and the surface structure of languages. Moreover, it is a conclusion which is in accord with a very traditional view of the grammatical structure of languages: 'Grammar is substantially the same in all languages, even though it may vary accidentally.' This is a famous quotation from the thirteenth-century philosopher Roger Bacon (1214–94). It is cast in the Aristotelian terminology of medieval scholasticism (cf. Lyons, *Introduction to Theoretical Linguistics*, pp. 15–16). But a very similar universalist view underpins the rationalist, Cartesian, theory of language of the seventeenth-century grammarians of Port-Royal, who have been seen by Chomsky as precursors of generative grammar and generativism.

It is a view which can be traced back, with the necessary terminological and conceptual adjustments, to the very origins of Western traditional grammar. And it is easy enough to reformulate it, on the basis of Chomsky's distinction between the deep structure and surface structure of sentences, indirectly and derivatively, as a distinction between the deep structure and the surface structure of languages. It will be instructive to do so and to use the resultant, more precisely formulated, hypothesis as a foil to Chomsky's very different universalist hypothesis.

Every language, let us say with Chomsky, is a set of sentences; to each sentence of any language that is generated by a standard-theory transformational grammar there is assigned, by the rules of the grammar, at least one deep structure and at least one surface structure; and sentences of the same language differ from one another in meaning if, and only if, they are derivable from two or more different, and semantically non-equivalent, deep structures. Let us now go on to say – as Chomsky does not – that the deep structure of a language is either (i) the set of deep structures from which its sentences are generated, considered in abstraction from the actual words supplied by the vocabulary, or (ii) the categorial rules of the grammar which (together with a rule of lexical insertion which makes reference to the vocabulary) generate the deep structures of the sentences; and let us, finally, declare or hypothesize that all natural human languages, being intertranslatable and generable from the same universal inventory of syntactic and semantic elements, share the same deep structure.

What I have just done is to reformulate, fairly precisely and in theoretically acceptable terms, a Chomskyan version of the hypothesis that all languages have the same deep structure. In the second of the two alternative formulations that I have here adumbrated, it was explicitly put forward, as *the universal-base hypothesis*, and defended, in conscious opposition to Chomsky's own theory, or hypothesis, of universal grammar in the late 1960s and early 1970s, by the breakaway group of generative grammarians known, misleadingly, as 'generative semanticists' (see p. 97 above).

The fact that the hypothesis that the deep structure of language is universal and innate can be satisfactorily reformulated within the framework of transformational grammar means that it cannot be dismissed as theoretically incoherent within this framework. Chomsky himself has never defended it and would challenge it as empirically unmotivated. But that is another matter. In my opinion, neither Chomsky's own theory of universal grammar (about the current version of which more will be said presently) nor the more traditional theory with which many scholars originally, and reasonably, thought Chomsky was associating himself is clearly preferable to its rivals on purely empirical grounds.

It is all too easy for non-specialists to get the impression from the arguments of Chomsky and his followers that the case for his version of universal grammar is very strongly confirmed by, rather than being more or less strongly supported by or merely compatible with, some of the findings of descriptive linguistics and of data which comes from the empirical investigation of the acquisition of language by children. It seems to me that in this area all options, apart from fairly radical behaviourism, are still open; and, as a linguist, one makes one's personal selection from the available options on metatheoretical and methodological, and more or less consciously philosophical, grounds.

The distinction between deep structure and surface structure no longer occupies the same position of prominence in Chomskyan generative grammar that it once did. As we saw in Chapter 8, the standard theory of transformational grammar, within which the distinction was originally formalized, was radically modified by Chomsky, in several relevant and important respects, more than a decade and a half ago; and the role of transformational rules has been successively reduced in the various Chomskyan and non-Chomskyan versions of generative grammar that have been developed since then. Indeed, as I will explain below in the section devoted to 'Government-Binding Theory', there is now, in Chomsky's own system, only one transformation (commonly referred to as 'Move alpha') and it has nothing like the status of the very heterogeneous transformational rules of either *Syntactic Structures* or *Aspects*.

The debate between the 'interpretivists' and (so-called) 'generativists', which raged throughout the late-1960s and early-1970s, is long over (see pp. 92ff.) It is generally said to have ended in victory for the former (of whom Chomsky was, of course, the principal champion). This historical judgement is fair enough. But, as I said in Chapter 8, both sides had more in common with one another than perhaps they realized. And it should not be thought that the influence of the 'generative semanticists' has disappeared without trace. Many of the issues that they raised have been recognized as relevant for linguistics, and some of their ideas have been absorbed and reinterpreted in modern Chomskyan work. As for the narrowly technical issue of the status of *Aspects*-type deep structures in an integrated syntactic and semantic account of the structure of natural languages, it is hard to say that either of two opposing sides was victorious.

Modularity of mind and language.

One of the currently fashionable terms in the vocabulary of those who are engaged in 'the generative enterprise' is 'modularity'. Though the term itself is new, being borrowed (in the sense in which it is now being used by psychologists, philosophers and linguists) from computer science (which, like aeronautics, had presumably borrowed it earlier from architecture and building technology), the idea with which it is associated is traditional enough and goes back many centuries to the very beginnings of the philosophy and psychology of mind. To say that something is modular – mind, language, a spacecraft, a building, a computer program, or whatever –

is to say no more than that it is composed of several structurally or functionally discrete, and more or less independent but interacting or interconnected, 'modules'.

One of the older terms for 'module' in the philosophy and psychology of mind is 'faculty', which has been used in the past, both technically (in various systems of so-called 'faculty psychology') and non-technically, to refer to such 'organs' or 'powers' of the mind as the intellect, the memory, the will and the emotions. As we have seen, it has been Chomsky's view from the early 1960s at least, that what until recently he called 'linguistic competence' (or 'grammatical competence') and is now referring to as 'I-language' is independent of other kinds of knowledge; that it develops in early childhood in the mind/-brain of the child (growing 'organically' under the control of a genetic program) independently of the development (or 'growth') of other mental capacities and that it must be ascribed to, or indeed identified with, a distinct mental 'faculty' (see pp. 126, 133 ff., 148 ff.). I have inserted the complex term 'mind/brain' in the preceding sentence, as Chomsky himself does on occasion, to remind the reader that Chomsky rejects the dualist approach to 'the body-mind problem'.

Chomsky's view that the language-faculty is a relatively independent mental 'organ' has not changed fundamentally over the last twenty-five years or so. It has, however, been successively clarified in some of the detail. In particular, he has made it clear in all his more recent publications on language and mind that, when he talks of linguistic competence (or the I-language) as a mental organ, he is not using the word 'organ' metaphorically. He denies that there is any distinction to be drawn, here or elsewhere, between the mental and the physical (in an appropriately extended sense of 'physical') and insists that linguistic competence is just as properly described as an organ which 'grows', or matures, in the human psycho-physical organism according to biologically pre-determined principles as is the liver or the heart.

Whether Chomsky's view of the modularity of mind has changed over the years is hard to say. He has always been concerned primarily with the language-faculty, and such references as he has made to other mental organs, or modules, have been incidental to this primary concern. As we have seen, his basic assumption, or hypothesis, is that linguistic competence is independent of other mental faculties or abilities, but interacts with them in the production and interpretation of utterances. His commitment to this assumption has certainly not changed.

What may have changed more recently is Chomskys view of the internal structure of the language-faculty. Since he has had little to say about this in earlier works, it is hard to be sure to what degree any changes that there may have been are merely changes of emphasis or focus (and he tends to present them as such) and to what degree they are more fundamental. What cannot be denied, however, is the fact that in all his work of the last decade or so – and most notably in *Knowledge of Language* (1986) – he has been arguing, as he did not before, not only that the language-faculty is one of the modules of the mind, but also that it is itself modular in structure. As before, he still sees it as the major task of theoretical linguistics to characterize the language-faculty by means of a generative grammar. But the kind of grammars with which he is currently working, as we shall see, are very different from those of the 'classical' or immediately 'post-classical' period. Indeed there are many who would deny that they are generative grammars in the sense in which Chomsky originally defined the term – or as I, following Chomsky, have defined it in Appendix 2. But that, in the present context, is irrelevant. Chomsky's interest in generative grammars as such has long been subordinate to his interest in grammar as a key with which to unlock 'the black box', as it were, and gain access to one part, or faculty, of the mind. For the moment, the point to note is that, for Chomsky, the grammar of any human language is now conceived, not as a single set of rules (operating upon a vocabulary), but as a system of relatively independent, but interacting, modules, each of which is of course a sub-module of the mind. How these sub-modules are currently conceived will be explained below. But first I must say something about modularity and the localization of particular modules of the language-faculty in different parts of the brain.

Modular neurolinguistic parallelism?

It as long been known that certain sensory, motor and mental functions are located in, or controlled by, particular regions of the brain. Two of these, discovered over a hundred years ago and named after their discoverers, are Broca's Area and Wernicke's Area, both of which are normally to be found in the left cerebral hemisphere (the former in the frontal lobe, the latter in the temporal lobe). Each of them plays an essential, but distinct, role in the neurophysiological processing of language and speech; and damage or disease in one or other of the two areas is associated with characteristically different kinds of aphasia. For this reason, and because their association with language and speech was established long before that of other regions of the brain, they are often popularly referred to as 'the language areas'.

The fact that they are located in the left hemisphere of the brain (in over ninety per cent of the population) is the consequence of what is called lateralization: the asymmetrical development of the two hemispheres of the human brain and the specialization in early childhood (under normal environmental and developmental conditions) of parts of the dominant hemisphere for particular functions. Lateralization and cerebral dominance (which for our purposes can be subsumed under the common term 'localization') are quite clearly controlled by a genetically transmitted program; and the role that they play in the acquisition of language is consistent with, and indeed can be seen as giving some degree of positive support to, a broadly Chomskyan view of the process.

Much faculty psychology of an earlier period was based on the assumption of psychophysiological parallelism: i.e., the assumption that every mental process or function can be matched with, and is dependent upon, a specific physiological process. This assumption does not of itself presuppose modularity or the localization of particular mental modules in particular areas of the brain. But it sits comfortably with both notions. Let me therefore combine it with them and refer to the resultant combination as the hypothesis of modular (neurolinguistic) parallelism. It is now natural to enquire, first of all, how Chomsky stands with respect to the hypothesis of modular parallelism (which, unlike certain traditional versions of psychophysiological parallelism, does not necessarily commit one to a dualist position on 'the mind-body problem') and, then, whether there is any empirical evidence currently available which supports the hypothesis.

The answer to the first of these two questions is quickly given. Chomsky's theory of the modularity of language is certainly consistent with the hypothesis of modular parallelism. He himself, however, would be agnostic about it. But he would not necessarily be hostile to it, provided that it is formulated in sufficiently general and abstract terms. Although Chomsky classifies linguistics as a branch of cognitive psychology, he himself is singularly uninterested in, not to say dismissive of, the theories and empirical findings of psychologists. Chomskyan linguistics has been since the early 1960s, and continues to be, one of the principal motive forces in the newly emergent cognitive sciences. Nevertheless, despite the much-vaunted 'cognitive turn', in linguistics as in other disciplines, when it comes to the description of natural languages, Chomskyan linguistics, as practised by Chomsky and most linguists (unless of course they describe themselves as sociolinguists, psycholinguists, ethnolinguists, neurolinguists, etc.), is no less 'autonomous' today than it was in the pre-Chomskyan structuralist period. This might seem to be somewhat paradoxical at first blush. Chomsky's view, however, which he has frequently reiterated, is that the psychological level at which he conceptualizes the storage and processing of language in the individual, though properly described as physical, is highly abstract. And he has always argued that the question 'What is linguistic competence?' must first be addressed and clarified by linguistics (operating 'autonomously') before other disciplines can profitably address the secondary question 'How is language competence stored and processed in the brain?'

As to the question of whether there is any empirical evidence to support the hypothesis of modular parallelism, the short answer would seem to that we are still a long way from being able to say that any particular form of this hypothesis is strongly supported or, alternatively, disconfirmed by empirical research. Scholars other than Chomsky have put forward more detailed modular theories of mind, most notably Fodor, whose book entitled *The Modularity of Mind* (1983) has done much to promote both the term and the concept. But no one of the currently competing modular theories of mind has won universal acceptance.

Considerable progress has been made recently in what has come to be called neurolinguistics: the neurophysiological and neuropsychological study of language and speech. It is now know for example that Broca's Area and Wernicke's Area are not the only regions of the brain in which language is stored or processed and that not all the processing of speech and language is carried out in the dominant hemisphere (or indeed by exclusively 'new-brain', neo-cortical, tissue). But there is still a very real sense in which the dominant hemisphere – and, moreover, certain identifiable regions of the dominant hemisphere, including, in particular, Broca's Area and Wernicke's Area – can be correctly described as having a specifically linguistic function. As far as the reception of speech is concerned, it seems that, whereas the verbal component of spoken utterance (i.e., what can be analysed phonologically as a succession of vowels and consonants) is usually processed by the dominant hemisphere, but that the non-segmental features of spoken utterances (e.g., stress and intonation) can be handled equally well by either hemisphere. Both hemispheres are involved in the grammatical and semantic processing of language-utterances; but, once again, there is some considerable degree of specialization, in that the non-dominant hemisphere is able to interpret expressions referring to concrete objects, but only the dominant hemisphere is capable of interpreting more abstract expressions. In short, certain of the long-standing generalizations made by neurophysiologists and aphasiologists have stood the test of time reasonably well, but have been refined and to some extent modified by more recent work based on new radiological techniques and careful study of the vastly increased clinical evidence.

It is not yet possible, however, to put the empirical findings of neurolinguistics (or experimental psycholinguistics) into correspondence with modular theories of mind and language except in such general terms that they do not speak clearly in favour of one model of language-structure or another. It may be added that, independently of the validity of the hypothesis of modular parallelism, neither Chomsky's modular theory nor any other Chomskyan or non-Chomskyan theory of the structure of language has yet been confirmed, or universally adopted as a basis for research, by psychologists, neurolinguists or cognitive scientists. It would be generally agreed, however, that the idea of modularity is currently a potent catalyst for progress in linguistics and related disciplines.

Universal grammar: principles and parameters; markedness; core and periphery.

As we have seen in earlier chapters, it has been Chomsky's view since at least the early 1960s that the structure of particular natural languages, such as English, Japanese, Arabic, Navaho, etc., is constrained by the principles and categories of universal grammar. Chomsky's general conception of the relation between universal grammar and the grammars of particular languages has not changed over the years. Nor has his view that universal grammar is strongly determined by (or indeed, in terms of the hypothesis of the modularity of mind and language, as it is currently formulated, is identifiable with) a genetically transmitted language-faculty, which plays an essential role (as what used to be referred to as LAD: 'the language-acquisition device') in children's acquisition of their native language (see p. 120).

Chomsky's thought, as I have been emphasizing throughout this chapter, is never static. As we saw in Chapter 8, the standard theory of *Aspects* (1965 was modified successively in the course of the 1970s as the 'extended standard theory' (EST) and the 'revised extended standard theory' (REST). Even more important modifications have been made in the last decade, as will be explained below in the section of 'Government-Binding Theory' (GB). Here I want to deal briefly with the major differences between the 'classic' Chomskyan view of universal grammar, which was outlined in *Aspects*, and the view which underpins Chomsky's current research and that of his followers.

The key-words, are 'principle' and 'parameter'. The first of these, of course, is not new. The standard theory of universal grammar, if I may so refer to it, was held to contain a set of formal and substantive universals, which, for present expository purposes, we can identify with principles and categories (see p. 120). One of the formal principles upon which Chomsky laid great stress at the time was that of structure-dependency (see pp. 129ff.). What may be called the general (or global) meta-theoretical principle of structure-dependency played a crucial role in the technical definition of 'transformation' in Chomsky's original formalization of transformational-generative grammar in the 1950s and continues to do so, presumably, even though current versions of transformational grammar, including GB, have greatly reduced the power and diversity of transformations.

Subsumed under the general principle of structure-dependency, in the standard theory and its successors, were a number of more specific principles, such as the 'A-over-A' principle, which was explained above (p. 130). All of these were of course hypothetical and provisional, and some of them have been modified or rejected in the light of new evidence. (The 'A-over-A' principle, for instance does not figure at all as such in GB.) In some cases, two or more principles of limited scope have been replaced with a single principle of wider import. For example, the 'specified-subject condition' and the 'tensed-sentence condition' of an earlier, post-*Aspects* but pre-GB, period have now given way to one of a set of *binding principles*, which is intended to cover the phenomena handled previously by both of them operating separately and at the same time to cover phenomena that were not handled previously by either. The terminological difference between 'condition' and 'principle' need not detain us here. Nor need we be concerned, at this stage, with the implications of the word 'binding' (see below).

What is of particular interest is the relatively new notion of *parametric variation*, which Chomsky introduced into his theory of universal grammar in the 1980s. (I say 'new', because it has been newly adapted to its present purpose: it has identifiable antecedents in earlier linguistic theory, Chomskyan and non-Chomskyan.) Universal grammar, as it is now conceived by Chomsky, is a (genetically-transmitted, modular) theory of *principles and parameters*, incorporating a sub-theory of *markedness*, which determines the acquisition of a core grammar and, somewhat differently and unpredictably from person to person, its extension to a *periphery*. Chomsky's formulation has varied to some degree in the several publications in which he has dealt with these questions during the 1980s. But the above formulation (with a certain amount of explanation) will serve to introduce the key concepts and to show how they fit together, in what turns out to be a rather more traditional – and, perhaps, a more attractive – theory of universal grammar than the 'classical' Chomskyan theory of *Aspects* and its more immediate post-*Aspects* successors. Parametric variation is invoked in order to account for such structural diversity as one undoubtedly finds, as a matter of empirical fact, in natural languages and to reconcile this diversity with the hypothesis of universality, by showing that it is highly constrained and predictable. The central idea is that some (or all) of the principles of universal grammar are associated (as part of the theory itself) with a 'parameter', which can be 'set' (during the process of language-acquisition) to one of a number of possible 'values' and that each such value will 'select' one typological feature rather than another. To take a simple example (which I will further simplify for expository purpose, both theoretically and in its empirical reference to particular languages): among the languages of the world there are those with a (relatively) free word order, such as Latin, and those with a (relatively) fixed word order such as English or Chinese. Let us now suppose that word order is determined 'parametrically' by one of the principles of universal grammar which 'allow' natural languages as it were, to 'select' for themselves either of the two possible word orders. This, as I say, is a deliberately simplified example. No such simplistic parametric 'word-order principle' of this kind has ever been proposed by Chomsky or his followers. But, with a little further development, our simple example will serve its purpose, without doing violence to the spirit of his proposals.

So, let us now suppose that this parametric 'word-order principle', initially of limited scope, is, first of all, generalized and made more abstract and, then, integrated within a system with other such fairly general principles, each empirically and independently motivated: principles which are similarly parametric (each with two or more 'values') and which, let us say, allow languages to have a relatively rich or a relatively poor inflectional system (or none at all); which allow pronouns (if the language has pronouns) to be optional or obligatory in certain grammatically definable positions; which allow the verb to agree (in person, number, gender, etc.) with its subject or with its object (or with neither); which allow verbs and prepositions to govern

their object in a distinct 'oblique' case (e.g. the accusative) different from that of the subject; and so on.
Chomsky's purpose, and that of those who follow him
in this direction, is to integrate a number of such principles (not formulated, as I have formulated them here,
in terms that are familiar from traditional school grammar, but more technically) both with one another and
with principles in other 'modules' of the grammar.
Ideally, such principles, interacting with one another,
will 'select' from the indefinitely large class of possible
languages a very much smaller subclass of possible *core
languages*.

Each such core language may be described as *structurally consistent* and *coherent*: consistent in that each principle
applies without exception throughout the language in
question; coherent in that all the principles which the
theory of universal grammar defines to be interdependent operate together as they are predicted to operate. These notions of structural consistency and coher-
ence, which have introduced, are not in fact Chomsky's,
but they derive naturally from his way of defining core
languages. They should make it easier for readers who
are not already familiar with Chomsky's recent work,
but have some knowledge of structuralist principles and
their application to typology to relate Chomsky's ideas,
in general if not in detail, to those of earlier structuralists
in the Saussurean and post-Saussurean tradition
(notably Hjelmslev). It is interesting that there should
be this point of contact, which, to the best of my knowledge, is both unconscious and unacknowledged. But then
it is noticeable that much of Chomsky's current thinking
can be brought into contact, at particular points, with
that of other twentieth-century schools of linguistics.

Few, if any, actual human languages are structurally
consistent and coherent. They have, not only a core,
but also a *periphery* consisting of a variety of historically

accidental 'irregularities'. For example, English being in general – i.e., in its core – a language which constructs the plural of nouns and the past tense of verbs by adding the appropriate suffix to the base-form is structurally inconsistent in respect of the forms *geese* or *mice* and *road* or *went*. Such forms (traditionally described as 'irregular') are said to be *marked*, rather than unmarked (in the linguist's sense of these terms): i.e., they deviate from what is the (unmarked) norm for an 'ideal' member of the relevant structural type. The acquisition, or learning, of such marked forms is also controlled, in Chomsky's view, by universal grammar 'but in somewhat different ways' – by the theory (or sub-theory) of markedness 'which permits the extension of [a] core grammar to a full grammar' as the child proceeds from 'the [innate] initial state of the language-faculty' to 'the more or less steady state' of full (adult) competence (in this or that natural language) 'under the triggering and shaping effect of experience' ('Knowledge of language: its elements and origins', 1981, p. 10). So far, so good.

It now has to be said, however, that Chomskys invocation of the notion of 'periphery' is open to the same kinds of criticism as was his earlier invocation of the notion of 'performance': that he uses it to cover a variety of phenomena which ought to be distinguished – phenomena which, quite reasonably, do not engage his interest, but which others, no less reasonably, do find interesting and worthy of study. Given his strongly individualist and realist view of the ontological status of languages, the peripheral part of a grammar will presumably be the structurally inconsistent part of a particular person's individual grammar stored in that person's mind/brain. Each person's peripheral grammar will differ, at least minimally and in some cases considerably, from every other person's. This is of course, not only a thoroughly defensible view, but one which, as far as it goes, is obviously correct. There is nothing especially novel in the observation that no two members of what is generally regarded as the same language-community speak exactly the same language or indeed exactly the same dialect: all members of any language-community have their own *idiolect*, which, in so far as it is systematic and rule-governed, has its own grammar distinct from the grammar of all other idiolects.

The fact remains that much of what is defined (by the notion of markedness) as peripheral in the idiolects of the members of a particular language-community will be shared by all of them or, at least, by all those who are held to be speakers of the same dialect. There is every reason, therefore, to continue to say (recognizing, as one always has recognized, that there is some degree of abstraction and idealization in saying this) that they are speakers of the same language (or dialect). To say, as Chomsky has been saying recently, that only grammars are real (and that languages are derivative, 'epiphenomenal' and theoretically uninteresting) smacks of undesirable reductionism. I will return to this point. As far as I can see, there is no incompatibility between commitment to the kind of 'principles-and-parameters' grammar of the kind that Chomsky is currently advocating and a rejection of his narrowly realist and individualist approach to the definition of 'language'. After all, the structuralist typology of languages to which I referred above was proposed within the framework of a thoroughgoing 'autonomous', or abstract, approach to the description of languages.

Chomsky's reductionist 'physicalism' and 'the unity of science'.

The heading that I have give to this section is deliberately, but I hope constructively, provocative.

It is a commonplace of the history of science (as also of political and social history) that those who see themselves, or are recognized by their peers, as revolutionaries usually take over from their predecessors far more than they reject and far more than they themselves realize. Chomsky is no exception to this generalization. In earlier chapters of this book, I have emphasized that Chomskyan generative grammar, in its original formulation, was in many of its details thoroughly 'Bloomfieldian' (or 'post-Bloomfieldian'). It has been suggested by many critics that, in doing this, I have overemphasized historical continuity and underemphasized what such critics see as radical and revolutionary discontinuity, of the kind that philosophers of science who follow T. S. Kuhn call a change of 'paradigm'.

In my view, there is no conflict here between, as it were, gradualism and catastrophism. I yield to no-one in my admiration of the visionary boldness of Chomsky's work both in linguistics and in the philosophy of mind and language. At the same time, I would still maintain that there is much, even now, in Chomsky's linguistics which derives very directly from its Bloomfieldian origins. But I do not wish to get into these technicalities here (see Appendix 1). What I want to do, instead, is to draw attention to what can be seen as another similarity between Bloomfield and Chomsky: their reductionist attitude towards linguistics and their commitment to the unity of science.

Of course, one must make due allowance for the fact that Bloomfield's notion of 'science' was formed more than half a century before Chomsky's: Bloomfield's physicalism (against which Chomsky reacted) is essentially that of the late-nineteenth and early-twentieth century, as was that of the 'unity of science' movement to which Bloomfield belonged (together with Carnap, Neurath, Nagel, Hempel, and other prominent scientific and logical positivists). Chomsky has a much more sophisticated, and what we currently see as 'modern', view of science.

Chomsky, it will be evident, adopts a 'reductionist' view of linguistics: he defines linguistics (or, at least, the part that interests him) to be a part of psychology and he defines psychology to be a part of biology. This is exactly the view that Bloomfield took; and between 1914 (when Bloomfield's earlier book was published) and the late 1920s, Bloomfield switched his allegiance from what we may now think of as the 'cognitive' or 'mentalist' psychology of Wundt to the behaviourist psychology of Watson (see Chapter 3). But his 'psychologism' did not change. Chomsky has long described himself as a 'mentalist'. However, as I noted at the end of Chapter 10, 'he might equally well be described as a "physicalist"' (p. 138). Given the line that Chomsky currently takes on what was traditionally called 'the mind-body problem', I think he is better described as a 'physicalist' than as a 'mentalist' (if we have to use one of these terms to the exclusion of the other). It is just that Chomsky has a different, more 'abstract', view of the physical sciences, including biology, than earlier 'physicalists' (and 'reductionists') had. Perhaps the best label for Chomsky's current position is 'abstract (reductionist) physicalism'. What is implied by this rather cumberson label (which is of course my own) should now be clear enough. Chomsky's abstract physicalism is not new; but it has now been more clearly (and more emphatically) articulated. So too has his reductionism; and he is noticeably more dismissive than he used to be of those 'parts of linguistics', as it is currently constituted, which do not interest him.

Chomsky's visionary reductionism – and I think this is the right way to characterized it – is undoubtedly exciting; and I, personally, find it philosophically inspiring. But, as I have been stressing throughout this chapter, it must be constantly borne in mind that there is at the moment very little hard empirical evidence to support it. It must also be appreciated that, just as Bloomfield's behaviouristic psychologism had very little effect on the description of languages that linguists who subscribed to it actually produced, so it is also with Chomskys very different psychologism (or cognitivism). Chomsky's linguistics, and most Chomskyan linguistics, as it is actually practised, is (like Bloomfieldian linguistics and most other kinds of descriptive linguistics) 'autonomous'; and, I would say, very properly so.

This is not the place to recite in full my own ontological *Credo*. But a briefer version is perhaps, not only permitted, but required, in order to supply a context for what I have referred to as Chomskys reductionism. (For details and supporting argument, reference may be made to the works listed in the Bibliography, in which various points made in this chapter are developed in full.)

Briefly, my position is one of ontological (and methodological) pluralism. The field of linguistics, as it is currently structured, can be divided in terms of at least four dichotomies: general linguistics vs. descriptive linguistics, synchronic linguistics vs. diachronic linguistics, microlinguistics (or 'core linguistics' – in a different sense of 'core' from that of Chomskys 'core languages') vs. macrolinguistics (psycholinguistics, sociolinguistics, ethnolinguistics, etc.) and theoretical linguistics vs. applied linguistics. Further refinements and subdivisions are possible. But these will suffice for the present purpose: that of placing the subfield of linguistics which interests Chomsky where, I think, it belongs and criticizing his dismissive and reductionist attitude towards other subfields of linguistics. And for this restricted purpose, I will not, and need not, explain the dichotomies that I have drawn. They are more or less generally accepted, though the terms in which they are drawn by different schools of linguists vary somewhat; and not everyone will distinguish 'general linguistics' from 'theoretical linguistics'. But, in my view, these four dichotomies are logically independent and serve to structure the multidimensional field of linguistics, as it is currently constituted, into a multiplicity of subfields, no one of which is to be identified, to the exclusion of the others with linguistics *tout court*. Admittedly the whole of linguistics (like most institutionalized academic fields of study) is at any one time, as Chomsky has said of the 'part of linguistics' which engages his particular interest, something of an 'artificially delimited discipline', part of whose subject matter will be absorbed in the course of time into neighbouring or more comprehensive disciplines. And it may well be that the subfield of linguistics which interests Chomsky – which I can now identify, within my classificatory scheme, as theoretical (synchronic, general descriptive) psycholinguistics – will disappear as other kinds of evidence become available that bear on questions with which it has been concerned' and will be absorbed into 'psychology, and ultimately biology'. But we are a long way from being able to predict confidently that this will happen.

The ontological status of natural languages (more precisely of the language-systems underlying natural languages) has been controversial ever since the publication of Saussure's *Cours* (1916). As we have seen, Saussure's own views are unclear and perhaps contradictory. At one time, he says that they are supraindividual social facts; at another time, that they are stored in the brains of individual members of the language community (*Cours*, 1916: 23–32). Much of the controversy that has surrounded the Saussurean distinction of 'langue' and 'parole' (or the Chomskyan distinction of 'competence' and 'performance') turns on the false assumption that there is only one kind of 'reality': that natural languages must be either psychological or social entities, or, in terms of an alternative dichotomy that they must be either physical or non-physical.

My view is that, if we take linguistics as it is at present structured, the several branches of linguistics each have their own legitimately different initial ('pre-theoretical' and more or less well-defined) notion of what a language is. Then, according to their own viewpoint, either 'autonomously' (in the case of microlinguistics) or 'non-autonomously' (in alliance with neighbouring disciplines), they each practice a particular kind of abstraction and idealization in the construction of their own ontologically (and methodologically) appropriate model of the underlying language-system.

Chomsky's 'individualistic-realist' (and 'abstract physicalist') notion of the language-system is eminently defensible for the sub-branch of linguistics that interests him. But it will not do for other sub-branches; and the way Chomsky lumps all other 'parts of linguistics' together, dismissively, by invoking an ill-defined and confusing concept of 'E-language' is unhelpful. Premature reductionism of whatever kind, generativist or physicalist, psycholinguistic or sociolinguistic, is detrimental to progress in linguistics. It is also detrimental, I think, to 'the generative enterprise' and to the philosophy of language and mind.

Rationalism, rationality and rationalization.

In the age-old dispute between philosophical rationalism and empiricism, Chomsky, as we have seen, is a self-proclaimed rationalist (Chapter 10). He has done more than anyone else in modern times to make the rationalist's doctrine of innate ideas and mental dispositions academically respectable with philosophers and psychologists of language. And, we have seen, he has brought up to date Plato's mythical notion of recollection and turned it into a thoroughly modern and eminently scientific theory of 'genetic anamnesis'.

But Chomsky is also a rationalist in the more popular sense of being 'rational': he is someone who applies to every issue that he addresses in his search for truth – in politics as also in linguistics, philosophy and psychology – what Cicero has called the 'dry light' of reason. And he does so with unusual consistency, intellectual intensity, doggedness of purpose and, as Peck has put it, 'unity of mind and outlook' (1988: ix). It is this remarkable unity of mind and outlook, evident in everything that he writes, says or does, which – together with his commitment to a belief in human freedom – unifies and integrates the totality of his thought and action.

Some would say that Chomsky's rationality – his commitment to reason and the pursuit of truth – is itself irrational in both the popular and the philosophical sense of the term. Nor is it clear that he himself would wish to rebut this charge or even to think it worth rebutting. He has on several occasions rejected the epistemologist's definition of knowledge as rationally-grounded or justified belief and he has denied that there is any sharp distinction to be drawn between various kinds of knowledge and belief. And he is on record as repudiating the suggestion that his rationality is sustained by an optimistic 'faith that truth will prevail if it becomes known' and as accepting that 'we have no alternative to proceeding on that assumption, whatever its credibility may be', because 'it's all we have' (Peck, 1988: 48).

Chomsky has often been criticized for selectivity in the use of evidence; he has also been criticized, sometimes rightly and sometimes wrongly, for his idealization of the data and for his readiness to simplify the issues.

Whatever the validity of these criticisms, there is no doubt that unless he had had this ability to select, to simplify and to idealize the data, as a precondition of the formalization of the structure of language-systems, he would not have succeeded in revolutionizing linguistics. Nor would he have been able to engage in debate with major philosophers of mind and language, more or less successfully, on the range of topics that I have subsumed under 'generativism' (or 'the generative enterprise').

This ability to select, simplify and idealize is one of his greatest strengths in any argument in which he chooses to offer battle, in print or orally. Another of his strengths – coupled with his powerful intellect and memory for relevant detail – is an all but unshakeable conviction that he is right and his opponents are wrong, both in logic and in what he sees as the point of the argument. This can be infuriating, and it makes of him a fearsome and invincible dialectician. Not surprisingly, he has aroused passions and created enemies.

Not surprisingly, too, his preparedness to speak out freely and fearlessly for what he takes to be a self-evident, valid principle, such as liberty of expression and self-determination, without trimming what he has to say for reasons of political expediency or to avoid causing offence, has provoked violent hostility. The most notable instance of this, perhaps, occurred in the 'Faurisson affair', which derived from his contribution of a Preface to the book by the French historian Robert Faurisson challenging the generally accepted account of the Nazi 'holocaust'. (For Chomsky's reaction to his critics: see the Bibliography for 1980/1981.)

As there is no necessary connection between philosophical rationalism and rationality of behaviour, so there is no necessary connection between either of these and what I am calling 'rationalization'. I am not using this word in the popular and pejorative sense, to mean something like the *post hoc* justification of one's actions by the invention of plausible or honourable motives. What I mean by the rationalization of a body of data or some field of enquiry is the exclusion from it of the non-rational or its reformulation and inclusion within the domain of the rational. And I am restricting my comments on Chomsky's rationalization to his ideas on language (though these comments may well apply more widely).

Chomsky's rationalization of linguistics, in which he is not alone, is evident, first, in his insistence that languages are essentially (cognitively-based) systems of representation rather than systems of communication and, second, in his attitude to semantics. Chomsky's argument, in several publications, that languages serve many non-communicative functions supports, amongst other things, the individualistic view that he has of them. Taken on its own terms and as far as it goes, like most of Chomsky's arguments, it cannot be faulted (see especially *Rules and Representations*, 1980, pp. 230ff.) At the same time, it is hard to deny that the grammatical structure of natural languages would not be as it is if they had not been used, over the millenia during which each of them has acquired its own structure, primarily, if not exclusively, for communication (in the broadest sense) among social beings. This has two discernible consequences: (i) that a good deal of the structure of most, if not all, human languages is dialogic (and their dialogic structure is put to use even in monologue and internal, or unspoken, soliloquy); (ii) that in many languages the social roles and status-based interpersonal relations that are operative in the society in which the language functions are encoded inextricably in its grammatical categories and their interdependencies.

As to Chomsky's views on semantics, he has never

developed these in detail. But I think it is fair to say that he has always (even in *Syntactic Structures*, 1957) given priority to propositional, or cognitive, meaning, in contrast with non-propositional (affective, instrumental, socio-expressive, etc) meaning. In other words (granted for the sake of argument that, as he says, the one basic function of languages is to serve for 'the expression of thought'), he is open to the criticism that (if I may use the vocabulary of traditional faculty-psychology) he has give priority to the expression of reason, rather than to the expression of will, desire, and the emotions. And it is noticeable that in his current system of grammar, 'Government-Binding Theory', the level of representation which he refers to as 'logical form' is given special status in the semantic representation that is assigned to sentences. This would seem to put Chomsky, to this extent at least, on the side of the formal, truth-conditional, semanticists, who were mentioned in Chapter 8 and whose influence has become even stronger, if not dominant, in Chomskyan and non-Chomskyan linguistics since 1977.

Government-Binding Theory

Chomsky's current version of principles-and-parameters generative grammar is commonly known as *Government-Binding Theory*. The term is unsatisfactory for two reasons. First, it throws too much emphasis on just two of the notions that are associated with Chomsky's modular grammar. Second, it might be held to imply that GB-theory (as I will henceforth call it) is the only theory of grammar which incorporates these notions. Both 'government' and 'binding', in much the same sense that they bear in GB-theory, are by now well established technical terms of modern grammatical theory. The former comes from traditional grammar (but has been give a broader interpretation in modern times); the latter, as I will explain below, has been taken over from formal logic (and reinterpreted).

There can be no question of going into the details of GB-theory here. As I have already explained, it is only one of many currently-competing Chomskyan and non-Chomskyan theories of grammar. Moreover, unlike some of its competitors (such as *generalized phrase-structure grammar* or *categorial grammar*, it has not won much support from researchers in neighbouring disciplines whose interest in theoretical linguistics is, quite rightly, restricted by their own more immediate goals. GB-theory is very much a theory for specialists in theoretical (including theoretical-descriptive) linguistics. This does not trouble Chomsky, of course, since he has always taken the view, as we saw in an earlier section, that theoretical linguistics (which, as he sees it, is part of theoretical cognitive psychology) operates, for the present and for the foreseeable future, at such a higher level of abstraction that it is pointless to seek to evaluate alternative theories of grammatical structure in terms of their putative psychological reality, their usefulness for teachers of languages or their technical exploitability in computer models of the processing of language and speech. Nor is it as easy as one might think to evaluate GB (at any stage of its development so far), as Chomsky taught us to evaluate theories (or grammars), in respect of power and either weak or strong adequacy and to compare it in these respects with its competitors.

First of all, there is the continuing problem of real or alleged 'notational equivalence' (see Appendix 1). Much of the notation and terminology used in different theories of grammar is unique to them (and at times unnecessarily idiosyncratic). But the differences of terminology do not always reflect genuinely different concepts or analyses. The problem is that few linguists (of whom I

am not one) have both a sufficiently specialized understanding of the several competing Chomskyan and non-
Chomskyan theories and, at the same time, a sufficiently
broad background in traditional and modern grammatical theory with reference to which to be able to compare
and evaluate them.

Second, the problem of evaluating GB has been aggra-
vated, ironically, by a relatively recent shift in Chomsky's attitude towards formalization. He still talks of GB
as a generative grammar. At the same time, he no longer
thinks of the generative grammarian's task as that of
constructing a fully formalized system of rules which
generates (in the mathematical sense of the term) all
and only the sentences of a language (see pp. 43ff and
Appendix 1). Not only does he nowadays play down the
importance of formalization, but over the last decade or
so, in what he describes as a 'shift of focus,' he has come
to lay much less emphasis on grammatical rules as such.
As he put it in 1981: 'the focus of attention has gradually
shifted from rule-systems to systems of principles such
as the binding theory and the projection principle'
('Knowledge of language: its elements and origins', p.
191). And he went on to cast doubts on the empirical
validity or applicability of 'most of the results of mathematical linguistics'. This 'shift of focus', as I have said,
has a certain – perhaps deliberate – irony to it. Chomsky's major contribution to theoretical linguistics has
been, and in my judgement continues to be, his formalization of part of linguistic theory.

Those who wish to study the details of GB-theory will
find guidance in the 'Suggestions for Further Reading'.
What I will do here is explain, as briefly and as non-
technically as I can, the concepts of 'government' and
'binding' as they are used in GB-theory (and more generally), and then say something, even more briefly (and
non-technically), about the various 'modules' currently

recognized by GB-theory and about the way in which they they relate to the modules (as we may now call them) of the standard theory. Readers who are not interested in linguistics as such should not be concerned if they find this section difficult or uninteresting. They can move on to the final section without loss. The general points that I am making here are that GB-theory can be seen as developing out of Chomsky's 'classical' and 'post-classical' systems of transformational-generative grammar; that it is far from having achieved definitive form; and that, considered from a historical point of view, it is (very properly) eclectic, linking up at various points with traditional grammar and also with several of the competing theories of grammar that emerged in the post-*Aspects* period (see Chapter 8).

The traditional sense of 'government' (and the verb 'govern') is exemplified in my formulation of one of the principles that I mentioned in the preceding section, to the effect that (in many European languages, including Latin, German, Russian and, to a limited degree, English, and in many other unrelated languages throughout the world) verbs and prepositions 'govern' their object in a particular 'case' which differs from the case of the subject. For example, the subject form of the first-person singular pronoun in English is *I* and its object-form is *me*: hence *I love Mary*, but *Mary loves me* and *Mary's love for me*. This traditional notion of government has been extended and generalized, not only in GB-theory, but also in other modern theories of grammar (notably dependency grammar). It has been extended in that: (i) not only verbs and prepositions are said to be governing categories; (ii) not only objects are said to be governed, or dependent, categories; and (iii) not only differences of case (*I/me*, etc.) are accounted for in terms of government. What is characteristic of the GB concept of binding, apart from its pervasive role throughout the system, is the way in which it is defined: in terms of phrase-structure configurations, rather than independently of constituent-structure, as it was in traditional grammar and in modern dependency grammar. Whether the GB-theory definition of government will survive in anything like its present form is no doubt questionable, but the fact that government (and its inverse, dependency) has been given a central role in GB-theory, as it was not in the standard theory of transformational grammar and its immediate Chomskyan successors, is very much to be welcomed. The government of one category by another does seem to be a genuinely universal property of natural languages.

The term 'binding', as I have said, comes originally from formal logic. But once again it has been adapted and generalized, and, in this case, familiarity with logical usage is not especially helpful. So I will not explain the connection. What we are concerned with is a phenomenon which is somewhat broader than, but for our purposes may be restricted to, the grammatically conditioned occurrence of pronouns and the way in which their reference is determined either directly or (*anaphorically*) by virtue of what is traditionally called an *antecedent*. For example, in both *When John came in, he was smiling* and *When he came in, John was smiling* the pronoun *he* can refer either to the same person as *John*, its antecedent, refers to (i.e., it can be co-referential with, and grammatically 'bound' to, its antecedent) or to some other person (who may or may not have been previously mentioned in the text); in contrast with this, in *He came in and John was smiling* the pronoun cannot be construed as being grammatically 'bound', or linked, to *John*.

This is a very simple example; and to simplify the exposition even more, I have generalized the use of the traditional term 'antecedent' to cover expressions which 'bind' pronouns regardless of whether the 'binding' expressions precede or follow the pronouns that they 'bind'. This, as I say, is a very simple example; and it is easy enough to formulate apparently satisfactory (and traditionally recognized) general conditions which account for the fact that in the one case the pronoun can be construed as being bound by an antecedent and in the other case not. Such conditions, expressed in traditional terms, would have to do with the fact that in one case we have a complex sentence (consisting of a main clause and a subordinate clause) and in the other a compound sentence (consisting of two main clauses joined by a co-ordinating conjunction), on the one hand, and, on the other, with the fact that in compound sentences a binding expression must precede the pronoun that it binds (i.e., it must be a genuine antecedent). Easy though it might appear to formulate conditions like this (and to reformulate them more satisfactorily in terms of modern syntactic theory, whether Chomskyan or not), it turns out to be remarkably difficult to formulate well-motivated and formally correct conditions which cover all cases. Furthermore, the 'binding' of pronouns when it is investigated in depth is found to be related to a large variety of phenomena in languages.

GB-theorists have probably devoted more effort to problems connected with (what is assumed to be sentence-internal, grammatically-controlled) pronominal reference than any other school of linguists. They, and – no less important – others challenging their theories and putting forward rival theories, have discovered a great deal more about the structure of languages than was known previously and a great deal more about the limitations of syntactic (in contrast with what are called 'pragmatic') explanations. But as yet the binding principles that have been proposed are far from being satisfactorily established either theoretically or empirically. Chomsky, of course, in his books and lectures, frequently uses problems of pronominal reference, explicated in terms of GB-theory at various stages of development, to support his arguments about innate knowledge of the principles (and parameters) of universal grammar. It must be borne in mind in the evaluation of such arguments that, not just this or that proposed binding principle is of questionable status, but that the whole approach is judged by many, rightly or wrongly, to be misguided. However, as far as progress in linguistics is concerned, and independently of Chomsky's own philosophical motivation, the intensive study of grammatically-controlled pronominal reference and related matters has already proved to be of great heuristic value.

Let me now say something, very briefly, about the modular structure of GB-theory in its current, or fairly recent, state of development; and what I have to say here, I would remind the reader, is not expected to be either interesting or comprehensible to the non-linguist. First of all, let us note that, although the term 'module' was not used at the time, the so-called standard theory of transformational-generative grammar of *Aspects* was in fact modular, in the sense in which this concept has been explained in the present chapter. This is clear from Figure 8 in Chapter 7, which shows four interrelated 'components', which we may now call 'modules' (one of which, the Base Component, contained, as sub-components, the Categorial Rules and the Lexicon). It is not easy to construct a similar schematic representation of the modular structure of GB-theory, which, as I have said, has not been formalized in any similarly 'standard' or (temporarily) definitive version. So, I will simply list the major modules that have been recognized and, where possible, relate them roughly to the 'components' or 'sub-components' of the *Aspects*-theory.

The *Lexicon* is now a separate module, not included within any of the syntactic modules as it was included in the Base Component in the *Aspects*-theory: this was a well-motivated change which took place in the immediate post-*Aspects* period.

The Phonological Component, renamed however as the *Phonetic Form* (PF) module remains where it was (as it were), and, though it operates differently, does much the same job: that of 'interpreting' S-structures – which may be identified without serious distortion with the surface structures of the *Aspects*-theory – and generating from them *Phonetic Representations*.

Roughly comparable with the Semantic Component of *Aspects*, we now have the *Logical Form* (LF) module, which provides a (partial) *Semantic Representation* of the sentence, namely that part which handles its cognitive or propositional meaning. The input to the LF-module, however, no longer comes from anything comparable with the deep structures of *Aspects*: it comes partly from the S-structure and partly from a new module, *Theta Theory*, which has been developed to handle what GB-theory calls 'thematic roles' (hence the Greek letter 'theta'): such roles as were recognized by traditional grammar (and many modern grammatical theories) as 'agent', 'patient' and 'goal'.

The Transformational Component of *Aspects*, as we have already noted, has been greatly simplified and indeed, in current versions of GB-theory, reduced to a single very general movement transformation ('Move alpha'). But it is still comparable to the Transformational Component of *Aspects*, in that it interrelates the S-structure and the D-structure of the sentence.

The categorical Sub-Component of the *Aspects* model, has been replaced by what is called *X-bar Theory*, supplemented by the *Projection Principle*, to which Chomsky frequently refers even in relatively non-technical presentations of his ideas on universal grammar. (Nothing written by Chomsky about linguistics is wholly non-technical!). The *X-bar Theory* module relates the syntax to the lexicon. But, as we noted in an earlier section, the syntax is no longer conceived as a set of rules, comparable with the categorial rules of *Aspects*, or the phrase-structure rules of *Syntactic Structures*. X-bar theory, in this respect and in others, has certain affinities with categorial grammar (see Appendix 1). In both cases the combinatorial possibilities are to some considerable degree derivable from the definition of the categories, and do not need to be stated in a set of rules. It is this property of categorial grammars which gives them their formal elegance and has made them especially attractive to formal semanticists and logicians (as well as to others familiar with one of the strands in the complex skein of theory and insight which we refer to as traditional grammar).

In addition to the modules mentioned so far, we have: the *Control-Theory*, the *Binding-Theory* and (not to be confused with it) the *Bounding-Theory*. The function of the Binding Theory, which consists of a number of interrelated principles, has been explained already (though not its mode of operation). All that needs to be said about the other modules is that very largely they serve to restrict and control the one remaining transformational rule and thus eliminate the need for other transformational rules.

This completes, then, my summary of GB-theory, the main purpose of which, as I have said, is to make clear its eclecticism and to indicate, if not to explain, the multiplicity of its connections (not always acknowledged by its adherents) with other modern theories and, not least with traditional grammar.

'The Chomskyan revolution': real progress or not?

In conclusion, I want to address briefly the two questions raised in the opening paragraphs of this chapter.

(1) What progress has the Chomskyan revolution made in linguistics and other disciplines (since 1977)?

(2) What contribution has the Chomskyan revolution made to progress in linguistics and other disciplines (since 1977)? We must still, no doubt, 'wait a generation' or so, 'before the owl of Minerva can take her flight', as Dell Hymes puts it in his review of the first edition of this book (see Appendix 2). But a further provisional and tentative assessment may be ventured.

The answer to the first of the two questions is readily given. The brash and quasi-Messianic triumphalism of the late 1960s and the early 1970s – which was character-istic, not of Chomsky's own work, but of that of several of his disciples and 'epigoni' – has all but disappeared from the scene. But that it is perhaps simply a conse-quence of the success of 'the Chomskyan revolution'. As will be evident from what has been said in the present chapter, the influence of Chomsky's thought continues to be dominant in any branch of linguistics that aspires to theoretical status. Evidence of this can be found in Frederick J. Newmeyer's recent four-volume *Survey of Linguistics* (1988). Admittedly, Newmeyer gives far less attention than he should to non-Chomskyan linguistics (and more or less neglects certain important trends in non-American linguistics). Nevertheless, his survey bears ample witness to the fecundity of Chomsky's ideas in the several sub-branches of linguistics, and not merely in the parts of linguistics that interest Chomsky.

But, in saying this, I must also emphasize that, not only Chomsky himself, but many others, have contri-buted to the success of the Chomskyan revolution within linguistics, including many who have challenged him, and continued to challenge him, on much of the technical detail. And, as I said at the outset, many, perhaps most, of these are not necessarily committed to 'the generative enterprise' and would, I think, be sceptical or agnostic about what Chomsky sees as the philosophical underpinnings of his theory of universal grammar. A good deal of Chomsky's own GB-theory, as I mentioned above, has developed from, and has incorporated, ideas from rival theories; and this is of course as it should be in any active branch of scientific research.

As to Chomsky's influence in other disciplines, this too is as strong as, or even stronger than, it was two decades ago. I have listed in the Bibliography several works of a philosophical nature which testify to this. But I should also mention the very large number of works that are now being published and are introducing the 'cognitive turn' into a wide variety of disciplines other than linguistics, psychology and philosophy. Chomsky, as we have seen, has been highly influential in the development of what might be called 'cognitivism', even though he himself has not been involved in any of 'the cognitive sciences' as such.

To turn now to the second of the two questions. One must be properly cautious about the 'Whiggist' term 'progress'. Progress implies directionality. It also implies a goal, and perhaps a series of goals, intermediate and ultimate. But it does not of course imply that the series is linear or constant in its directionality. Nor does it imply that what are seen retrospectively (and 'Whiggishly') as the determinant short-term goals of the participants at any one time are recognized as such, at that time, by the participants themselves. It is often easier to be sure of the ultimate goal and to know whether one has come significantly closer to it than one's predecessors were than it is to know whether one has made significant progress towards one's declared intermediate, short-term, goals or whether their achievement, if they are achieved, will be retrospectively identified as marking the path of progress.

That said, I think that there can be no doubt but that the Chomskyan revolution has contributed to long-term progress in linguistics. Few branches of linguistic theory, other than grammatical theory, have yet been satisfactorily formalized: i.e., formulated in mathematically precise terms. But at least a start has been made; and Chomskys formalization of generative grammar has pointed the way for branches of linguistics other than so-called '(autonomous) core linguistics'. As we have seen, Chomsky himself has recently been expressing doubts about the necessity of formalization, or mathematicization, as a condition of scientific progress. I, for one ('more Catholic than the Pope'!), am still attached to the older Chomskyan faith, as I (and, I am sure, others) understood it in earlier days; and I should like to think that there is no going back in this respect. Chomsky may of course be right to question the universal importance of formalization.

But whether or not this is so, the Chomskyan formalization of generative grammar has already proved its worth, not only in the insights that it has provided for theoreticians, but also in the contribution that it has made to the relatively non-theoretical day-to-day description of languages. Anyone who doubts that this is so has only to look at recently produced reference grammars, especially of English, but also of other major languages, and to compare them with what counted as authoritative a generation ago. Whole areas of grammar are now dealt with which were not mentioned before; and the rules that are given, whilst they may not be absolutely precise, are considerably more precise than they used to be. Much, if not all, of this increased coverage and increased precision can be attributed, directly or indirectly, to the Chomskyan revolution in theoretical linguistics.

I cannot pretend to assess the contribution that the Chomskyan revolution has made to long-term progress in disciplines other than linguistics. What can be safely said is that his work has inspired, and continues to inspire, an immense amount of research and discussion in any and every discipline that bears at all on the nature of language and mind. And there are few disciplines which do not! Granted that one can measure progress in the empirical sciences in terms of the accumulation of knowledge and in increased abstractness and generalization, it is not so clear that these concepts are applicable, in the same way or to the same degree, in disciplines such as philosophy. Nor is it clear that by these measures (in so far as they are applicable) the Chomskyan revolution has contributed to long-term progress in the philosophy of mind and language. Chomsky himself has in any event consistently emphasized the similarity between his ideas and those of the great rationalist philosophers of the past. But if philosophy is rightly defined, as it has been, as a 'set of footnotes to Plato, most of them written by Aristotle', Chomsky can surely claim, at the very least, to have written one or two of the most interesting footnotes in modern times.

In this chapter, I have tried to give a balanced account of why Chomsky's ideas on language and mind continue to be as widely influential as they are. Such criticisms as I have made have been made with greater or less confidence according to the topic being dealt with. But none of them should be interpreted as implying anything other than admiration for Chomsky's astonishing achievement and gratitude for what 'the Chomskyan revolution' has taught us about language and perhaps also about the human mind.

Appendices

Appendix 1:
Formal Languages and Formal Grammars

The purpose of this Appendix is to provide, for students of linguistics and others who might be interested in such questions, a rather more technical account of the basic concepts of Chomskyan generative grammar than I have thought proper to include in the main body of the book. Many of the terms that are defined below—'sentence', 'language', 'grammar', 'rule', etc.—have been employed freely in the preceding chapters, where I have not been as careful as I shall be here to establish and maintain a distinction between formal languages and natural languages. In what follows we shall be concerned primarily with formal languages; and the term 'language' will be defined in such a way that whatever satisfies the definition will count as a formal language.

The relation between formal languages and natural languages (English, Turkish, Chinese, Swahili, etc.) is a matter of controversy among linguists. The view taken here is that, whether natural languages are or are not formal languages, they have certain properties (duality of structure, recursivity, grammatical ambiguity, etc.) which they share with particular kinds of formal languages. In so far as natural languages and formal languages share the same structural properties, formal languages may usefully serve as *models* of natural languages. It is important to realize, however, that the notion of a formal language is totally independent, in principle, of the notion of a natural language. It is also, as we shall see, a much more general notion. Such terms as 'sentence' and 'vocabulary', which we shall use in our definition of 'language', must be understood to have as general a sense as the definitions in which they occur allow them to have.

We may begin by defining a *language* (i.e. a formal language) to be a set of sentences and a *sentence* to be a finite sequence, or *string*, of elements, each of which is drawn from a finite *vocabulary*. More precisely, we can say that sentences consist of *tokens* of the elements which exist as *types* in the vocabulary. For example, given that the vocabulary, V, of the language, L, is the two-member set $\{a, b\}$, L might have as its members not only a, b, ab and ba but also aa, aba, bba, etc. The strings aa and aba each contain two tokens of the same type, a; the string bba contains two tokens of the type b; and so on. For the moment, we will simply take for granted this notion of type-token identity, in terms of which we can say that several tokens, or instances, of the same element can occur in several different strings or at several different places in the same string, although the vocabulary from which the elements are drawn contains only one element of the type in question. If σ (sigma) is a string of tokens whose types are members of V, then σ is said to be a string *over* V. Any set of strings over V is a language over V.

The *length* of a string is determined by the number of elements (i.e. element-tokens) of which it is composed. For example, given that $V = \{a, b\}$, *aa* is a string of length 2 over V, *bab* is a string of length 3 over V, and so on. Strings may be finite or infinite in length; but sentences, as we have seen, are defined to be of finite length. Not only sequences of two or more elements, but also single elements are said to be strings: they are strings of length 1. We will also introduce as a member of every set of strings over any vocabulary the *empty string* or *null string*, which we will symbolize as o (zero) and define to be of length zero. All strings other than the empty string are *non-null*.

In saying that strings are sequences, rather than sets, of elements, we imply that they have the property of *linearity*: that each of the elements in a string occupies a particular position (and no two elements occupy the same position). In all strings of whatever length, there will be one (and only one) element that is the successor of no other element, and this we take to be the first element in the string. The position of all other elements (in strings of length i, where $i \geq 2$) may be defined in terms of the relation of succession: the second element is the element that immediately follows the first, and in general the $n + $ 1th element is the one that immediately follows the nth element in the string. All finite strings will have not only a first element but also a last element, definable as the element that has no successor. (In strings of length 1 the last element will of course be identical with the first element. We need not go into the question of how the notion of being the first or last element in the string applies to the empty string.) Two strings are *identical* if, and only if, they consist of exactly the same elements in exactly the same order.

Strings are formed by means of the binary operation of *concatenation*. Using the Greek letters ϕ, χ, ψ as variables, we can say then $\phi^\frown\chi$ (i.e. the result of concatenating ϕ and χ) is also a string. Concatenation, like the ordinary arithmetical addition, is *associative*: $(\phi^\frown\chi)^\frown\psi = \phi^\frown(\chi^\frown\psi)$. Unlike the operation of addition, however, it is *non-commutative*: $\phi^\frown\chi \neq \chi^\frown\phi$. The empty string serves as an identity-element with respect to concatenation (as zero serves as an identity-element with respect to ordinary arithmetical addition): thus $\phi^\frown o = o^\frown\phi = \phi$. Given that V is a finite vocabulary and that V* is the set of all finite strings over V, V* is *closed* under the operation of concatenation: in the sense that, if ϕ and χ are in the set V^*, then $\phi^\frown\chi$ is also in V^*.

If there are m elements in the vocabulary—i.e. $V = \{v_1, v_2, v_3, \ldots, v_m\}$—there will be exactly m strings of length 1 in V^*, m^2 strings of length 2, and in general m^i strings of length i. The set of all strings of length i over V may be referred to as V^i. Thus: V^0 will be the one-member set of strings of length zero; V^1 will be the m-member set of length 1; V^2 will be the m^2-member set of strings of length 2; and so on. V^* will therefore be the *union* of all V^i: $V^* = V^0 + V^1 + V^2 + \ldots$ If $V = $ finite and no upper bound is set to i, there will be an infinite (but *denumerably infinite*) number of strings in V^*. (To say of any set that it is *denumerable* is to say that its members can be put into correspondence with the natural numbers $\{1, 2, 3, \ldots\}$. There are higher orders of infinity than denumerable infinity.)

Every finite or infinite subset of V^* is a language (and there is a non-denumerable infinity of them). Using the letter L to refer to the set of all languages over V (i.e. to all the subsets of V^*), we can distinguish one member of L from another by means of a non-numerical subscript. Thus: $L = \{L_a, L_b, L_c, \ldots\}$. (These non-numerical subscripts, it should be noted, are to be distinguished, in terms of their function, from the numerical superscripts introduced above to refer to sets of strings of a particular length. V^0, V^1, V^2, etc. are members of L, since they are all subsets of V^*; but there are many [infinitely many] members of $L_a, L_b, L_c, \ldots$ that are not members of $\{V^0, V^1, V^2, \ldots\}$.) Any string in L_x (where L_x is some arbitrary member of L) is a sentence of L_x: it is a grammatically *well-formed* string; it has the property of *grammaticality*. Any string over V that is not a string in L_x is *ill-formed*, or *ungrammatical*, with respect to L_x, though it may very well be a grammatical sentence of some other arbitrary language over V— of L_y, let us say. It follows that every sentence of L_x or L_y is grammatical in L_x or L_y, respectively.

Any finite specification of the sentences of L_x (i.e. any device, or set of rules, for determining the membership of L_x) is a grammar of L_x: it *generates* L_x. Some languages, if not all, are such that they are generated by more than one grammar. We will use the expression $G(L_x)$ to refer to the set of all the grammars that generate L_x. If $G(L_x)$ contains more than one member, we can distinguish them, one from another, by means of arbitrary numerical subscripts: $G_1(L_x)$, $G_2(L_x)$, etc. (The use of numerical subscripts is not to be understood as implying that the grammars of a language can be ordered, by whatever principle, in a series. As we shall see presently, there is at least a partial hierarchical ordering among grammars based upon their relative power.) Any two (or more) grammars that generate the same language, e.g. L_x, are said to be *(weakly) equivalent*. Given that $G_1(L_x)$ and $G_2(L_x)$ are equivalent (in this sense of equivalence), but not identical, we can ask what are the formal properties that differentiate them.

Some formal languages are more interesting than others—both intrinsically, in some intuitively clear sense, and as potential models for the description of natural languages. If L_x is finite, it will always be possible in principle to specify the sentences of L_x by listing them: i.e. by constructing what may be referred to as a *list-grammar*. If L_x is an infinite language, it will be impossible to specify its sentences by listing them. List-grammars are intrinsically uninteresting. Furthermore, they are uninteresting as models for the description of natural languages, which, whether they are infinite or not (see Chapter 5), are certainly not learned as lists of sentences by native speakers. Many of the languages that can be specified by list-grammars can be specified by intrinsically more interesting grammars. But any language that cannot be specified otherwise than by listing the sentences that it contains is, for our purposes at least, by virtue of that very fact, uninteresting.

Hardly more interesting than the languages generated by list-grammars are the members of V^t. As far as we know, there is no natural language whose sentences are all strings of length 2, or of length 7, or of length 109, or of any fixed length. But even if it is the case that all the sentences of some natural language are strings of fixed length, we can be sure that their length will not be the only property that distinguishes them from non-sentences (i.e. ungrammatical strings over the same vocabulary). All sentences might be of length 6, but not all strings of length 6 will be sentences.

Without going further into this question, let us simply say that of the indefinitely many languages over any finite vocabulary V some, but not others, will be intrinsically interesting in terms of their formal properties; and that of those that are intrinsically interesting some, but not others, will be interesting as models for the description of natural languages—namely, subsets of V^* (given that V is of the same order of magnitude as are the vocabularies of natural language) which have at least some of the same formal properties as English, Turkish, Chinese, Swahili and other natural languages. We will concentrate, therefore, as Chomsky did in his early work, upon particular subclasses of formal languages; and we will talk about them, and about the grammars that generate them, within the same theoretical and terminological framework that Chomsky used.

The most powerful type of formal grammar is what is called an *unrestricted rewriting system*—a system of rules each of which has the form $\phi \rightarrow \chi$ ('rewrite ϕ as χ') with no restriction being imposed upon the values of the variables ϕ and χ. This is more powerful than various kinds of *restricted rewriting systems* in that there are certain kinds of languages which are generated by unrestricted rewriting systems (over a given vocabulary V), but which are not generated by restricted rewriting systems (over the same vocabulary V). It has been shown by Chomsky and others that within the class of restricted rewriting systems there are some that are more powerful than others. It has been shown, in fact, that within the class of grammars formalized as rewriting systems there is a hierarchy with at least four levels. At the top of this hierarchy are unrestricted rewriting systems—grammars of Type 0; at the bottom (less powerful grammars than this being of no interest as potential models of natural languages) we have finite-state grammars (informally discussed in Chapter 5)—grammars of Type 4. The languages generated by Type 4 grammars are known, for historically irrelevant reasons, as *regular languages*. (The term is unfortunate in that it can be easily misunderstood as implying that only regular languages are subject to rule.) The general principle governing the hierarchical classification of grammars in terms of their power is that of inclusion as a relation holding between the languages generated by the grammars in question. That is to say: the languages generated by grammars of Type 4 are properly included as a subclass of the languages generated by grammars of Type 3; the languages generated by grammars of Type 3 are properly included in the languages generated by grammars of Type 2; and, in general, the languages generated by grammars of Type i are also generated by grammars of Type i-1, but not conversely. Grammars of Type 3 include *context-free phrase-structure* (CF) grammars and grammars of Type 2 include *context-sensitive phrase-structure* (CS) grammars. The languages generated by Type 3 and Type 2 grammars, respectively, may be referred to as CF-languages and CS-languages (or, more fully, as context-free languages and context-sensitive languages). The languages generated by Type 1 grammars are known as *recursive* languages and they constitute a proper subset of *recursively enumerable* languages, which are generated by Type 0 grammars.

The difference between recursive sets and recursively enumerable sets, upon which the difference between the languages generated by Type 1 and Type 0 grammars ultimately depends, is one whose mathematical implications need not concern us. (A recursive set is a recursively enumerable set whose complement is also recursively enumerable.) The important point is that there is an identifiable class of formal languages which properly includes CS-languages and is properly included in the class of recursively enumerable languages. The question for the theoretical linguist is whether formal grammars of one type rather than another will serve best as models for the description of natural languages. As we have seen in the main body of the book, Chomsky has argued strongly for the view that it is impossible, in principle, to describe the syntax of natural languages by means of a grammar that is less powerful than a CF-grammar (Type 3).

CF-grammars differ from the more powerful class of CS-grammars (Type 2) in that the latter, but not the former, permit the use of context-sensitive rules: i.e. rules of the form

$$\phi \to \chi/\alpha - \beta$$

('ϕ is rewritten as χ in the environment of a preceding α and a following β') where ϕ, χ, α and β are all variables ranging over strings. Both CF-grammars and CS-grammars make use of the distinction between *auxiliary symbols* and *terminal symbols*. We can make this distinction apparent, notationally, by using capital italic letters, $\{A, B, C, \ldots\}$, for the former, and small italic letters, $\{a, b, c, \ldots\}$, for the latter. For example, the rule

$$A \to a/\text{B}-\text{C}$$

would be interpreted to mean that the auxiliary symbol A is replaced by the terminal symbol a when, in the string to which the rule is applied, A is preceded by B and followed by C. CF-grammars are of course a proper subclass of CS-grammars, in that a context-free rule is but the special case of a context-sensitive rule in which no specific values are assigned to the contextual variables α and β.

The rules of both CF-grammars and CS-grammars are subject to certain restrictions. Neither ϕ nor χ can be the identity-element (i.e. the empty string); ϕ cannot be a terminal symbol; ϕ cannot be a string containing more than a single symbol and χ cannot properly or improperly include ϕ (as a sub-string). CF-grammars and CS-grammars are both *phrase-structure* (PS) grammars; and, as we saw in Chapter 6, they have the property that (associated with certain conventions) they not only generate strings of terminal symbols, *terminal strings*, but they assign to each such terminal string a particular kind of *structural description*—an analysis of the terminal string in terms of a *labelled bracketting*. To assign such a structural description to the terminal strings that they generate is the function of the auxiliary, or non-terminal, symbols. The effect of the restrictions listed at the beginning of this paragraph is to reduce considerably the power of the class of grammars that the restrictions, in part, define. For example, it can be proved that a phrase-structure grammar with deletion rules (i.e. rules of the form $\phi \to 0$) has the power of an unrestricted rewriting system. Taken together (and formulated rather more precisely than they have been here), the restrictions listed above also ensure that each terminal string has a determinable structural description.

PS-grammars, as we saw in Chapter 6, consist of sets of rules (each of the form $\phi \rightarrow \chi/\alpha - \beta$). The rules can be *ordered* or *unordered*. If they are unordered, any rule that is applicable to a string (by virtue of the occurrence in that string of a symbol corresponding to the symbol on the left-hand side of the rule) may be applied to the string in question, regardless of whether some other rule in the set has been applied (if applicable) or not. If they are ordered, a rule that is ordered later in the set cannot be applied before a rule that is ordered earlier in the set has been applied (if it is applicable). The question of rule-ordering is important because the set of languages that is generated by ordered PS-grammars is not identical with the set of languages generated by unordered PS-grammars. The sample CF-grammar given in Chapter 6 was unordered.

But the particular *derivation* that was referred to in the discussion of the sample CF-grammar in Chapter 6 was different from alternative derivations of the same terminal string; and if the reader works carefully through some alternative derivations he will see that the derivations differ (when they differ) by virtue of a difference in the order in which the rules are applied. This does not mean that the grammar is ordered in the same sense in which the term 'ordered' is being used here. There is some degree of *intrinsic ordering*: (iv) cannot apply unless (ii) has applied; (vi) cannot apply unless (iii) has applied; and so on. But there is no *extrinsic ordering*; and this is what is usually meant when the term 'ordering' is used in the classification of grammars. A distinction must be drawn between the ordering of rules in the grammar and the order in which they are applied in a given derivation. As far as the sample grammar of Chapter 6 is concerned, and this holds true of all CF-grammars that are subject to the restrictions listed earlier, the *phrase-markers* (i.e. the structural descriptions assigned by a grammar to the terminal strings that it generates) are not to be identified with particular derivations, but with equivalence-classes of alternative derivations.

Given that the vocabulary of a particular PS-grammar includes both a set of non-terminal (or auxiliary) symbols, $V_N = \{A, B, C, \ldots\}$, and a set of terminal symbols, $V_T = \{a, b, c, \ldots\}$, such that V is the union of V_N and V_T (i.e. $V = V_N + V_T$), we can see that a derivation will be a sequence of strings over V, each string in the sequence being *derived* from its predecessor in the sequence by some rule in the grammar. The first member in a sequence has no predecessor; the *initial string* of a derivation cannot therefore be formed, by a rule $\phi \rightarrow \chi/\alpha - \beta$, from some preceding string in the derivation. Our PS-grammar will have associated with it a statement telling us what members of V* are to count as initial strings: e.g. $\varSigma = \{B \frown a, b \frown C \frown c, \ldots\}$, where $\varSigma$ is the set of initial strings. The initial strings are, as it were, the *axioms*; and each string that can be derived from one of the initial strings by the application of one or more rules is comparable with a theorem provable in a formal system. The last member of any derivation will be a string over V_T—i.e. a string consisting of only terminal symbols. A PS-grammar will generate, therefore, both terminal strings (a subset of the strings over V_T) and non-terminal strings (a subset of the strings over V containing at least one element from V_N). By our definitions of 'language' and 'sentence', both terminal and non-terminal strings are sentences of the language generated by a PS-grammar. In using PS-grammars as models for the description of natural languages we can readily restrict the definition of 'sentence' so that only terminal strings will be recognized as sentences.

I have deliberately chosen as examples of initial strings, or axioms, strings from V* that contain both terminal and non-terminal symbols: $B^\frown a$ and $b^\frown C^\frown c$. There must be at least one non-terminal symbol in any initial string that serves as the first member of a derivation. It is important to realize, however, that the initial strings are not necessarily single elements: i.e. members of V_N. The initial string in Chapter 6 was the symbol *Sentence*; but no explicit statement, $\Sigma = \{Sentence, \ldots\}$, was made to this effect. Generally speaking, in the applications that linguists have made of PS-grammars, they have explicitly or implicitly restricted the set of initial strings to one-member sets containing some particular member of V_N. By convention, the symbol S (in works written in English) is usually reserved for this purpose; and this symbol may be thought of as being mnemonically connected with the term 'sentence'.

One other symbol must now be mentioned: the *boundary-symbol*, #. If we add to V the symbol # and then, whether by rule or convention, ensure that the initial string contains as both the first and the last element in the string a token of #, we shall be able to write context-sensitive rules of the form

$$\phi \to \chi / \#\alpha - \beta$$
$$\text{or} \qquad \phi \to \chi / \alpha - \beta\#$$

(where, as always, α and β may be either null or non-null), in order to indicate that ϕ must occur at the beginning or end of a string or more generally, at some specified number of positions from the beginning or end of the string, if the rule that converts it to χ is to be applicable.

Given that the initial string is $\#^\frown S^\frown \#$ and, further, that no other boundary-symbols are introduced into the strings generated by the grammar, every terminal string will contain just two tokens of #, one as the first and one as the last element of the string. (In view of our earlier definition of 'terminal string', it now follows that, if the boundary-symbols are to count as elements in terminal strings, #

must be added to V_T. But this is a technicality of relatively minor importance. All that was said earlier was that $\#$ is a member of V.) Let us suppose, however that our grammar contains rules of the form

$$\phi \to \chi^{\frown}\#^{\frown}S^{\frown}\#^{\frown}\psi/\alpha - \beta$$

i.e. rules which introduce tokens of the initial string into strings derived by other rules from the initial string. First of all, it will be observed, such rules are *recursive*; and, as we saw in Chapter 5, there is reason to believe that any formal grammar that is to serve as a model for the description of a natural language must contain at least one recursive rule. This does not mean, of course, that the recursive rule, or rules, that appear in the grammar must necessarily have on the right-hand side of the arrow an instance of the initial string. But Chomsky has throughout held to the view that there is no sub-sentential recursion in natural languages.

Furthermore, in an *Aspects*-type transformational grammar it is not just S, but $\#^{\frown}S^{\frown}\#$, that is *embedded* by means of the recursive rules of the base-component (see Chapter 6). The string-internal boundary-symbols are then erased by means of a convention associated with the operation of certain *cyclical* transformations (provided that these rules, which are extrinsically ordered, have been applied in the proper order). It thus becomes possible to use the presence or absence of sentence-internal boundary-symbols in strings (or, more generally, in phrase-markers), to *filter* out a certain class of ill-formed surface-structures. The importance of this rather technical point (which cannot be developed in full here) derives from the fact that filtering of the kind that an *Aspects*-type grammar permits has now been shown to increase the power of a transformational grammar to the point that transformational grammars that have this property and are otherwise unconstrained are weakly equivalent to Type 0 grammars. It is generally agreed that any formal grammar that is as powerful as this is far too powerful as a model for the description of natural languages. As we have seen in Chapter 7, current work in the development of Chomskyan transformational grammars is directed towards an empirically motivated reduction of their power.

No more will be said here about the technicalities of transform-ational grammars. All the general points that need to be made about formal grammars as models for the description of natural languages can be made with reference, in the first instance, to PS-grammars. It suffices to remind the reader that the formalization of transformation-al grammars and the investigation of the properties of the languages that they generate (on the assumption that the grammars in question are so constrained that they generate a proper subset of the recursively enumerable languages over some large, but finite, vocabulary V) are far more complex than is the formalization of PS-grammars, and more especially CF-languages, which are well now understood.

One important distinction that can now be drawn is the distinction between *weak equivalence* and *strong equivalence*. As we have seen, two grammars, $G_i(L_x)$ and $G_j(L_y)$, are weakly equivalent if, and only if, they each generate exactly the same language; and $L_x = L_y$, it will be recalled, if and only if they both contain exactly the same set of terminal strings over a common vocabulary V_T. (We have adjusted the definition of weak equivalence to take account of the distinction subsequently introduced, of terminal and non-terminal strings. The sentences of L_x and L_y are now the terminal strings generated by grammars of L_x and L_y.) Two grammars, $G_i(L_x)$ and $G_j(L_y)$, are strongly equivalent if, and only if, they generate the same *structures*. To illustrate: the structures generated by PS-grammars are phrase-markers (i.e. labelled bracketings). Two PS-grammars will therefore be strongly equivalent if, and only if, they both generate the same phrase-markers. A terminal string is a part of every well-formed phrase-marker in the set of phrase-markers (over the terminal and non-terminal vocabulary) generated by a grammar; and a phrase-marker may be regarded as structural description of the terminal string that it contains. What has just been said can therefore be understood to imply that two grammars are strongly equivalent, if they not only generate the same sentences, but assign to each sentence the same set of structural descriptions. As far as PS-grammars are concerned, they will be strongly non-equivalent if the structures that they generate differ with respect to either the labelling or the bracketing (or both). As we saw in Chapter 6, the fact that different labelled brackettings can be assigned to the same terminal string means that one kind of *structural ambiguity* that is found in natural languages is readily identifiable (under a certain interpretation of the correspondence that holds between formal and natural languages) with one of the properties of CF-languages (and CS-languages).

Other kinds of formal grammars—notably *categorial grammars* and *dependency grammars*—have been proved to be at least weakly, and perhaps strongly, equivalent to PS-grammars. The reason why I say 'perhaps' is that when it comes to the consideration of what are taken to be comparable structures it is not always clear what counts as a significant difference and what is no more than *notational variation*. Both categorial grammars and dependency grammars assign to the strings that they generate structures that can be treated as labelled brackettings. To this extent, therefore, a given categorial grammar or a given dependency grammar might be held to be strongly equivalent to a given PS-grammar. It might be argued, however, that, in so far as the non-terminal vocabulary of a categorial grammar consists of both basic and derived categories and the principle whereby the derived categories are constructed out of basic categories directly reflects the distribution and syntactic function of each derived category, the labels are more than simply notational variants of the non-terminal symbols, $\{A, B, C, \ldots\}$, in a PS-grammar.

Categorial grammars have been mentioned here (though not explained) because they play an important role in certain current alternatives to Chomsky's own system of transformational-generative grammar (see Chapter 8).

We now turn to a brief consideration of the question of relating formal languages to natural languages by taking the former (or a subclass of the former) as *models* of the latter. The term 'model' has several senses. In the sense in which it is being used here, a model is a deliberately restricted and abstract representation of the phenomena whose structure or behaviour is being investigated. The construction of such models by the physicist, the economist or the linguist necessarily involves some degree of idealization. If the model is to have any explanatory value or predictive power, however, it must contain elements and relations which can be put into *correspondence* with elements and relations of the system that is being modelled.

So far we have talked of natural languages rather than of natural language. We will proceed on the working assumption that all natural languages share certain properties, such that it is reasonable to expect that their grammatical structure will be describab'e in terms of a formal grammar of the same general type and the same power. This, as we have seen, is an assumption that Chomsky makes. Indeed, the way in which he formulates that assumption and makes it mathematically precise is an essential part of the 'Chomskyan revolution', independently of the philosophical and psychological conclusions that he draws from it (see Chapter 11).

The natural-language correlates of the well-formed terminal strings of a formal language are, of course, sentences. But what are the natural-language correlates of the members of V_T?

All known natural languages have at least two *levels* of structure: the phonological and the syntactic (see Chapter 2). The lower-level units are *phonemes*; the higher-level units are *forms* (of which words—more precisely, word-forms—are a subclass). Forms are composed of phonemes; but the distribution of a form is, in general, not predictable in terms of its phonological composition. Minimal forms are *morphemes* (under one interpretation of the term 'morpheme'). It might seem reasonable, therefore, to take the natural-language correlates of the members of V_T—the syntactic *primes* of natural languages—to be morphemes. Several problems arise immediately.

(i) In all natural languages, utterances differ from one another significantly, not only in terms of the forms of which they are composed, but also in terms of their *prosodic contour* (i.e. stress-pattern and intonation-pattern). It is pre-theoretically unclear how much of this systematic prosodic variation is to be treated as being part of the sentence. But some of it would normally be so treated by linguists. This means that natural-language sentences are not just strings of morphemes. In order to put natural-language sentences into correspondence with the terminal strings of some concatenating formal language, we must represent what is essentially non-linear by means of elements which, whether arbitrarily or not, are given a certain position in a string of morpheme-correlates.

(ii) In all natural languages, there is a greater or less degree of homonymy: i.e. a single form may have two different (and unrelated) meanings (cf. *bank* in English). More important than the difference of meaning, in the present connection, is the fact that the same form may belong to several different syntactic classes (cf. *down* in English). Do we correlate a single natural-language form with several formal-language elements? The answer is pre-theoretically unclear; and there is no clear and unequivocal answer provided by current linguistic theory.

(iii) More serious is the fact that morphemes (in the sense of minimal forms) are not as readily identifiable in certain natural languages (e.g. Latin) as they are, generally speaking, in English. It is arguable that the sentences of such languages do not consist of strings of morphemes and that, by putting them into correspondence with the terminal strings of a concatenating formal language (i.e. in a one-to-one, morpheme-to-element, order-preserving correspondence), we necessarily introduce so high a degree of arbitrariness as to constitute distortion.

There are problems then with the assumption that morphemes are, in all natural languages, the correlates of formal-language elements on the syntactic level of representation. These problems can always be resolved at the price of arbitrariness or, alternatively, by postulating the existence of rather more abstract forms and complicating the relationship between the phonological and the syntactic level (as this is represented in the model). It may well be that there are empirically valid and discoverable, reasons for postulating the existence of more abstract minimal forms. We will not go into this question. The point being made here is that in some, if not all, natural languages, the relationship between syntax and phonology is far more complex than the simplest statement of the principle of duality, in terms of phonemes and morphemes, might suggest.

And it is not just a matter of relating the two levels of syntax and phonology in our models of natural languages. Whether there should be sub-levels within phonology (sub-levels at which such units as syllables and phonological words are identified) is perhaps debatable. There can be no question but that there are various sub-levels to be recognized within syntax. The most obvious of these is the sub-level whose primes are words (or, more precisely, word-forms). In some languages, words are readily identifiable as strings of morphemes; in other languages they are not. In some languages word-order plays a significant grammatical role; in others its function is stylistic, rather than grammatical. Once again, we have what appear to be important structural differences among natural languages. It is arguable that our models should directly reflect such differences. Formal languages of the kind that we have been considering in this Appendix are, by definition, sets of strings over vocabularies of elements, or primes. But a case can be made for the view that, in some natural languages at least, sequential position plays no part at all at the higher sub-levels of syntax (i.e. at the sub-levels of words and phrases). This point is controversial and will not be pressed. It is but one of several that could be made to emphasize the complexity and diversity of the formal structures that we find in natural languages.

The reader will have noted that there is nothing in the definition of formal languages to say that the elements in their vocabularies or the strings of elements that constitute their sentences should be meaningful. Indeed, there is nothing in the definition of 'language' that makes reference to communication or any particular function of the system whose grammatical structure we may be studying. Formal languages may be treated either as *interpreted* or *uninterpreted* systems. There are various ways in which a *semantic interpretation* may be assigned to the elements and sentences of a formal language. We need not go into this. It is important to realize, however, that the syntax of a formal language is describable without reference to any interpretation that might be assigned to the elements or combinations of elements; and a formal language might serve as a model, in principle, for all sorts of systems that have nothing to do with communication and would never be described as languages in the everyday sense of the term. The goal of theoretical linguistics can be described as that of constructing a class of formal languages, all of whose members share certain general properties and each of whose members can be put into correspondence with some actual or potential natural language. It is as yet unclear whether this goal can be achieved.

Appendix 2:

An Alternative View of Chomsky and His Background

Since the appearance of the first edition of this book, *The Logical Structure of Linguistic Theory* has been published and in it an Introduction, dated 1973, in which Chomsky explains the 'rather unusual status' of his manuscript (*LSLT*) and sets it in its historical context. He points out that, apart from the original 1955 version (which was left unfinished), there is a partially edited and revised version of January 1956. Of these versions, the first was both duplicated and microfilmed and the second was microfilmed. In 1956, Chomsky began to revise the manuscript for publication, but he abandoned this task when the MIT Press, to whom he submitted parts of the manuscript, rejected it 'with the not unreasonable observation that an unknown author taking a rather unconventional approach should submit articles based on this material to professional journals before planning to publish such a comprehensive and detailed manuscript as a book'. The one article on generative grammars that Chomsky had submitted to a linguistics journal 'had been rejected, virtually by return mail' and, as far as he could determine, whilst lecturing at various universities, 'there was little interest in these topics among professional linguists'.

It was at the suggestion of Morris Halle, to whom he showed some of his 'lecture notes for an undergraduate course at MIT', that he approached the editor of Mouton's *Janua Linguarum* series. What subsequently appeared as *Syntactic Structures* was a 'slightly revised version' of the lecture notes, containing 'a sketchy and informal outline of some of the material in *LSLT*, along with some material on finite-state grammars and formal properties of grammars from 1956'.

What Chomsky has to say here about the origin of *Syntactic Structures* and the unpublishability of *LSLT* should be read by anyone who has access to the now-published version of *LSLT* and is puzzled by my footnote on p. 63. Chomsky also explains in his Introduction to the 1975 version of *LSLT* that his adoption of the 'methodological', rather than the 'psychological' interpretation of the linguist's task was determined by his feeling that it would have been 'too audacious' for him to have raised the issue of justifying grammars in psychological terms at that time. As he points out, R. B. Lees did raise this issue in his provocative, but influential, review of *Syntactic Structures* (see Bibliography). Chomsky says that 'the "psychological analogue" to the methodological problem of constructing linguistic theory', though not discussed in *LSLT*, 'lay in the immediate background' of his thinking; and, in preparing *LSLT* for publication a second time in 1958-9 (a task that was, once again, abandoned, due to the pressure of other commitments), he presented the alternative psychological interpretation 'as the framework for the entire study'. He has continued to do so ever since. (The 1975 published version of *LSLT* is an amalgamated version based on the 1955 version and the two 1956 versions. It does not contain anything from the 1958-9 revision and thus sets generative grammar within the earlier non-psychological framework.)

Chomsky's Introduction to *LSLT* contains much that is of historical importance. But there is nothing else, I think, that would lead me to revise my classification of his early work as being essentially 'Bloomfieldian' in spirit. It now appears, however, that it was deliberately given this character by Chomsky himself. It was *Syntactic Structures* that first made Chomsky's ideas known to linguists. If this, being deliberately 'watered down', was interpreted differently by different groups of linguists, it is hardly surprising. I, for one, thought that Lees, in his review, read into it much that was not there. On the other hand, by virtue of my own background, I immediately related Chomsky's notion of generative grammar to the ideas of Saussure and Von Humboldt, whereas it was only much later that Chomsky himself became aware of the connection.

In his detailed and informative review of the first edition of the present work, Dell Hymes criticizes many aspects of my account of the context and development of Chomsky's work and of my assessment of Chomsky as an intellectual figure. I cannot comment here upon all the points that he makes. But I will mention the most important and give some indication of my response. (For Hymes's review, see Bibliography; page references are to the reprinted version.)

Hymes suggests, as many have done, that in my presentation of Chomsky's early work I have exaggerated its 'Bloomfieldian' character (pp. 324-7). If this is so, the reason, as will now be clear, is that Chomsky himself deliberately suppressed in publication what would have been, in 1957, an excessively 'non-Bloomfieldian' appeal to the native speaker's intuitions, to the 'psychological analogue' and to the integration of syntax with semantics. Hymes had the advantage of being present, at the time, at conferences and meetings at which it became clear earlier than it is in published work that Chomsky was less of a 'Bloomfieldian' than he appears to be as he presents himself in *Syntactic Structures*. I concede, therefore, that the view that I give of Chomsky's early work is perhaps limited by the fact that I (like most non-American linguists) knew nothing of the 'non-Bloomfieldian' element in Chomsky's thought until much later. Indeed, I cannot now recall being made aware of this during the year 1960-1, which I spent in the United States (though not in direct contact with Chomsky). But by then I had long been fixed in my own opinion of Chomsky's theory of grammar; and I may simply have assumed that it was shared by others. However that may be, I hope that Hymes is wrong when he says that, in my account of Chomsky's early work, I have been guilty of a 'soft-pedalling, to the point of inaudibility, of any note of the dramatic impact' that this had at the time. The impact of Chomsky's work upon my thinking and upon that of other linguists with whom I was discussing it in 1957 was certainly dramatic enough; and I am sorry if this does not come out clearly in my book.

Hymes takes me to task for saying that there has never been a 'Sapirian' school of linguistics. He submits 'that in the 1930s there was at the very least a Sapir tradition, and a group of younger scholars whose work was thoroughly informed by it' (p. 321). I accept this point entirely—the more readily as Hymes himself is probably the most eminent living representative of that tradition. But there is a difference beteen a 'school' and a 'tradition'; and we are both agreed that there was never a 'Sapirian' orthodoxy. What Hymes makes clear in his review (and I do not in Chapter 3) is that the 'Bloomfieldian' school was largely the creation, not of Bloomfield himself, but of a group of men 'who took a certain conception of Bloomfield as its symbol'. As he suggests, the climate of American linguistics might have been very different if Sapir had not died in 1939. There is much else in Hymes's discussion of my account of American linguistics in the pre-Chomskyan period (notably his comments on the role of Boas and his suggestion that the appeal of 'various forms of operationalism, positivism, and behaviourism, at least as a style and ideology' had a great deal to do with the 'scepticism and even cynicism as to traditional concepts and rationalism in all fields' in the period after the First World War: p. 320) that I cannot deal with here. What Hymes has to say is extremely interesting; and I would refer the reader to the review itself and to other works of his own that Hymes cites therein.

I accept that 'it is ideological confidence rather than empirical knowledge' (p. 318) that leads me and other linguists to say (as I do in Chapter 2) that all languages are 'of roughly equal complexity'. I also accept that 'to say that every language has sufficiently rich vocabulary for the expression of all the distinctions that are important in the society using it is to beg a host of questions' (p. 317). Whether it is true that this brand of 'functional optimism' (which Hymes attributes to the uncritical acceptance by 'most linguists' of 'a liberal humanist ideology formed earlier in the century': p. 318) would or 'would not pass muster for a moment in the political circles in which Chomsky figures' (p. 317). I do not know. But I still believe that, until we have more evidence than there is at present to decide the issue otherwise, it is preferable for the linguist to emphasize, as I have done, the fact that no language is more 'primitive' than any other. But I do agree with Hymes that one should try to study, empirically and without ideological prejudice, the possiblity of there being some kind of correlation between language and culture.

The most serious criticism that Hymes makes of my book is that, in not dealing with Chomsky as a political figure, I have failed to show how 'the impact of Chomsky, as of other men, has been jointly a product of the man, the work and the times' (p. 323). I freely admit that this is a limitation of the book. I simply did not feel that I could do justice to Chomsky's political commitment. In his review, Hymes goes a long way towards supplying this deficiency of my book. He talks of another kind of 'Chomskyan revolution', different from the one to which I refer in the final paragraph of my book—a revolution which has as its goal 'the realization of an alternative form of social order, as necessary to the realization of human values'—and of Chomsky as 'a dramatically successful scholar who would put his mind and to some extent his body on the line for causes that matter—a man who publicly and committedly broke with the age-old tradition of trahison des clercs' (p. 329). This is indeed a very important element in the impact that Chomsky made in the 1960s and early 1970s. How lasting this impact will be, I do not know. 'Perhaps', as Hymes puts it in his final sentence, 'one must always wait a generation, for memoirs, retrospection and the like, before the owl of Minerva can take her flight.'

In conclusion, I would draw attention to Hymes's suggestion that, 'if Chomsky established grammaticality as an effective criterion, as against occurrence in a corpus, the next step in linguistics would appear to be to establish appropriateness and acceptability'. As I have explained in the final chapter of the present edition, there has recently been a noticeable shift of interest, within linguistics, towards the social and the behavioural. I should mention here that Hymes has played a major role in bringing this about. Though I do not myself consider that there is, as yet, any good reason to abandon the Chomskyan idealization of linguistic competence, I would agree, with Hymes, that language should also be studied as human activity, within a framework to which ethnography and social psychology make an essential contribution. Hymes's *Foundations in Sociolinguistics* (see Bibliography) is an excellent starting-point for anyone who wishes to pursue this approach.

Biographical Note

Avram Noam Chomsky was born in Philadelphia, Pennsylvania, on 7 December 1928. He received his earlier education at the Oak Lane Country Day School (where he was happy, it being an 'experimental progressive school') and the Central High School, Philadelphia, (where he was unhappy and demotivated, it being a highly competitive, 'college oriented' school). He then went on to the University of Pennsylvania: he seriously considered 'dropping out' of college after one year, but (having come under the influence of Zellig Harris, Professor of Linguistics) he returned to study linguistics, mathematics and philosophy. It was at the University of Pennsylvania that he took his Ph.D., although most of the research that led to this degree was carried out as a Junior Fellow of the Society of Fellows at Harvard University between 1951 and 1955. Since 1955, he has taught at Massachusetts Institute of Technology, where he held the Ferrari P. Ward Chair of Modern Languages and Linguistics from 1966 to 1976 and, since 1976, has been an Institute Professor. He is married, with two daughters and a son. His wife, Carol Schatz Chomsky (whom he married in 1949), is also a linguist, who has worked in phonetics and subsequently in the acquisition of language.

Chomsky's work has been widely acclaimed in academic circles since the middle 1960s, and the honorary doctorates and other honours that he has been awarded throughout the world are by now too numerous to list in full. They include honorary doctorates from the University of London (1967), the University of Chicago (1967), Swarthmore College (1970), Loyola University, Chicago (1970), the University of Delhi (1972), the University of Massachusetts (1973), the University of Visva-Bharati, West Bengal (1980) and the University of Pennsylvania (1985). He has been awarded the Distinguished Scientific Contribution Award of the American Psychological Association (1984) and the Kyoto Prize in Basic Science

(1988). He is a member of the National Academy of Sciences, the American Academy of Arts and Sciences, a Corresponding Fellow of the British Academy, and an Honorary Fellow of the British Psychological Society, etc. He is also a Member of the Council of the International Confederation for Disarmament and Peace. He has given a large number of special lectures in several countries, including the Shearman Lectures, London (1969), the John Locke Lectures, Oxford (1969), the Bertrand Russell Memorial Lectures, Cambridge, (1971), the Nehru Memorial Lectures, New Delhi (1972), the Whidden Lectures, McMaster University (1975), the Huizinga Memorial Lectures, Leiden (1977), the Woodbridge Lectures, Columbia University (1978), the Kant Lectures, Stanford University (1979). And he has held visiting appointments, etc., at several universities in the United States.

Chomsky first made his academic reputation in linguistics. He had learned something of the principles of historical linguistics from his father, William Chomsky, who was a well-known Hebrew scholar, whose publications include, most notably, *Hebrew: The Eternal Language* (Philadelphia: Jewish Publication Society of America, 1958). Chomsky himself did some of his earliest linguistic research, for the degree of MA, on modern spoken Hebrew. But the work for which he first became famous in linguistics, the construction of a system of generative grammar and the working out of its implications for linguistic theory, developed out of his interest in modern logic and the foundations in mathematics, and was only subsequently applied to the description of natural languages. Of considerable importance in Chomsky's intellectual development was the influence of Zellig Harris (Professor Linguistics at the University of Pennsylvania, referred to above); and Chomsky himself has explained, on several occasions, that it was really his sympathy with Harris's political views that led him to work as an undergraduate in linguistics. There is a very real sense, therefore, in which it was politics which brought him into linguistics. And he is now, of course, at least as widely known for his political writings and his political activity as he is for his work in linguistics.

Chomsky has been interested in politics since his childhood. His views were formed in what he refers to as 'The radical

Jewish community in New York and have always tended towards socialism or anarchism. He describes himself these days as a libertarian socialist. In the 1960s, he became one of the leading critics of American foreign policy; and his book of essays on this topic, *American Power and the New Mandarins* (1969) was widely recognized as one of the most powerful indictments of American involvement in Vietnam to have been published on the subject at that time. It was followed by several other books on political issues: *For Reasons of State* (1973), *The Backroom Boys* (1973), *At War with Asia* (1970) and *Peace in the Middle East* (1974), *Human Rights and American Foreign Policy* (1978), *Radical Priorities* (1981), *Towards a New Cold War* (1982), *Fateful Triangle: the United States, Israel and the Palestinians* (1983), and several other works. Throughout the 1970s and 1980s he has been a constant critic of the involvement of the United States in Central America, the Middle East, Cambodia, and elsewhere; and, early in 1991, he gave a series of broadcasts and wrote articles critical of the role of the United States, Britain and other Western powers in the Gulf War and in the events which led up to it.

Bibliography

The Bibliography is arranged in two sections. Section A contains a representative (though not fully comprehensive) selection of works by Chomsky in the fields of linguistics, philosophy and politics. Section B contains a small number of works by other authors, including all those to which reference is made in the Suggestions for Further Reading.

A. SELECTED WORKS BY CHOMSKY

1951 'Morphophonemics of Modern Hebrew'. Unpublished Master's thesis, University of Pennsylvania.

1953 'Systems of syntactic analysis'. *Journal of Symbolic Logic* 18, 242-56.

1955 'Logical syntax and semantics: their linguistic relevance'. *Language* 31, 36-45.
'The Logical Structure of Linguistic Theory'. Mimeographed, MIT Library, Cambridge, Mass. (Now published, with revisions and an important and informative Introduction; New York & London: Plenum, 1975. See below.)
'Transformational Analysis'. Ph.D. dissertation, University of Pennsylvania.
'Semantic considerations in grammar'. Monograph No. 8, 141-53; Washington, D.C.: Georgetown University Institute of Languages and Linguistics.

1956 'On accent and juncture in English', with M. Halle and F. Lukoff. In M. Halle, H. Lunt, and H. MacLean (eds.), *For Roman Jakobson*; The Hague: Mouton.
'Three models for the description of language'. *I. R. E. Transactions on Information Theory*, Vol. IT-2, 113-24. Reprinted, with corrections, in R. D. Luce, R. Bush and E. Galanter (eds.), *Readings in Mathematical Psychology*, Vol. II; New York: Wiley, 1963.
'Logical structures in language'. *American Documentation* 8, 284-91.

1957 *Syntactic Structures*. The Hague: Mouton.
Review of C. F. Hockett, *Manual of Phonology*. In *International Journal of American Linguistics* 23, 223-34.

Review of R. Jakobson and M. Halle, *Fundamentals of Language*. In *International Journal of American Linguistics* 23, 234-42.

1958 'Finite state languages', with G. A. Miller. *Information and Control* I, 91-112. Reprinted in R. D. Luce, R. Bush and E. Galanter (eds.), *Readings in Mathematical Psychology*, Vol. II; New York: Wiley, 1963.

Review of I. Belevitch, *Langage des Machines et Langage humain*. In *Language* 34, 99-105.

1959 Review of B. F. Skinner, *Verbal Behavior*. In *Language* 35, 26-58. Reprinted in J. A. Fodor and J. D. Katz, *The Structure of Language*.

Review of J. Greenberg, *Essays in Linguistics*. In *Word* 15, 202-18.

'On certain formal properties of grammars'. *Information and Control* 2, 137-67. Reprinted in R. D. Luce, R. Bush, and E. Galanter (eds.), *Readings in Mathematical Psychology*, Vol. II; New York: Wiley, 1963.

'A note on phrase structure grammars'. *Information and Control* 2, 393-5.

1960 'The morphophonemics of English', with M. Halle. *Quarterly Progress Report* No. 58; Cambridge, Mass: Research Lab. of Electronics, 275-81.

1961 'On the notion "rule of grammar"'. In R. Jakobson (ed.), *Structure of Language and its Mathematical Aspect*, 6-24; Providence, R. I.: American Mathematical Society. (Reprinted in J. A. Fodor and J. D. Katz, *The Structure of Language*).

1962 'Explanatory models in linguistics'. In E. Nagel, P. Suppes and A. Tarski (eds.), *Logic, Methodology and Philosophy of Science: Proc. of the 1960 Int. Congress*; Stanford, California: Stanford University Press.

'Context-free grammars and pushdown storage'. *RLE Quarterly Progress Report* No. 65; Cambridge, Mass.: MIT.

'A transformational approach to syntax.' In A. A. Hill (ed.), *Proceedings of the 1958 Conference on Problems of Linguistic Analysis In English*, 124-48; Austin, Texas. (Reprinted in J. A. Fodor and J. D. Katz, *The Structure of Language*.)

1963 'The algebraic theory of context-free languages', with M. P. Schutzenberger. In P. Braffort and D. Hirschbert (eds.), *Computer Programming and Formal Systems*, 119-61; Amsterdam: North-Holland.

'Formal properties of grammars'. In R. D. Luce, R. Bush, and E. Galanter (eds.), *Handbook of Mathematical Psychology* II, 323-418; New York: Wiley, 1963

'Introduction to the formal analysis of natural languages',

with G. A. Miller. *Ibid*, 269-322.

'Finitary models of language users', with G. A. Miller. *Ibid*, 419-91.

1964   *Current Issues in Linguistic Theory*. The Hague: Mouton.

'Formal discussion: the development of grammar in child language'. In Ursula Bellugi and Roger Brown (eds.), *The Acquisition of Language* (Monographs of the Society for Research in Child Development, 29); Lafayette, Indiana: Purdue University.

1965   'Some controversial questions in phonological theory', with M. Halle. *Journal of Linguistics* 1, 97-138.

Aspects of the Theory of Syntax. Cambridge, Mass. & London: MIT Press.

1966   *Cartesian Linguistics*. New York and London: Harper & Row.

Topics in the Theory of Generative Grammar. The Hague: Mouton. (Also in T. A. Sebeok (ed.), *Current Trends in Linguistics* III: Linguistic Theory; The Hague: Mouton.)

'The current scene in linguistics: present directions'. In *College English* 27, 587-95. Reprinted in D. A. Reibel & S. A. Schane, *Modern Studies in English*; Prentice-Hall, 1969.

1967   'The formal nature of language'. Appendix to E. H. Lenneberg, *Biological Foundations of Language*; New York: Wiley. Reprinted in the 1972 edition of Chomsky, *Language and Mind*.

'Some general properties of phonological rules'. *Language* 43, 102-128.

'The general properties of language'. In P. L. Darley (ed.), *Brain Mechanisms Underlying Speech and Language* (Proceedings of a Conference held at Princeton, N.J., 9-12 November 1965), 73-81; New York: Grune & Stratton.

1968   *The Sound Pattern of English*, with M. Halle. New York and London: Harper & Row.

Language and Mind. New York and London: Harcourt Brace.

1969   'Linguistics and philosophy'. In S. Hook (ed.), *Language and Philosophy*; New York University Press (New York University Institute of Philosophy Symposium). (Reprinted in 1972 edition of Chomsky, *Language and Mind*.)

'Knowledge of language'. (Excerpted from the first John Locke Lecture, Oxford, 29 April 1969.) London: *Times Literary Supplement*, 15 May.

'Form and meaning in natural language'. In John D. Roslansky (ed.), *Communication*; Amsterdam: North-Holland.

'Quine's empirical assumptions'. In D. Davidson & J. Hintikka, *Words and Objections*; Dordrecht: Reidel.

'Some empirical assumptions in modern philosophy of

language'. In S. Morgenbosser *et al* (eds.), *Philosophy, Science and Method*; New York: St Martin's Press.

American Power and the New Mandarins. New York: Pantheon; London: Chatto & Windus (paperback: Penguin Books).

1970 'Remarks on nominalisation'. In R. Jacobs and P. Rosenbaum (eds.), *Readings in Transformational Grammar*; Waltham, Mass.: Blaisdell. (Reprinted in Chomsky, *Studies on Semantics*, 1972.)

'Phonology and reading'. In H. Levin and Joanna P. Williams (eds.), *Basic Studies in Reading*; New York: Basic Books.

'Problems of explanation in linguistics'. In R. Borger and F. Cioffi (eds.), *Explanations in the Behavioural Sciences*; London & New York: Cambridge University Press.

'Deep structure, surface structure and semantic interpretation'. In R. Jakobson and S. Kawamoto (eds.), *Studies in General and Oriental Linguistics*; Tokyo: TEC Corporation for Language Research. (Reprinted in Chomsky, *Studies on Semantics*, 1972.)

'Some observations on the problems of semantic analysis in natural languages'. In A. J. Greimas *et al.*, *Sign, Language, Culture*; The Hague: Mouton.

At War with Asia: Essays on Indochina. New York: Random House.

1971 *Problems of Knowledge and Freedom*. New York: Basic Books; London: Barrie & Jenkins (paperback: Fontana).

1972 *Language and Mind*. Enlarged edition; New York: Harcourt Brace Jovanovich. (Page references in this text are to the first edition, 1968.)

Studies on Semantics in Generative Grammar. The Hague: Mouton.

'Some empirical issues in the theory of transformational grammar'. In S. Peters (ed.) *Goals of Linguistic Theory*, 63-130; Prentice-Hall. (Also in Chomsky, *Studies on Semantics*, 1972.)

1973 'Conditions on transformations'. In S. R. Anderson & P. Kiparsky (eds.), *Festschrift for Morris Halle*; New York: Holt, Rinehart & Winston.

For Reasons of State. New York: Pantheon; London: Fontana.

The Backroom Boys. New York: Pantheon; London: Fontana.

1974 'Dialogue with Noam Chomsky'. In P. Parret (ed.), *Discussing Language*; The Hague: Mouton.

Peace in the Middle East? New York: Vintage; London: Fontana.

'What the linguist is talking about', with J. J. Katz, *Journal of Philosophy* 71, 347-67.

'On innateness', with J. J. Katz *Philosophical Review* 84, 347-67.

1975   'Knowledge of Language'. In K. Gunderson and Maxwell (eds.), *Minnesota Studies in Philosophy of Science* 6; Minneapolis: University of Minnesota Press.
'Questions of form and interpretation'. *Linguistic Analysis* 1, 75-109.
The Logical Structure of Linguistic Theory. New York & London: Plenum.
'Conditions on rules of grammar'. Unpublished.

1976   *Reflections on Language*. New York: Pantheon; London: Temple Smith (paperback: Fontana).

1977   *Essays on Form and Interpretation*. Amsterdam and New York: Elsevier/North Holland.

1978   *'Human Rights' and American Foreign Policy*. Nottingham: Spokesman Books.

1979   'The ideas of Chomsky'. In Bryan Magee (ed.), *Men of Ideas: Some Creators of Modern Philosophy*. London: BBC Publications.
After the Cataclysm: Postwar IndoChina and the Reconstruction of American Imperial Ideology (with Edward S. Herman). (*Political Economy of Human Rights*, vol. 2.) Boston: South End Press; Nottingham Spokesman Books.
Language and Responsibility: Based on Conversations with Mitsou Ronat. New York: Pantheon Books. (Translation, with revisions by Chomsky, of *Dialogues avec Mitsou Ronat*. Paris: Flammarion, 1977.)
The Washington Connection and Third World Fascism (with Edward S. Herman). (*Political Economy of Human Rights*, vol 1.) Boston: South End Press; Nottingham: Spokesman Books.

1980   'On binding'. *Linguistic Inquiry* 11, 1–46. (Reprinted, with comments and discussion by others, in Frank Heny, ed., *Binding and Filtering*, London: Croom Helm; Cambridge, Mass.: MIT Press, 1982.)
'On cognitive structures and their development'. In M. Piattelli-Palmarini (ed.), *Language and Learning: The Debate between Jean Piaget and Noam Chomsky*, London: Routledge & Kegan Paul; Cambridge, Mass.: Harvard University Press. English version of *Théories du langage*, Paris: Seuil, 1979.)
'On opacity'. In Sidney Greenbaum, G. Leech and J. Svartvik (eds.), *Studies in English Linguistics: For Randolph Quirk*, London and New York: Longman.
'Quelques commentaires élémentaires sur le droit de la liberté d'expression'. Preface to Robert Faurisson, *Mémoire en défense contre ceux qui m'accusent de falsifier l'histoire: la question des chambres à gaz*. Paris: La Vieille Taupe.
'Linguistic perspectives on language development' (with

David Caplan). In David Caplan (ed.), *Biological Studies of Mental Processes*, Cambridge, Mass. and London: MIT Press.
Rules and Representations. Oxford: Blackwell; New York: Columbia University Press.

1981 'The Commissars of literature'. *New Statesman* (14 Aug. 1981) pp. 13–14. [Reply to Gitta Seremy's criticism of Chomsky's role in 'The Faurisson case' in 'The Nazi record on trial', *New Statesman* (10 Apr. 1981), p. 4.
'The Faurisson affair: his right to say it'. *The Nation* (Feb. 28, 1981) pp. 231–35. Chomsky's reply to several critics of his preface to Faurisson's book: see above.) (Reprinted as 'His right to say it: The Faurisson affair', *Social Alternatives* (2 Feb. 1982) 45–8.)
'Knowledge of language: its elements and origins'. In Longuet-Higgins *et al.* (eds.), *Psychological Mechanisms of Language*. pp. 9–20 (See Section B for fuller reference.)
Lectures on Government and Binding. Dordrecht: Foris.
'Markedness and core grammar'. In Adriana Belletti, L. Brandi and L. Rizzi (eds.), *Theory of Markedness in Generative Grammar*. Pisa: Scuola Normale Superiore.
'Principles and parameters in syntactic theory'. In N. Hornstein and D. Lightfoot (eds.), *Explanation in Linguistics: The Logical Problem of Language Acquisition*. London and New York: Longman, pp. 32–75.
Radical Priorities (edited with Introduction by Carlos Otero). Montreal: Black Rose Books. (2nd enlarged edn, 1984.)

1982 *[Noam Chomsky on] The Generative Enterprise: A Discussion with Riny Huybregts and Henk van Riemsdijk*. Dordrecht: Foris.
'The ideas of Chomsky'. In B. Magee, *Men of Letters*, Oxford: Oxford University Press, pp. 173–93.
'Reply to Erika Apfelbaum on "Forgetting the past" '. *Partisan Review* 3 (1982). 474–7. [On the Faurisson affair.]
Some Concepts and Consequences of the Theory of Government and Binding, Cambridge, Mass: MIT Press.
Towards a New Cold War: Essays on the Current Crisis and How we Got There. New York: Pantheon Books.

1983 *The Fateful Triangle: The United States, Israel and the Palestinians*, London: Pluto Press.
'Some conceptual shifts in the study of language'. (The Lionel Trilling Lecture, Columbia University, 4 November 1982.) In Leigh S. Cauman *et al.* eds., *How Many Questions? Essays in Honor of Sidney Morgenbesser*. Indianapolis: Hackett.

1984 *Modular Approaches to the Study of Mind*. San Diego: California State University Press.

Réponses inédites à mes détracteurs parisiens. Paris: Spartacus.

1985 'Censorship and twentieth-century culture'. *New Criterion* (New York) 3, 81–4 (Jan. 1985). (Letter to the Editor replying to Geoffrey Samson 'Censorship and twentieth-century culture', in *New Criterion* 3, 7–16, (Oct. 1984).
Turning the Tide: US Intervention in Central America and the Struggle for Peace. London: Pluto Press.

1986 *Barriers.* (*Linguistic Inquiry Monograph,* 13.) Cambridge, Mass.: MIT Press.
Knowledge of Language: Its Nature, Origin and Use. New York and London: Praeger.

1987 *The Chomsky Reader* (edited by James Peck). New York: Pantheon Books; London: Serpent's Tail (1988).
Generative Grammar: Its Bases, Development and Prospects. (Special Issue of the Bulletin of the English Department.) Kyoto, Japan: Kyoto University.
Language in a Psychological Setting. (*Sophia Linguistica, 22.*) Tokyo: Sophia University.
On Power and Ideology. Boston: South End Press.

1988 *The Culture of Terrorism.* Boston: South End Press and London: Pluto Press.
Language and Problems of Knowledge. Cambridge, Mass.: MIT Press.
Manufacturing Consent (with Edward S. Herman). Boston: South End Press.

1989 'Mental constructions and social reality'. Paper delivered at conference on knowledge and language held in Groningen. May 1989.

1990 'On formalization and formal linguistics'. *Natural Language and Linguistic Theory* 8, 143–7.

1991 *Deterring Democracy.* London: Verso.
'Language and mind'. In P.N. Johnson-Laird (ed.), *Ways of Communicating.* London: Cambridge University Press.

B. OTHER WORKS

Aarsleff, Hans, *From Locke to Saussure.* London: Athlone, 1982.
Aitchison, Jean, *The Articulate Mammal: An Introduction to Psycholinguistics,* 3rd edn, London: Unwin Hyman, 1989.
Akmajian, A., Demers, R. A. & Harnish, R. M., *Linguistics: An Introduction to Language and Communication,* 2nd edn, Cambridge, Mass.: MIT Press, 1989.

Allen, J. P. B. & Van Buren, P. (eds.), *Chomsky: Selected Readings*. London: Oxford University Press, 1971.

Atkinson, Martin, Kilby, D. & Roca, I., *Foundations of General Linguistics*, 2nd edn, London: Unwin Hyman, 1988. (1st edn, 1982).

Bach, Emmon, 'Structural linguistics and the philosophy of science'. *Diogenes* 31 (1965) 111–128.

Bach, Emmon, *Syntactic Theory*. New York: Holt, Rinehart & Winston, 1974.

Bloomfield, Leonard, *Language*. New York: Holt, 1933; London: Allen & Unwin, 1935.

Botha, Rudolf P., *Challenging Chomsky: The Generative Garden Game*. Oxford: Blackwell, 1989.

Bracken, H., *Mind and Language: Essays on Descartes and Chomsky*. Dordrecht: Foris, 1984.

Brown, (E.) Keith, *Syntax Today*. Cambridge: Cambridge University Press, 1992 (revised and updated version of *Linguistics Today*, London: Fontana/Collins, 1984.)

Caplan, David, *Neurolinguistics and Linguistic Aphasiology*. Cambridge: Cambridge University Press, 1987.

Clarke, H. H. & Clarke E. V., *Psychology and Language: An Introduction to Psycholinguistics*. New York: Harcourt Brace Jovanovich, 1977.

Cook, Vivien, J., *Chomsky's Universal Grammar: An Introduction*. (Applied Language Studies) Oxford: Blackwell, 1988.

Crystal, David, *Listen to Your Child: A Parent's Guide to Children's Language*. Harmondsworth, Middlesex: Penguin, 1986.

D'Agostino, Fred, *Chomsky's System of Ideas*. Oxford: Clarendon Press, 1986.

Dinneen, F. P., *An Introduction to General Linguistics*. New York: Holt, Rinehart & Winston, 1967 (includes excerpts from the writings of Boas, Sapir, Bloomfield and early Chomsky, with exposition).

Elliot, Alison, *Child Language*. Cambridge: Cambridge University Press, 1981.

Fletcher, Paul & Garman, M., *Language Acquisition*. 2nd edn, Cambridge: Cambridge University Press, 1986.

Fodor, Janet A., *Semantics: Theories of Meaning in Generative Linguistics*. New York: Cromwell, 1977.

Fodor, Jerrold A., *The Modularity of Mind: An Essay on Faculty Psychology*. Cambridge, Mass.: MIT Press, 1983.

Fodor, Jerrold, A., 'Some Notes on what linguistics is about'. In J. J. Katz, *The Philosophy of Linguistics* (see below), pp. 146–60.

Fodor, Jerrold A. & Katz, J. J., *The Structure of Language: Readings in the Philosophy of Language*. Englewood Cliffs, N.J.: Prentice-Hall, 1964.

Fromkin, Victoria & Rodman, R., *An Introduction to Language*. 4th edn, New York: Holt, Rinehart & Winston, 1988.

Gazdar, Gerald, 'On syntactic categories'. In Longuet-Higgins *et al* (eds.), *Psychological Mechanisms* (1981), pp. 53–69.

Gazdar, Gerald, 'Generative grammar'. In Lyons *et al* (eds.), *New Horizons in Linguistics 2* (1987) pp. 122–51.

George, Alexander, *Reflections on Chomsky*. Oxford: Blackwell, 1989.

Greene, Judith, *Psycholinguistics: Chomsky and Psychology*. Harmondsworth, Middlesex and Baltimore: Penguin, 1972.

Hall, Robert A., *Linguistics and Pseudo-linguistics: Selected Essays 1965–1985*. Amsterdam: John Benjamins, 1987.

Harman, Gilbert, *On Noam Chomsky: Selected Essays*. New York: Doubleday, 1974.

Harris, Zellig S., *Methods in Structural Linguistics*. Chicago: University of Chicago Press, 1951.

Harris, Zellig S., 'Transformational theory'. *Language* 41 (1965), 363–401.

Hockett, Charles F., 'Sound change'. *Language* 41 (1965), 185–205.

Hockett, Charles F., *The State of Art*. The Hague: Mouton, 1967.

Horrocks, Geoffrey, *Generative Grammar*. London and New York: Longman, 1987.

Hoenigswald, Henry M., ed., *The European Background of American Linguistics*. Dordrecht: Foris, 1979.

Huddlesdon, Rodney D., *Introduction to English Transformational Syntax*. London: Longmans, 1976.

Hymes, Dell, Review of First Edition of Lyons' (Noam) *Chomsky*, in *Language* 48 (1972): 414–427. (Reprinted in Harman, *On Noam Chomsky*, pp. 316–33).

Hymes, Dell, *Foundations in Sociolinguistics*. Philadelphia: University of Pennsylvania Press, 1974.

Hymes, Dell & Fought, J., 'American structuralism'. In T. A. Sebeok, ed., *Current Trends in Linguistics*, vol. 13., The Hague, Mouton, pp. 901–1176. (reprinted separately with 'Epilogue, 1979'. The Hague: Mouton, 1981).

Ingram, David, *First Language Acquisition: Method, Description and Explanation*. Cambridge: Cambridge University Press, 1989.

Joos, Martin, ed., *Readings in Linguistics*. Washington, D.C.: American Council of Learned Societies, 1957. (Republished as *Readings in Linguistics 1*. Chicago: Chicago University Press, 1966).

Kasher, Asa, ed., *The Chomskyan Turn*. Oxford: Blackwell, 1991.

Katz, Jerrold J., *Language and Other Abstract Objects*. Oxford: Blackwell, 1981.

Katz, Jerrold J., ed., *The Philosophy of Linguistics*. Oxford: Oxford University Press, 1985.

Koerner, Konrad & Tajima M., eds., *Noam Chomsky: A Personal Bibliography 1951–1986*. Amsterdam: John Benjamins, 1986.

Lees, Robert B., Review of Chomsky, *Syntactic Structures*, in *Language* 33 (1957), 375–407. Reprinted in Harman, *On Noam Chomsky*.

Lightfoot, David, *The Language Lottery*. Cambridge, Mass.: MIT Press, 1982.

Longuet-Higgins, H. Christopher, Lyons, J. & Broadbent, D. E., eds., *The Psychological Mechanisms of Language*. Proceedings of a Joint Symposium of the Royal Society and The British Academy, 11–12 March 1981. London: Royal Society & British Academy, 1981.

Lyons, John, *Introduction to Theoretical Linguistics*. London and New York: Cambridge University Press, 1968.

Lyons, John ed., *New Horizons in Linguistics*. Harmondsworth Middlesex: Penguin, 1970. (Reissued as *New Horizons in Linguistics, 1*. 1987.

Lyons, John, 'The last forty years: real progress or not?' *Georgetown University Round Table on Languages and Linguistics 1989*. Washington, D.C.: Georgetown University Press, pp. 13–38.

Lyons, John, *Language and Linguistics*. Cambridge, New York, etc: Cambridge University Press, 1981.

Lyons, John, *Language, Meaning and Context*. 2nd edn, London, New York, etc.: Cambridge University Press, 1992, (1st edn, London: Fontana/Collins; New York: Viking, 1970.)

Lyons, John, *Natural Language and Universal Grammar: Essays in Linguistic Theory*, vol. 1. Cambridge: Cambridge University Press, 1991.

Lyons, John, 'Linguistics and law: The legacy of Sir Henry Maine'. In Alan Diamond, ed., *The Victorian Achievement of Sir Henry Maine*. Cambridge: Cambridge University Press, 1991.

Lyons, John, Coates, R., Deuchar, M. and Gazdar, G., (eds.), *New Horizons in Linguistics 2*. London: Penguin & New York: Viking Penguin, 1987.

Lyons, John and Wales J., (eds.), *Psycholinguistics Papers*. Edinburgh: Edinburgh University Press.

Matthews, Peter H., Review of Chomsky, *Aspects of the Theory of Syntax*, in *Journal of Linguistics* 3 (1967), 119–152.

Matthews, Peter H., *Generative Grammar and Linguistic Competence*. London: Allen & Unwin, 1979.

Matthews, Peter H., 'Distributional syntax', in Theodora Bynon & F. R. Palmer, (eds.), *Studies in the History of Western Linguistics*, Cambridge: Cambridge University Press, 1986, pp. 245–77.

Matthews, Peter H., 'Language as a mental faculty: Chomsky's progress, in N. E. Collinge, ed., *An Encyclopaedia of Language*, London & New York: Routledge, 1990, pp. 112–38.

Modgil, S. and Modgil, C., (eds.), *Noam Chomsky: Consensus and Controversy*. Barcombe, Sussex: Falmer Press 1987.

Newmeyer, Frederick J., ed., *Linguistic Theory in America: The First Quarter Century of Transformational Grammar*. New York Academic Press, 1980.

Newmeyer, Frederick F., ed., *Linguistics: The Cambridge Survey*, 4 vols. Cambridge: Cambridge University Press, 1988.

Oldfield, R. C. & Marshal J. C., (eds.), *Language*. Harmondsworth: Penguin, 1968.

Partee, Barbara H. *et al*, *Mathematical Methods in Linguistics*. Dordrecht: Kluwer Academic Publishers, 1990.

Pateman, Trevor, *Language in Mind and Language in Society*. London: Oxford University Press, 1987.

Percival, W. Keith, 'The applicability of Kuhn's paradigms to the history of linguistics'. *Language* 52 (1976), 285–294.

Radford, Andrew, *Transformational Grammar: A First Course*. Cambridge: Cambridge University Press, 1988.

Robins, Robert H., *A Short History of Linguistics*. 2nd edn, London: Longman, 1979. (1st edn, 1967.)

Salkie, Raphael, *The Chomsky Update: Linguistics and Politics*. London: Unwin Hyman, 1990.

Sampson, Geoffrey R., *Schools of Linguistics*. London: Hutchinson; Stanford, Calif.: Stanford University Press, 1982.

Sapir, Edward, *Language*. New York: Harcourt, Brace and World, 1921.

Skinner, B. F., *Beyond Freedom and Dignity*. Harmondsworth, Middlesex: Penguin, 1973.

Smith, Neil V. and Wilson, Deirdre, *Modern Linguistics: The Results of Chomsky's Revolution*. Harmondsworth, Middlesex: Penguin, 1979.

Steinberg, Daniel D. and Jakobovits, L., (eds.), *Semantics: An Interdisciplinary Reader in Philosophy, Linguistics and Psychology*. Cambridge and New York: Cambridge University Press, 1971.

Suggestions for Further Reading

My main purpose in writing this book, as I have said in the Preface, is to provide readers with enough of the historical and technical background, in linguistics and to some extent also in philosophy and psychology, for them to read Chomsky's own works with some degree of critical understanding.

Chomsky is an enormously productive writer, and the publications listed in Section A of the Bibliography are but a small part of his output. To the best of my knowledge, there is as yet no definitive or absolutely comprehensive published bibliography of his writing. But the wok by Koerner and Tajima (1986), which I have listed in Section B of the Bibliography, will amply suffice for most purposes, as far as Chomsky's own writings are concerned (for the period that it covers). It draws (with acknowledgement and references) upon other partial bibliographies and, usefully, lists most of the important reviews of Chomsky's major books.

Though far from comprehensive, Section A of the Bibliography is fully representative of Chomsky's work, not only in linguistics, philosophy and psychology, but also in politics. The problem for the reader coming fresh to Chomsky's own work is where to start. Much of what he has published in books started life in the form of talks and lectures for many different kinds of audience. This means, first of all, that there is a good deal of repetition and restatement over the years and, second, that there are, in many cases, different levels of generalization or simplification in different chapters of the same book. Moreover, as I mentioned in the Preface, Chomsky's ideas have been more or less continuously modified and refined since the mid-1960s: he does not always signal these modifications and revisions or make it clear when alternative formulations of what is substantially the same theoretical point or the same example represent anything more than a change of emphasis or focus or a difference in the provenance of the original upon which the printed version is based. Finally, because so much of what he has published is based on talks given earlier, and at different times, the chronological sequence of his publications does not reflect at all faithfully the progressive modification and refinement of his thought to which I have referred.

For those who are interested in the wider philosophical and psychological implications of Chomsky's work, there is still something to be said for starting with the enlarged edition of *Language and Mind* (1972) and moving on directly from there to *Language and Problems of Knowledge* (1988). But one could equally well read these two works in reverse order; each illuminates the other. In either event, it is probably unnecessary (though of course it would considerably improve one's understanding of Chomsky's evolving ideas) to read his widely reviewed *Reflections on Language* (1976). At that point, what is so far Chomsky's most systematic and most substantial account of his recent ideas (which I have covered very briefly in Chapter 12), *Knowledge of Language* (1986), should be reasonably accessible. Also worth picking out for special mention are *Language and Responsibility* (1979) and *The Generative Enterprise* (1982), which, being based on interviews with Chomsky, contain a lot of information and commentary which is not readily available elsewhere.

As far as Chomsky's work in linguistics as such is concerned, it may still be the case that one should start with the so-called 'standard theory' of what I have been calling the 'classical' period. *Topics in the Theory of Generative Grammar* (1966) gives a clearer account of this than does *Aspects of the Theory of Syntax* (1965), which, in many ways, is a very confusing book. *Syntactic Structures* (1957) is perhaps no longer to be read in detail, except for historical reasons; but, if it is read (as I explain in Appendix 2), it can now be interpreted in the light of the Introduction to *The Logical Structure of Linguistic Theory* (1975). Excerpts from *Syntactic Structures, Topics in the Theory of Generative Grammar, Aspects of the Theory of Syntax* and other works of the 'classical' period are conveniently brought together, with a linking editorial commentary in Allen and Van Buren's *Chomsky: Selected Readings* (1971). For Chomsky's more recent work in linguistics reference may be made, once again, to *Knowledge of Language* (1986), to *Barriers* (1986) and to *Some Concepts and Consequences of the Theory of Government and Binding* (1982), and to the articles by Chomsky listed in Section A of the Bibliography. But it will probably be necessary to read these later works in conjunction with some of the expository works listed in Section B of the Bibliography.

The works by authors other than Chomsky, listed in Section B, have been chosen for their relevance to the topics dealt with in this book and, with one or two exceptions, for their accessibility. Three rather different, but equally reliable, introductions to transformational grammar of the 'classical' period have been mentioned: Huddleston's (1976) is perhaps the most readable (and, in my view, rather better than the others for the general background); Akmajian & Heny's (in the 1975 edition) is the most comprehensive; Bach (1974) is good on the formalism, without being excessively technical.

Smith & Wilson (1979) gives a good account (from a highly committed point of view) of Chomskyan grammar in the immediately 'post-classical' period. Janet D. Fodor (1977) provides a clear and readable treatment of the work that was done in semantics within the framework of 'classical' and, to a certain extent, 'post-classical' Chomskyan generative grammar and is especially good on the philosophical background.

For the later period, the following more or less introductory works may be recommended (each of which has its own merits): Akmajian *et al*, *Linguistics*,(3rd edn, 1990); Atkinson *et al.*, *Foundations* (2nd edn, 1989); Brown, *Syntax Today* (1992); Radford, *Transformational Grammar* (1988); Horrocks, *Generative Grammar* (1987). Also useful as a relatively non-technical introduction to 'Government-Binding Theory' (though lacking in historical perspective and, at times, unnecessarily imprecise, even for non-specialists) is Cook, *Chomsky's Universal Grammar* (1988), which also explores the implications of Chomsky's theory, as it is currently formulated, for first-language acquisition and second-language learning. As I pointed out in Chapter 12, recent introductory textbooks tend to confuse generative grammar, as such, with 'the generative enterprise', and none of the books that I have listed here (except Brown, *Syntax Today*) is above criticism in this respect. Some, however, are more partisan than others, and this will quickly be evident to the discerning reader.

I have also included in Section B a number of background works, for both the earlier and the later period. In most cases, their relevance will be clear from their titles. The Fodor & Katz (1964) and the Steinberg & Jakobovits (1971) collections contain important articles from the earlier periods of generative grammar. They are both intended to bring out the philosophical and psychological implications of Chomskyan linguistics. Of the other collections from an earlier period: Harman's (1974) volume is more specifically philosophical in orientation, Oldfield & Marshall's (1968) is psychological, and Lyons, ed., *New Horizons 1* (1970) is focused more particularly on linguistics (broadly conceived): it is now of course somewhat dated, but it has a good bibliography and, unlike most other anthologies, is made up wholly of articles written for non-specialists. It has recently been supplemented with Lyons *et al*, (eds.), *New Horizons 2* (1987), which also has a comprehensive bibliography. More recent collections of articles include: Modgil & Modgil, *Noam Chomsky* (1987) (which is designed to give full representation to both pro-Chomsky and anti-Chomsky points of view), George, *Reflections on Chomsky* (1989) and Kasher *The Chomskyan Turn* (1990).

I have listed several works on psycholinguistics. Of these, the most readily accessible for non-specialists are Greene, *Psycholinguistics*

(1972), for the earlier period, and Aitchison, *The Articulate Mammal* (3rd edn, 1989), for the later.

Published works critical of Chomsky's ideas are not lacking. Many of them are based on fairly elementary misunderstandings, and I have not listed them in the Bibliography. Hockett's *State of the Art* (1967), though arguably distorted by a certain amount of misunderstanding, is nonetheless well worth reading; and Hockett, with Zellig Harris, can fairly claim to have prepared the way for Chomskyan generative grammar with his partial formalization of Bloomfieldian concepts. Some of the most challenging criticisms of generative grammar (and 'the generative enterprise'), from a well-informed point of view are to be found in Matthews, *Generative Grammar and Linguistic Competence* (1979). Other criticisms, from within linguistics, will be found in Moore & Carling, *Understanding Language* (1982).

Mention should also be made, finally, of Salkie, *The Chomsky Update* (1990), which usefully complements my own, in that it concentrates upon Chomsky's more recent work in linguistics and, unlike my book, also deals with his politics, in both cases from Chomsky's own point of view. (It is, however, in my view rather uncritical in its presentation of Chomsky's views and arguments.) Peck's *Chomsky Reader* (1987) is devoted almost exclusively to Chomsky's political writings, and it is also especially valuable for the biographical information which is reproduced in the editor's published interview with Chomsky and upon which I have drawn in my own 'Bibliographical Note'.

The Rise and Fall of the Political Press in Britain

Stephen Koss

In this magisterial book, Stephen Koss traces the evolution of the relationship between journalists, proprietors and politicians from the late eighteenth century to the end of World War Two. He follows the progress of the political press from control by the state through the age of the press barons to the arrival of the mass media and modern market forces. He draws on a mass of manuscript sources, many never previously consulted, to provide a thrilling and vivid account of the history of that most influential and Byzantine of political institutions, the British Press.

'Exceptionally well-written . . . its mind and references are broad enough for it to be enjoyed by the general reader who will frequently read amazed . . . There is nothing but pleasure and instruction here . . . A study of major importance.'

Michael Ratcliffe, *The Times*

'Professor Koss never puts a foot wrong, his scholarship is impeccable and he writes with wit, elegance and humour.'

Robert Black, *Illustrated London News*

'This book is indispensable reading for politicians of all parties.'

Asa Briggs, *New Society*

'Professor Koss knows the ambitions and foibles of every back-bench MP, the hopes and fears for his future of every editor, and half his staff a well, the cheque book stubs, not only of every major proprietor, but of every minor plutocrat who aspired to influence, and maybe towards ennoblement too, through newspaper owner-ship, in almost terrifying depth.'   Roy Jenkins, *Sunday Times*

FONTANA PRESS

Whitehall

Peter Hennessy

'The thinking man's *Yes Minister*.'

Lord Hunt, ex-secretary of the Cabinet

'Mr Hennessy has at last produced his magnum opus – more than 800 pages chronicling the history of Whitehall from the Norman Conquest to Norman Strauss. Along the way we also get an analysis of present-day ministries, a reform tract and a succession of the Great and Good . . . It is the best account of the British Civil Service ever produced. More than that, it is also, to use Edward Bridges' favourite word, enormous fun.'

Robert Harris, *Observer*

'The most thorough examination of the civil service and her ways yet published. It is ambitious in intent, sweeping in scope, meticulous in detail and penetrating in analysis. His judgements are fair, and sure to disappoint the ideologies of both left and right. Whitehall looks set to beome the standard work on the ways and byways of a hugely important and underexposed part of national life.'

Jeremy Paxton, *Independent*

'This is an outstanding book by a political historian and journalist who has himself become something of a national institution . . . Present and future ministers, whether seeking to alter the machine or merely to comprehend its puzzling idiom and culture, are certain to regard Hennessy's brilliant investigation as the indispensable guide.'

Ben Pimlott, *Sunday Times*

'*Whitehall* is much the best book on the British civil service ever to appear. Everyone who claims the slightest acquaintance with British government will have to read the book, indeed own it.'

Anthony King, *Economist*

FONTANA PRESS

Fontana Paperbacks
Non-fiction

Fontana is a leading paperback publisher of non-fiction. Below are some recent titles.

- ☐ All the King's Men *Robert Marshall* £3.50
- ☐ War Papers *Virgil Pomfret* £10.99
- ☐ The Boys and the Butterflies *James Birdsall* £2.95
- ☐ Pursuit *Ludovic Kennedy* £3.50
- ☐ Malta Convoy *Shankland and Hunter* £2.95
- ☐ We Die Alone *David Howarth* £2.95
- ☐ The Bridge on the River Kwai *Pierre Boulle* £2.95
- ☐ Carve Her Name With Pride *R. J. Minney* £2.95
- ☐ The Tunnel *Eric Williams* £3.50
- ☐ Reach for the Sky *Paul Brickhill* £3.50
- ☐ Rommel *Desmond Young* £3.95

You can buy Fontana paperbacks at your local bookshop or newsagent. Or you can order them from Fontana Paperbacks, Cash Sales Department, Box 29, Douglas, Isle of Man. Please send a cheque, postal or money order (not currency) worth the purchase price plus 22p per book for postage (maximum postage required is £3).

NAME (Block letters) _____

ADDRESS _____

_____

_____